Jane Roberts
PSYCHIC
POLITICS

An Aspect Psychology Book

PRENTICE-HALL, INC., ENGLEWOOD CLIFFS, N.J.

Books by Jane Roberts

THE SETH MATERIAL

SETH SPEAKS
The Eternal Validity of the Soul

THE EDUCATION OF OVERSOUL 7

THE NATURE OF PERSONAL REALITY
A Seth Book

ADVENTURES IN CONSCIOUSNESS
An Introduction to Aspect Psychology

DIALOGUES OF THE SOUL
AND MORTAL SELF IN TIME

PSYCHIC POLITICS
An Aspect Psychology Book

THE "UNKNOWN" REALITY
A Seth Book (in two volumes)

THE WORLD VIEW OF
PAUL CÉZANNE

Psychic Politics: An Aspect
Psychology Book by Jane Roberts
Copyright ©1976 by Jane Roberts
All rights reserved. No part of this book may be
reproduced in any form or by an means, except
for the inclusion of brief quotations in a review,
without permission in writing from the publisher.
Printed in the United States of America
Prentice-Hall International, Inc., London
Prentice-Hall of Australia, Pty. Ltd., Sydney
Prentice-Hall of Canada, Ltd., Toronto
Prentice-Hall of India Private Ltd., New Delhi
Prentice-Hall of Japan, Inc., Tokyo
Prentice-Hall of Southeast Asia Pte. Ltd., Singapore

10 9 8 7 6 5 4

Library of Congress Cataloging in Publication Data
Roberts, Jane.
    Psychic Politics
    Includes index.
    1. Psychical research.   I. Title.
BF1031.R633   158'.1   76-22751
ISBN 0-13-731745-X

Contents

PART THREE / *Toward a New Politics of the Psyche,
and an Alternate Model for Civilization
to Follow*

Part One

THE LIBRARY
AND AN INTRODUCTION
TO THE SUPER-REAL

Chapter 1
The Library

We've just moved into a house, and now our Water Street quarters are vacant. As I write, I no longer hear the bridge traffic at the corner intersection or watch the pigeons on our roof above the parking lot. It was in that large living room that the Seth sessions first began. In the beginning there was just Rob and me, artist and writer, husband and wife, experimenting as millions do with a Ouija board. By the time we left those apartments, nearly forty students were crowding the living room each Tuesday; Seth, my "trance personality," had dictated two books and was nearly finished with another one; and I'd written three of my own. More than that: When I walked into that apartment house for the first time, I was thirty-one; and when I left for the final time, I was forty-five. The Seth sessions began when I was thirty-five.

In the beginning years we were very secretive about the sessions, telling only a few close friends but not the neighbors. A couple of times, Seth's booming voice carried through the night air. Once a neighbor came to investigate. It was summer; the windows were open, and he must have been struck by the odd quality of Seth's voice: deep, masculine-like, and accented in a strange fashion we've never been able to categorize. Anyway, when the knock came at the door, Rob turned on the television—loud. And our neighbor saw just the two of us, innocently sitting there. The man tried to explain about the voice he heard. Rob said, "It must have been the television program," and our neighbor went away, shaking his head.

In a way, Seth *is* like a television program, in that I'm tuned in to another channel of reality during sessions so that Seth's "program" plays over my own, or temporarily supersedes my own official station of consciousness. Sometimes I think that Seth is like some public education channel; invisible dials whirl in my head, and he clicks on. Other times I think of Seth as a director of some multidimensional communications network with me lucky enough to possess a unique set to pick up his stations. Certainly he seems to direct many of my other excursions into realms of consciousness beyond the norm.

More and more "stations" seem available to me all the time, yet always Seth is the general "commentator": the master of ceremonies, the newscaster, the genial guide through jungles and deserts and mountains of the inner mind.

In other words, one way or another, I get signals from strange lands. I always have, though when I was growing up I just labeled everything as inspiration and let it go at that. Finally inspiration had a voice of its own and a personage, Seth, to boot. So Seth writes his books and I write mine, and each succeeding stable alteration of consciousness brings new messages from these alien yet somehow familiar inner lands of reality.

Listening to these messages, translating them, writing them down is life to me. Seth says that being is its own justification, and for a while I thought that perhaps I wrote to justify my life. It took some time for me to realize that being *is* writing to me. When I'm not "turned on" in my own particular fashion, my being seems dimmer. I become glum. So when I've finished one book, I can't wait to begin another.

When I completed *Adventures in Consciousness*, then, my last book, I went around in a huff for a while. Nothing contented me, although Seth was dictating *The "Unknown" Reality* in our twice-weekly sessions. The days disappeared into weeks and I grew more restless. I felt disconnected from my being. So I began the series of steps I usually take whenever I want to contact deeper levels of my own consciousness. I did some watercolor painting, but *that* didn't seem to work. Then one afternoon early in October I wrote the following poem, half angrily, depicting my situation.

Invitation

Ah love this stubborn mortal self,
once more trying to contact its soul,
and wondering on an autumn afternoon
how best to trick it from its high domain.

The mortal self says, "Dear soul,
The earth is beautiful this time of year
and certainly some part of you is touched
by the leaves dizzily falling everywhere,
and by the misty autumn dusk
that swirls around the neighborhood
like a ghost on a treasure hunt.
But if you aren't,
isn't it enough that I'd like to talk?
You're my soul, after all,
so I don't see why I need an appointment
to get a moment of your time.

"I'll meet you any place at all,
though some structure seems to help,

so I'm offering this poem
which is flexible enough to bear
the weight of even the heaviest dialogue.
First of all, I'd like to know
if you've heard a thing
I've had to say so far.
So before I really begin,
would you kindly give me some sign
that you're listening?"

With this, the mortal self gets up,
makes some coffee, then comes back
and sits down again to wait.
It wonders: who knows about the soul's world
except the self who surely doesn't know enough,
and if the soul did speak, who'd know
except its earthly counterpart?
Suspense. The moments pass.
The cat meows.
The mortal self says,
"I feel like such an ass.
Either I'm using the wrong approach,
or my soul doesn't act
as if it knows that I'm alive."

There were actually many other verses to the poem, but these contain the main request: I wanted to feel in touch again, and I wanted an uprush of inspiration and energy. The mortal self—me, of course—went on rather quarrelsomely to say that it was only too ready to do whatever it was supposed to do next, providing the soul would be kind enough to inform it of its next "project." Having written the poem, I rested my case and waited, though not too graciously.

But what energy that poem set into action, and how it propelled me into new excursions! Because of it this book is being written and my exterior life changed, so that now the Water Street apartments where all this began are now a memory. More than that, I became familiar with new dimensions of being and began to learn more about the alternate realities that wind in and out of this one all the time.

Actually, I worked on the poem off and on for nearly a week, adding new verses as I thought of new arguments in my own favor. But still I received no answer, as far as I could tell. No new insights, dreams, or ideas came to me. Great, I thought ironically, and I'd do another verse asking "the soul" where it was, and what was wrong, and repeating my request for a kind of communication that I could understand.

Each morning I'd sit at least briefly at my desk—waiting. About a week and a half later, on October 25, 1974, I plunked myself down as usual. By then I'd nearly forgotten the poem itself. There wasn't an idea in my head. Then, suddenly, my next project was presented to me so clearly that I could have no doubts. All at once the image of a library was transposed over the southeast corner of the living room, and in it I saw my own image. At the same time, two paragraphs sprang to life within my mind. Excited, I wrote them down and then described the experience itself as it began to unfold. By then I knew that the notes were themselves the beginning of a new book.

These are my original notes. The first two paragraphs are arranged exactly as I saw them in my mental vision—I imagine that this was to set them off and let me know that new material was involved. Even later, that precise arrangement was significant to me.

> "No man is an island unto himself,"
> but each person contains an inner
> civilization of the self which he
> learns to govern with a psychic
> politics that is the framework for
> the outer world of government and
> law.
>
> The ego rises from the civilization
> of the psyche just as the ruler, king, queen,

president, or dictator rises from the masses
of the people; appointed, chosen, or taking
control according to an inner politics first
existing within the greater inner mind.

"The above two paragraphs affect me most strangely, with a force difficult to describe. I feel that they exist
somewhere else and have for centuries, that they are inevitable, and that the book in which they appear has already
been written, though I am just beginning to transcribe it. The
book is a classic, known as such somewhere or in some other
time. The two paragraphs above are just the beginning, yet
they come to me with an impeccable sense of their rightness.
Suddenly I'm sure that I'm meant to "write" that book, that
it represents "my path" and is a part of my destiny. I don't
mean that I feel forced to do this, but that I recognize in
some odd manner the utter rightness of this path, this book
and what it represents, to me. The book is to be called
Psychic Politics.
  "Certainly I've been writing these years, and no
one else, I'm convinced, could produce *The Seth Material* or
maintain the kind of relationship that I have with Seth, but
this new book strikes me in an even more intimate fashion.
Yet a sense of distance operates; the distance that still separates me from the complete manuscript in our time, for I am
pulling it to me or it is pulling me to it, one or the other, in
the most natural fashion.
  "There seems to be a path between me and the
book that strikes me more than anything else in my life so far
as 'my way', so that I find myself wondering if I've already
written it in some other place or time. It might have been
written by someone else. But in any case I feel that I'm the
one meant to transcribe it, and that this act brings the book
alive in three-dimensional reality, even though it exists outside of that context and is being translated into it.
  "Part of the book, the main part, represents certain
principles and dynamics of the psyche that have always been
known at certain levels. Yet what I add in terms of fresh
examples and experience will make the book applicable in

our time. Again, I feel strongly that this is a classic, perhaps lost from libraries that were destroyed in other civilizations.

"I recognize this sense of perfect rightness only now as something I've been searching for for years, that would bring its own high assurance and psychic aptness; as if I've been casting my consciousness out in all directions, probing, and that sooner or later I'd have to find this clear circle or path to a particular source. And somehow I kept myself off-balance in the meantime, in that I continued searching when it seemed that I should be satisfied; because I wouldn't know what it was I wanted until I found it.

" 'It,' the book, may only be one of many, but I seem to sense it as if it is the first of many in a great library, bound in gold, a collection of classics that are somehow echoed in other ways within the private and mass psyche. The image of the library may be symbolic, of course, yet on another level I can see myself standing there by those volumes, nearly weeping, thinking that I've finally come home.

"I feel that my destiny is to transcribe these invisible books, sifting them through my psyche as it lives in our time, and therefore re-creating the books by imbuing them once more with life. They have to be translated through the flesh, and they grow through its medium, even while the transcriber has to have the most perfect affinity for them on other, psychic levels. This was the next step waiting for me, that I was to follow, and perhaps all the others have been leading to this one.

"I don't know where Seth fits into all this. Through me, he's been writing his books for years, but I don't feel any conflict between this new work of mine and his. Instead, they are connected. Seth's books represent one unique personality addressing other unique personalities. These other new books seem to be something else entirely—apart, aloof, finished in one sense: principles that will come alive through my private experience. And I feel that the books and my life will interweave, so that each adds to the other."

Just as I finished writing the above, there was a

knock at the door. I thought it was the paper boy and yelled, "Come in." Instead, to my complete surprise, a young man came striding into the living room, his arms confidently swinging, his eyes shining, moist—and determined. I'll call him Lyman.*

I nearly groaned in disbelief. I'd met him only the night before when he'd attended my expansion of consciousness class. He'd identified himself by phone earlier that day as a "budding parapsychologist," speaking with great erudite phrases. After class, though, he wanted me to tell him what to do with his life, as if it was my challenge instead of his. I took nearly an hour to talk to him, hopefully to reinforce his confidence in himself.

Apparently I'd succeeded, but not in the way I thought, because here he was, unannounced. With one brisk gesture he had his jacket off, his tape recorder on the table beside me, next to the pile of Kleenex soggily sitting there—I had a cold—and he attacked me with his energetic eyes. With no preamble he started in. He'd phoned another psychic, enthusiastically telling me how he'd tracked the woman down to her hospital bed. "Then, though the call cost me twenty dollars, it was worth it," he said. "I told her all about you and your class and found that she'd read your books; and I asked her to comment on your ideas."

I just sat looking at him, and at the Kleenex.

"You say there isn't going to be a holocaust," he said. "And all the other psychics, including Cayce, say there will be. She said that the holocaust won't come in the year 2000, but any day now. What have you got to say to that?" He turned on his recorder.

"Not a damned thing," I said.

He plunged on. "And *she* says there *is* a hierarchy in the Astral plane, and that only seven people have access to the Akashic records, and she's one of them. The others charge huge prices and only tell about one life, where for far less, only fifty dollars, she gives a reading that includes all the

---

*Throughout this book, names and personal details have been changed to protect the privacy of those involved.

lives you've had in other times that affect this one. But *you* say that there aren't any Akashic records to begin with, that they're only a symbol for something else. So how do you explain that?"

His appreciation of his own astute abilities as a psychic detective was almost too much for him to bear. I let him go on for another fifteen minutes before I asked quietly enough, "What did you come here for?"

He was eloquent. He gestured grandly. "I wanted you to ask Seth to comment on the discrepancies between what he says and what others say. I wanted you to ask—"

"I couldn't care less," I said, with a very quiet but studied ungraciousness.

"What?" he asked.

I stared at him and blew my nose, dirtying another Kleenex.

"But Seth may care," Lyman said, scandalized.

"I doubt that he does," I said. There was silence for the first time since Lyman barged in on me. I said, quietly enough, "You could have apologized for just coming here without calling first."

He didn't even blush. "I thought you wouldn't see me; that you'd be busy," he said, obviously impressed with his own daring. "So I just came anyway."

"I just started a new book, as you came in," I said, "and I still have supper dishes to do, and a Seth session in an hour."

"Can I bum one of those?" he asked, picking up my pack of cigarettes.

The phone rang. I answered it. A young man asked to attend one of my classes, but what he really wanted was help in making a decision. "It's a spiritual, mental decision," he said three or four times, in three or four different mixed-up ways. He wanted me to tell him what to do. I took a few minutes to talk to him, saying that getting other people to make your decisions for you was no way to learn how to make decisions, and was no training at all for any kind of development. I gave him a few simple techniques for clearing his mind, and hung up. Mr. Junior Parapsychologist was still sitting there.

"You're still here because I'm trying to figure out *my* reasons for your visit, as apart from yours," I said. I meant, but didn't say, "How come this guy came to bug me just when I felt that I'd just found my own "true path"? As much as I disliked the pat phrase, it seemed completely apt.

"You mean there's another reason?" Lyman was instantly excited. "Like I've known you or Seth in a past life or something? I knew it. I have to admit that I knew it; another psychic told me so."

"I'm afraid that's not what I mean at all," I said, but he was all wound up again. Visions of grandeur and hope tensed his muscles. He leaned forward so abruptly that the piles of Kleenex quivered.

Startled, I looked up; and suddenly I saw my reasons for Lyman's visit. I realized that through the entire interview, from the instant he'd walked through the door, Lyman had been bigger than life somehow; at least as far as I was concerned. Super-real. I'd been presented—or he'd presented me—with the first character for my book. He was so himself, so impeccably what he was that I could only marvel at his uniqueness whether he bugged me or not. It was as if he arrived freshly out of space and time, self-delivering himself as a package of which he was, of course, supremely proud, but a package that I'd be bound to look at with my own eyes. And he was a fantastic package tied with glowing bands of enthusiasm. I just didn't like the contents.

And I saw why. He was a living presentation of some of my own old fears and ideas, coming just when I thought I'd just given them up. I'd always scorned the idea of Akashic records as a psychic convention, representing something else perhaps. Certainly I didn't believe that some super score sheet of our lives was written out there in space somewhere for anybody to read. On the other hand, before Lyman's visit I'd found myself in a library at another level of reality, and felt it "my destiny" to transcribe and re-create some of the books there.

I'd been doing all this thinking, staring at the freshly minted Lyman, when I realized that he was waiting for me to speak, leaning forward with his great intent anticipatory stare. "Seth and I *are* related, then," he shouted, unable to bear it for another moment. "I had to retain some skepticism, but I've known it all along—" He reached for another of my cigarettes; nervously, as if sure that the revelations of the ages were about to fall upon his shoulders and he wanted to be prepared.

"No, you and Seth aren't related," I said as gently as I could. But I thought: Of course—Lyman was representing my own ideas about something else too; the overly gullible people who parade as skeptics. All many of them need is a word that they've been some big shot in a past life, or known some famous person, and presto, they're confirmed "believers." People like that—like the boy on the phone—never trust their own vision. And up to now I hadn't completely trusted mine either, I thought. Every time I was presented with a Lyman or the Akashic records or spiritual name-dropping, I'd think: Those people trust their visions and look at them. Some kind of integrity is missing from their lives. So I watched my own visions with a stern questioning eye. But I'd been wrong. Those people relied on dogma, not visions at all.

I had to get rid of Lyman so I could figure it all out. He looked disappointed but still determined to stay forever. You could almost hear him crowing later to his friends, "I just hung in there, boy!" To me he said, "You have to understand. I have to track the famous psychics down and compare what they say, and note the discrepancies." His voice rang with conviction. It was an invigorating, exciting sport to him; but he wasn't going to run around my track anymore.

"Great," I said. "You do what you have to do. Enjoy yourself, if that's your thing. But it isn't *my* thing. Okay?" I was grinning. "I still have a session tonight." This time my voice was firm.

He stood up. "You *do* understand?" he asked.

"You bet I do," I said. "Do your thing, Lyman. Just not here, if you don't mind."

But I was laughing, because I realized that in the past I'd often doubted my own vision just because I didn't trust other people's visions. I'd begun to feel that visions themselves were at best untrustworthy, and that the more you believed in your own, the blinder you become to the reality of others. Now, in fact, I saw that there was no need to judge visions at all. They simply are. You accept or reject them. But thank God, I no longer felt that I must be responsible for the reliability of *all* visions, or for how others use or misuse them. I'm only responsible for my own.

And what *about* my own? I wondered when Lyman finally left. What about the library that I'd sensed so briefly before the interruption? What about the book? Was I, as I suspected, at the beginning of a new creative and psychic adventure, or would I back off? I could see myself saying, "I've got this, uh, library in the sky—"

And me answering, "Sure you have, baby. Don't worry, it's *all right*!" Then I thought: Symbolic or not, real in our terms or unreal, a part of my psyche or separate, there's something there and I'm going to find out what it is.

When Lyman left, it was already past 8:00 P.M. Seth was dictating his own book, The *"Unknown" Reality*, in our twice-weekly private sessions. One was due in about an hour. Years ago we'd mutually settled upon 9:00 P.M. Monday and Wednesday. This was particularly advantageous in the beginning—people weren't as apt to drop in during the middle of the week—but beside this, I'm a night person. I can't imagine holding sessions regularly in the morning or afternoon, for example. My mind wasn't really on having a session that night, though. I was thinking about the day's experiences for one thing, and I still had the supper dishes to do. (Rob and I divide our household chores. I get meals— except breakfast—and do dishes, plus some of the cleaning: he does the wash and the rest of the cleaning.) Anyway that day I'd stacked the lunch dishes too. So I went out to the kitchen, finished my chores, and finally sat down with Rob for our session.

My own experiences vary at such times. Usually when Seth is dictating a book, I simply alter my own consciousness, and let Seth "go to it." He takes my glasses off, begins to dictate after a few remarks to Rob, and continues, with a few rest periods, for the next two or three hours. That night things began to happen the minute I sat down for the session. Luckily, Seth described one of my experiences, and I was able to tell Rob about others on the spot, because later, I didn't remember what happened at all.

This was our 714th official session, Wednesday, October 23, 1974. I can imagine how Rob looked, sitting there grinning, because I had a cold; I'd been excited over the "library," and after Lyman came I'd wondered aloud about having a session at all. But here Seth was, coming through almost as soon as we sat down. Almost at the same time, I sensed an odd pyramid effect over my head; a subjective phenomenon that I experience now and then with psychic work. Another fairly familiar sensation accompanied the pyramid effect. I felt physically massive. I'd no sooner told Rob about this when Seth came through:

"This is somewhat of a momentous evening for Ruburt [as Seth calls me]. As I speak, he is experiencing certain sensations in which his body feels drastically elongated; the head reaching out beyond the stars; the whole form straddling realities. Now in a sense, the physical body does this always; that is, it sits astride realities, containing even within itself dimensions of time and being that cannot be verbally described.

"The unknown reality and the psyche's greater existence cannot be separated from the intimate knowledge of the flesh, however, for the life of the flesh takes place within that framework. As earlier mentioned, generally the conscious self focuses in but one small dimension. That dimension, however, is experienced as fully as possible, its clear brilliance and exquisite focus possible only because you tune in to it and bring to it the foremost of your attention. When you understand how to do this, then you can begin to tune in to other 'stations' as well."

As he continued, Seth used my experiences to point up the existence of the "unknown reality" and to discuss other ways of exploring it. "There are inner conventions, then, as there are outer ones," he said. "As the outer mores try to force you to conform to generally accepted ideas, so the inner conventions try to force you to make your inner experience conform to preconceived packaging. There are good reasons for conventions. Generally they help organize experience. If they are lightly held to and accepted, they can serve well as guidelines. Applied with a heavy hand, they become unnecessary dogma, rigidly limiting experience. . . .

"Ruburt has thus far insisted upon his private vision and his unique expression of the unknown reality as he experiences it, so he brings back bulletins that do not agree with the conventional psychic line."

Seth spoke for nearly an hour about "psychic guided tours" and the various kinds of dogmas that can program inner experience. Then we took a rest period. The feeling of massiveness Seth described was still with me. I felt as if my head would go through the roof when I stood up. At the same time, I knew quite well that I retained my usual physical size even though I was experiencing it differently at one level. So when I *did* stand up, one part of me walked around in my usual fashion while another part of me felt as if my head reached far above the earth.

Actually, our break only lasted about ten minutes, then Seth returned and continued dictating his own book. He spoke for half an hour, then said, "Give us a moment." Instantly I went into a series of experiences that I forgot almost at once. I tried to describe them to Rob on the spot, and here I'll have to give excerpts from Rob's notes taken at the time. Even now, as far as I'm concerned on a conscious level, the experiences might as well have happened to someone else. Only the sense of "knowing" and certainty remains. The events themselves vanished almost as soon as they happened.

Rob's Notes
" 'If I can get this, it'll be something, I'll tell you,' Jane said, lighting up a cigarette. She sipped a beer. 'Bob, what I'm getting is . . . quick beautiful sounds that I can't duplicate—very quick, very musical—connected with the spin of electrons and cellular composition. The spin of electrons is faster than the cellular composition. The faster speed of the

electrons somehow gives the cells their boundaries. And
there's something that's in a trance, say, in crystals, that's
alive in the cells.

" 'Wait a minute. What I'm getting is a fantastic
sound that's imprisoned in a crystal, that speaks through
light, that's the essence of personality. I'm getting almost
jewel-like colored sounds. Wait—I'll see what I can get with it.
I want to get it in verbal stuff and I'm getting it so fast. . . .

" 'As the seed falls blown by the wind in any
environment, so there's a seed of personality that rides on the
wings of itself and falls into worlds of many times and places.
Falling with a sound that is its *own true tone*, struck in
different chords.

" 'These sounds are aware of their own separateness, gloriously unique, yet each one merging into a symphony. Each sound recognizes itself as itself, striking the
dimensional medium in which it finds its expression, yet it's
aware of the infinite multitudinous sounds it makes in other
realities—the instruments through which it so grandly plays.
Each cell 'strikes' in the same fashion, and so does each self,
in a kaleidoscope in which each slightest variation has
meaning and affects the individual notes made by all. So we
'strike' in more realities than one, and now I hear those notes
together yet separately, perhaps as raindrops, and attempt to
put them together and yet hear each separate note. . . . And
suddenly I heard my own true tone, which I'm bound to
follow.' "

After the first part, my delivery had been so steady
that Rob wondered if I'd gone back into a Seth trance, minus
Seth's usual voice effects and manner. I'd spoken so quickly
that Rob had trouble taking notes. Yet all I could say when I
was done was, "It's like a note finds its own true tone. But
once you strike it, you know that's it. You've got it made.
You know your own meaning in the universe, even if you
can't verbalize it."

When it was over, I *felt* entirely different, even
though whatever happened had vanished from my conscious
mind. I *knew*, even though I no longer remembered what I

knew. All in all, Seth actually said little about the library itself, but I immediately connected the "true tone" with my feelings when I first glimpsed the library, and with my certainty that I'd "come home" when I saw the books there. I said to Rob, "It's strange. I feel that no matter which way I turn, there's a path laid out for me, and I never felt that way before." Seth didn't come through any more that evening. I've only quoted the portions of the session that directly related to my own experiences. The rest of the session appears in context in Seth's own book.

The library, though, began to assume a reality of its own. The next day as I sat at my desk, I suddenly "knew" that it was only part of a much larger establishment. Then I found myself there, facing a floor-to-ceiling bookcase. It didn't occur to me to turn around to see what was behind me. To my left, though, I glimpsed a library table of light-colored wood. Far to my right was a window with a southern exposure and outside were lush green grounds, though it was autumn and the trees were bare in the world that I knew. Several times that day I suddenly found myself standing in the library, always in the same place.

Later toward evening I put sausage and spaghetti on the stove to cook for dinner and sat down to work at my desk for a few moments before calling Rob for our evening meal. I was looking out our wide bay windows at the street below. With no preamble, I was aware of the library once again and saw myself drinking a golden-colored elixir of some kind. I knew that the drink, taken *there*, was something like an overall tonic, toning up the entire physical body and specifically purifying the blood. I got the impression that this elixir was given to anyone from here who went there, and that it also provided the necessary energy needed for work at hand. As I drank the liquid in the library, at my table here I thought that it looked like honey, only not as thick; and my head, here, suddenly felt very relaxed and loose.

I just remembered something else: While doing the supper dishes later I had the feeling that you could look out that library to our world, and at my particular corner of

Walnut and Water streets—and it seemed that our world was a part of the library grounds.

I also knew, or thought I knew, that some kind of system of study was being set up for me. I wasn't to spend all of my time in the library but would also be outside, in the field so to speak.

My feeling even then was that at some other level of reality I'd entered a college or community of scholars, perhaps for a course of study. In the past I've had no great love of libraries, except that they provide a needed service. That is, I used to think of them as places that had "Silence, please" signs. But "my" library didn't strike me that way at all. More than that, I kept thinking "I've come home" whenever I found myself there.

It's quite possible, of course, that someone else might see flashes of lights instead of books, or experience that same environment in a different fashion. But for me from the beginning there was a library at another level of experience; and I knew I'd be transcribing books from it and re-creating them, and that while I went about my work here, I'd be making my way there at the same time.

Chapter 2

A Private View of the "Super-Real." Models for Physical Reality and Psychic Structures

The next morning, Friday, October 25, I sat down at my desk, feeling that some material "was ready for me" from the library. This time I didn't see the books or the table at all. Instead I felt lethargic and very relaxed. The words that came to me didn't seem to be dictated by anyone. In an almost mechanical fashion, they were transplanted from the library into my head; at least, that's how it felt. The passage wasn't long; I wasn't even sure that I knew what it meant, yet once again I was struck by that sense of perfect aptness. This is the passage:

From the Library

MODELS FOR PHYSICAL REALITY

There are ever-changing models for physical reality, transforming themselves constantly in line with new equations instantly set up with each new stabilization, eternally forming with a blinding rapidity of motion. Yet any one model, whether for a molecule or an entire civilization, never vanishes once it is impressed in the medium of probabilities. We tune in to these models, and our interactions with them alter them at any given point, causing new dimensions of actuality that then reach out from that new focus.

Past plus present equals future. 1 plus 1 equals 2. So it seems, but the 1, 1, and 2 exist at the same time and so do the past, present, and future, though not necessarily in that order.

When I was finished I stared at what I'd written, but the passage didn't really register. It was lunchtime, so I left my desk to do some chores, since I'd planned to go downtown with Rob after lunch. In the meantime I kept growing more and more relaxed, so that I almost decided to stay at home. Certainly some part of me must have known what was going to happen that afternoon, but it was only at the last moment that I changed my mind, got my jacket, and told Rob that I'd go with him after all.

As I stepped off the downstairs porch out into the backyard, I was struck intensely by the beauty of the day—lawn full of autumn's brown-green leaves, each seeming amazingly separate and alive. Most of all, I felt enveloped by the incredibly spicy odors of the earth; the smell of rotting pears fallen from the tree outside Rob's studio, and certain scents rising from the ground itself; evocative yet impossible to categorize. I didn't notice anything else until we'd driven several blocks and parked in front of an office supply store. I waited in the car while Rob went inside, and as I sat there, my body began to feel silky, smooth, and strangely mobile inside as if my mind were skating on an inner ice pond.

Then, between one moment and the next, the world literally changed before my eyes. The transformation was astonishing—all the more because while everything was different, everything was also the same, so that it took me a minute to realize what was happening. The physical street with the parking lot hadn't really changed: The office supply store still sat in its place, and people walked up and down the sidewalk. On the other hand everything that I saw was more than itself, imbued with an extra reality almost beyond description.

We almost always keep a pad and pencil in the car, but I rummaged through the glove compartment automatically, muttering under my breath with impatience, to no avail. I had no idea how long the experience was going to last, and I wanted to write it down while it was still happening. Part of me didn't want to bother taking notes at all, though, only to luxuriate in this strangely altered version of the world, so I just sat there, staring, till Rob came back to the car.

My words fell one over the other as I tried to describe what was happening—and we still had to go to the grocery store. So Rob ran into the drugstore next to the market, bought a pen and pad, and left me alone while he did the shopping. I started to take notes, but at the same time I hated to take my eyes away from the windshield. I could hardly believe what I was seeing. We'd shopped at the same supermarket for years, for example, but the plaza was so qualitatively different that . . . while it looked the same in one way . . . it was difficult to believe that it was the same place.

For one thing, the air and everything else sparkled. Each piece of paper on the walk, or blade of grass, or grocery cart glistened, stood apart with an almost miraculous separateness, even while it was something else . . . beside itself. While Rob did the shopping, I kept looking and looking and looking. My notes were so scribbled that I had trouble deciphering them that night when I finally typed them up. This is what I wrote:

"Suddenly the world appears different. I'm viewing it from an entirely different perspective. It seems far more real than usual, more solid and better constructed. Really, it's a different world than I've seen before and I'm in it in a new fashion. It's like the old world but infinitely richer, more 'now', built better, and with much greater depth.

"Words aren't describing this at all, but people seem fantastic in their uniqueness. No one is bland or 'just a person' in old terms and each person is ... more solid and whole in the weirdest fashion. Each person who passes the car is more than three-dimensional, super-real in this time but part of a 'model' of a greater self; one version of it that adds dimension to any given individual person—or building, or blade of grass, or anything.

"This particular scene with cars parked and others pulling in and out is all imbued with a greatness in itself, yet the scene exists beyond itself at the same time. I don't know how I'm perceiving this, but I actually 'see' this extra reality over the reality we know, so everything in my view *is* super-real and each person's reality is obviously and clearly more than three-dimensional. I know I'm repeating here, but I want to get this down in case I forget; though it seems inconceivable that I could ever forget this moment. It's as if before I've only seen a part of people or things. The world is so much more solid right now that by contrast my earlier experience of it is like a shoddy version, made up of disconnected dots or blurred focus.

"It's as if all the people I see are versions of the same people, say, that were painted centuries ago by the old masters; new versions, yet unique variations of themselves, their own originality altering the models even while their existence rises from them. The city streets seem more solid, as if they fit more firmly on the earth, but the people capture my attention most of all—again, so super-real, each so individual yet part of greater models of themselves which they are constantly changing."

As I watched, I knew that each person had free will, yet each motion was inevitable, and somehow there was no contradiction. This was a physical perception—physically felt—but difficult to describe; but looking at each person I could sense his or her "model" and all the variations, and see how the model was here and now in the person; while the particular version of the model I saw was also present in all of the other versions. I saw these people as True People in the meaning of whole people. Usually we just respond to the current earth person. These people were "more here," fuller somehow, more complete. The sensed inner support of the model gave them additional vitality.

My own physical senses responded accordingly: The world *was* richer, more real, and so forth, because it was also supported by these inner dimensions which filled it out. The streets, for example, were all city streets, built according to an inner model, yet uniquely *these* city streets, sparkling in their peculiarities—Elmira, New York, at a particular corner and no other, precisely because of the model and the variations of it.

People seemed to be classics of themselves. As I sat in the car in front of the supermarket, I faced a group of shops and saw these also as models and their variations; as Arab stalls and Indian bazaars; each variations of models. And the Halloween pumpkin in a window display was fantastic as itself, and as the fulfillment of a model. The same applied to everything I saw.

One small corner by a parking lot I remember in particular. It was lined with small trees. A man stood there, dressed in suspenders, shirt, trousers too short and tight in the crotch. His clothes were old and faded, but he wore brand-new brown shoes. He was smoking, standing there watching the corner, and the sun glittered on his reddish-brown wispy hair. He had a noncommittal yet somehow bold face. I was too far away to see his features clearly, but it was his pose and clothes that got me. He was utterly himself, yet he was a classic in that he could have emerged in any century; yet he appeared here—the model and himself together.

I thought: I'm being filled to the brim; and for a moment I even wondered if it was possible that I'd been fitted with a spectacular new pair of glasses and had forgotten. I knew this was ridiculous, but in that instant it was almost easier to believe *that* than to accept the fact that the world could suddenly be so different from the way it had been less than an hour earlier. It was an effort to write the notes to begin with. I wanted to just look forever.

It wasn't until I finished typing my description of the experiences late that night that I looked at the "library material" notes that I'd jotted down that morning. Then they'd made little sense, and if they were supposed to be part of a book, I hadn't the slightest idea where or when they'd fit into any manuscript. As soon as I reread them, I thought: Of course! The same contents of the world don't add up to one particular sum, but to a series of sums according to how you unite them. And I knew that I'd hopped over a certain series of sums, into another.

I was really surprised, though, that I hadn't connected the morning's library material with my experience at once, because it was obvious that I'd perceived the models that were described; and experienced them, so that they had suddenly become a part of my conscious knowledge. I'd had my first "lesson," backing up the library material, though I didn't quite understand that then.

Immediately I began to make new connections, which I scribbled down at once: "When you get the feeling of the model and your own creative version of it changing the whole thing, then you really sense your own power. You tune in to a fuller version of the world. You're also aware, then, of the power of the model and able to use it. Then, like a magnet, zoom! the two get pulled together, pulled into line, you and your model. A whole new orientation results, with the world and with others. There's suddenly evidence for things that before you had to take on faith—if you accepted them at all.

"The model is the basis for what we think of as the self-image. We keep building our own model in the private psyche to correspond to this sensed greater one, and use it as a working plan. Yet we sense the model also as it exists apart from us almost in classic terms. Once you sense the model, then your own 'rightness' and 'aptness' is instantly apparent, and in an odd way, physically perceivable. You also understand and perceive the aptness and rightness of each other person—or thing.

"It's as if a series of alignments had occurred, or as if the visible world were suddenly lined up with its invisible counterpart, and you realize that before you'd only seen half of reality; half of people's existence. Now the invisible portion fleshes out the exterior to its fullest and supports it. Driving home with Rob, for example, I felt the earth support the road which supported the tires and the car. I felt this physically, in the same way that we sense, say, temperature; a positive support or pressure that held the road up and almost seemed to push up of its own accord in a long powerful arch, like a giant animal's back."

That night and the next day, my own daily habits and domestic ways seemed triple-real to me too. They struck me as immensely immediate even though, or perhaps because, I kept sensing another part of myself in the library. And my library self would think: Of *course*, that's what I do in the world, and that's what I'm like there. So my most habitual gestures seemed familiar and surprising at once.

Had I somehow joined a part of myself who'd been at the library waiting for me? I kept wondering about it, and the library's reality was constantly with me, though in the background, as I went about my day. Insights about it kept coming into my mind. I knew that when you went into the library from our world, normal life was imbued with new dimensions when you returned. I kept wanting to explore the library grounds, to "get there" more clearly and completely. And of course, I wondered how long the whole thing would last. How permanent was the library, for example?

As we ate dinner that evening, I saw myself for a moment sitting at a refectory-type table in the library, drinking that elixir again, and for a moment my own coffee tasted like honey. I sensed my image *there*, my model image, I supposed: My hair was cut in a pageboy style with straight bangs. I wore a shirt, the kind of jeans that I usually wear, but I was several pounds heavier than I am and my body moved with almost instant agility. I also saw an older model. She wore a cowl-type shirt but with slacks of some sort; she was a courier between worlds. Would I look like her in ten years? I wondered.

I remembered "Mr. Junior Parapsychologist" and

how super-real he'd seemed. Had the day's experience actually begun then? And I couldn't get over it, because everyone was like that; classics of themselves. It was as if before, I'd only seen prints of the world, and not the original.

But what about the shift of focus that had tuned me in to the new world? How many other such focuses were there? The world perspective at any time could contain infinite focus variations, from "poorest" to "clearest," each distinctly different, and maybe each one focused on entirely different aspects. How much else was there in the world that I wasn't seeing; what other shifts of awareness possible of which I was ignorant?

In a way, I thought, people alive in our time and space could be experiencing the world in such various fashions that some of them might have more in common with someone from another planet or another reality. A pauper at some hypothetical Focus 3 could find the world richer and more fulfilling than a king at, say, Focus 1. I didn't like the implications of "better or worse" focuses, but I had to admit that my new perspective was far superior to the way I usually viewed and experienced the world. Reincarnational lives, so called, could deal with the same kinds of shifts, I saw, only with alterations great enough to alter time perspective entirely.

As I thought about all this I was vaguely conscious of myself going about my business at the library, and it occurred to me that part of me was as focused there, as "I" was in my reality. I also knew that the two worlds were synchronized in some fashion. But would my perception of the library broaden or deepen? How long would this great new richness last? Would it become the norm, so that I forgot what my old life had been like? With the contrast gone, how would I remember? Or would the whole thing dwindle away in time?

Testing, I went for a walk, and the physical world outside seemed to be an extension of the grounds outside the library so that inner and outer realities were connected in the strangest way. Walnut Street was full of traffic. Usually I walked in the backyard instead, and sometimes in the parking lot that had once been our garden. Now, though, the road and cars and houses all seemed more solid, and even the mountains beyond, which always seemed substantial enough, had an added substance and full brilliance. I walked around the corner and briefly visited a friend. We had a glass of beer and some crackers, and as we sat there chatting, I felt that I was also visiting someone at the library at the same time. Returning home, I felt more solidly in the world myself, a part of the environment in a new way. I used to feel as if I were staring out at whatever scene was before me. Now I was a portion of the scene, moving through itself, yet I retained my own prime focus.

As I stepped back into my workroom, I realized that while I was out, that other part of me had done some exploring at the library which, I suddenly knew, was actually a learning center, fairly well populated. It was a world of mind, or state of mind, where all of the others were in their own way at the same level as myself; a "place" where these invisible colleagues and I would work together. We would eventually be completely in focus with this inner environment, and hence with our exterior ones. We would have one clear focus in which we could learn and do our work. And I knew that though we might be out of phase with other levels, here we were at home. I found myself thinking: Tomorrow I'll really get settled in, and I was as excited thinking about it as if I'd physically arrived at some advanced university. Yet I knew, of course, that the library wasn't physical in our terms, and that it represented a certain place in the psyche which was being materialized at least to some extent in our world.

Others have provided maps for the psyche, but I've never trusted them. Those maps carried the marks of too many name-places in this reality. When you travel through the psyche, you necessarily journey through your own deepest mind—and as you travel into inner realities, this means that you move into another kind of atmosphere, as you would if you were traveling in outer space. In the past, others have projected phantoms of their own minds there, then acted as if these were natural signposts. In my journeys I refused to follow those paths, feeling that they were not safe or dependable and fearing that they might cloud my own view or make me lose my way. These distortions are like debris left behind by physical spaceships: bits of broken flags or discarded equipment that then might orbit out in space.

Only the debris I'm speaking about is psychic. Much of it probably served a purpose at one time (again like discarded space "junk" that once was workable). But to follow it in space would only take you where others had gone already.

Yet I'm literal-minded too, like most of my kind—earth people who deal with objects and the evidence of their senses—and the idea of uncharted space, inner or outer, probably makes us feel dwarfed. Or you think: Traveling into inner reality, what shall I look for? What kind of features? Will what I see really be there? Or will my experiences be a response to features that can't be viewed directly?

I'm reminded of a line of a poem I wrote when I was a freshman in college: "I make my own sidewalk." Perhaps in a way each of us makes our own path, and our own psychic structure that is then flung out into inner space in the same way that a spaceship is launched from the earth. This makes certain exquisite sense: The vehicle for space travel is made of physical stuff, suited to its environment, highly equipped to perceive particular kinds of data in a specific system.

So we also construct a mental framework or vehicle to transport us to inner space, and in my case perhaps the library is like a floating satellite well equipped with earthlike environment that makes me feel at home away from home. It's just as efficient and real as any spaceship and just as practical. And—let me hasten to add—it exists as surely as the spaceship and is just as dependable.

In a way it is even more sophisticated, because I'm sure that its coordinates line up with our reality, and what I see and experience *there* is translated to me here, whether or not I translate the message at once. It's also quite possible, I suppose, that while the library represents my structure, my path, it also correlates with the structures of others at the same level or state, so that in certain terms the library grounds are fairly permanent, constantly created in changed form through the eons.

I was so curious about the library, in fact, that when Monday night came, I was nearly tempted to try to explore it further instead of having our regular Seth session. After all, I was more or less sure of Seth, but for all I knew the library would vanish entirely, never to be "seen" again. If we haven't had Seth sessions for a while for one reason or another, *then* I get uneasy, and I have one just to make sure that Seth is still "here" or at least, still accessible. But after having sessions week in and week out, I completely forget that I was ever uneasy. Besides, I knew that Seth was in the middle of his own book, and he wasn't about to bow out in the middle of it.

Seth hadn't said very much about my library experiences in the last session, though, and I was also curious about his reactions. It seemed to me that he was oddly reticent, and I wondered why. Only after the session did I realize how tricky he'd been, in his own way, and how tricky I'd been, in mine.

The following excerpts are taken from *"Unknown" Reality*, and I've included only those passages in which Seth refers to my library experiences or related ones. Since this was book dictation, it was directed to the reader (rather than to Rob) and the material not given here was devoted to a discussion of altered states of consciousness.

Excerpts from Session 715, October 28, 1974

"I said at our last session that the evening was momentous for Ruburt, and that is true for many reasons. This book [Seth's *"Unknown" Reality*] deals with the unknown reality, and Ruburt began a different excursion into other dimensions last week.

"I hope in these sessions to show the indivisible connections between the experience of the psyche at various levels and the resulting experience in terms of varying systems—each valid, each to some extent or another bearing on the life you know.

"Ruburt has allowed a portion of his this-life consciousness to go off on a tangent, so to speak, on another path into another system of actuality. His life there is as valid as his existence in your world. In the waking state, he is now able to alter the direction of his focus precisely enough to bring about a condition in which he perceives both realities simultaneously. He is just beginning, so as yet he is only occasionally conscious of that other experience. He is, however, aware of it now in the back of his mind more or less constantly. It does not intrude upon the world that he knows, but enriches it.

"The concepts in this book [*"Unknown" Reality*] will help expand the consciousness of each of its readers, and the book itself is presented in such a manner that it automatically pulls your awareness out of its usual grooves, so that it bounces back and forth between the standardized version of the world you accept, and the unofficial versions that are sensed but generally unknown to you.

"Now as Ruburt delivers this material, the same thing happens in a different way to him, so that in some respects he has been snapping back and forth between dimensions, practicing with the elasticity of his consciousness and in this book more than in previous ones, his consciousness has been sent out further, so to speak. The delivery of the material itself has helped him to develop the necessary flexibility for his latest pursuits.

"Clear understanding or effective exploration of the unknown reality can only be achieved when you are able to leave behind you many of the "facts" that you have accepted as criteria of experience. This book is also written in such a way that it will, hopefully, bring many of your cherished beliefs about existence into question. Then you will be able to look even at this existence with new eyes. Ruburt is taking this new step from your perspective, and from that standpoint he is doing two things.

"He is consciously entering into another room of the psyche and also entering the reality that corresponds to it. This brings the two existences together so that they coincide. They're held, however, both separately and in joint focus. As a rule you use one particular level of awareness, and this correlates all of your conscious activities. I told you that the physical body itself was able to pick up other neurological messages beside those to which you usually react. Now let me add that when a certain proficiency is reached in alterations of consciousness, this allows you to become practically familiar with some of these other neurological messages. In such a way Ruburt is able to physically perceive what he is doing in his 'library'. . . .

"He first saw his library from the inside last Wednesday. He was simultaneously himself here in this living room, watching the image of himself in a library room, and he was the self in the library. Before him he saw a wall of books, and the self in the living room suddenly knew that his purpose here in this reality was to re-create some of those books. He knew that he was working at both levels. The unknown and the known realities merged, clicked in, and were seen as the opposite sides of each other.

"He had been working with me for some time in your terms, yet I do not 'control' his subjective reality in any way. I have certainly been a teacher to him. Yet his progress is always his own challenge and responsibility, and basically what he does with my teaching is up to him. (Humorously:) Right now I give him an A. . . .

"Ruburt's library exists as surely as this room does. It also exists as *unsurely* as this room. It is one thing to be theoretically convinced that other worlds exist and to take a certain comfort and joy from the idea. It is quite another thing to find yourself in such an environment, and to feel the worlds coincide. Reality is above all practical, so when you expand your concepts concerning the nature of reality, you are apt to find yourselves scandalized, appalled, or simply disoriented. So in this book I am presenting you not only with probabilities as conjecture, but often showing you how such probabilities affect your daily lives, and giving examples of the ways in which Ruburt's and Joseph's lives have been so touched. . . .

"Many of you are fascinated by theories or concepts that hint of the multidimensionality of your being, and yet you are scandalized by any evidence that supports it.

"Often you interpret such evidence in terms of the dogmas with which you are already familiar. This makes them more acceptable. Ruburt was often almost indignant when presented with such evidence, but he also refused to cast it in conventionalized guise, and his own curiosity and creative abilities kept him flexible enough so that learning could take place while he maintained normal contact with the world you know.

"He has had many experiences in which he glimpsed momentarily the rich otherness within physical reality. He has known heightened perceptions of a unique nature. Never before, however, has he stepped firmly, while awake, into another level of reality, where he allowed himself to sense the continued vivid connection between worlds. He hid his own purpose from himself, as many of *you* do. At the same time, he was pursuing it, of course, as all of you are working toward your own goals.

"To admit his purpose, however; to bring it out into the open, would mean for Ruburt a private and public statement of affiliation such as he was not able to make earlier. The goals of each of you differ. Some of you are embarked upon adventures that deal with intimate family contact, deep personal involvement with children, or with other careers that meet 'vertically' with physical experience. So journeys into unknown realities may be highly intriguing and represent important sidelights to your current preoccupations. These interests will be like an avocation to you, adding great understanding and depth to your experience.

"Ruburt and Joseph chose to specialize, so to speak, in precisely those excursions or explorations that are secondary to others. . . .

"I have told you that your consciousness is not stationary, but ever-moving and creative so that through your life, each of you moves through your psyche, and your physical experience is correspondingly altered. During these years, then, Ruburt's position within his psyche has gradually shifted until he found a new, for him, better, firmer point of basis. From this new framework he can more effectively handle different kinds of stimuli and form these together to construct an understandable *model* of other realities. I will continue to speak from my own unique viewpoint, but in your terms Ruburt is one of you, and his explorations, taken from your perspective, can be most valuable."

Rob read me the session when it was over. I was honestly astonished to discover that my latest experiences were connected with Seth's *"Unknown" Reality.* At the same time, I could hardly understand my surprise because the connections were now so clear. Seth's book is devoted to exercises geared to develop flexibility of consciousness. There are whole sections dealing with methods of perceiving other kinds of reality, and after all, trance or not, I'd delivered that material myself. Yet I'd kept Seth's book and my own library experiences separate. Instead, I was exploring my own unknown reality in my own way, while Seth was writing his book about it. My personal encounters were the other side of Seth's manuscript in some way impossible to describe.

Seth had said that *his* book would show the reader how unknown realities affected personal life, and told us that he would sometimes use us as examples. That I understood. But I had a funny suspicion that more was involved. I'd just begun this book and I was beginning to wonder if Seth's *"Unknown" Reality* was somehow a trigger that was setting all of these new experiences of mine into motion. Unknown reality, indeed! I could imagine Seth smiling almost smugly from some hypothetical cloud nine, beckoning me on, only to find *that* framework dissolving into another, and another . . in some kind of merry chase to find the nature of reality.

Chapter 3
Models and
Beloved Eccentrics

The next morning was bright and clear, with October leaves falling everywhere. I sat down at my table in front of the bay windows to write. The pigeons were feeding on the roof, their feathers ruffled by the wind. It came in bursts, hitting the side of the house and rattling the old windows with their ancient sashes. In between the gusts, everything seemed relatively quiet. In one of those silences, there was a sudden dry rustling sound of crunchy leaves swirling across the parking lot below. All at once I saw myself sitting in the library, looking at an open book, only the pages were flying open and the leaves outside the window were the sounds that the pages made in the library. They flew open by themselves, it seemed. For a moment the two experiences clicked together so smoothly that I accepted their unity without question. Only an instant later did I wonder: How could the real wind outside rustle the pages of a book in a nonphysical library? But for me, the inner and outer experiences coincided with an almost breathtaking symmetry.

For some reason, only then did I remember the poems I'd written the week earlier asking for inspiration and realize that I was getting a whole new book in answer to the poems' request. The library was a gift from the psyche, uniting my experience, focusing it in a fresh direction. I remembered how glum I'd been then, yet in my new creative state I'd completely forgotten my earlier request. I hate to write thank-you notes, but when the soul was concerned, my lack of thanks seemed like some sort of metaphysical *faux pas*. So, filled with gratitude, I wrote the following poem. In it I've made some points about the nature of inspiration that are quite difficult to make in prose. At the time, though, I just sat there and wrote the poem spontaneously as an expression of thanks, filled with wonder at the psyche's ability to regenerate us just when we need it most. As I wrote, fresh bursts of October wind rattled the windows: the pigeons rose in a flurry of feathers and I kept seeing the image of myself in the library. Now and then that self smiled and looked back at me as I sat at my desk.

> *Dear soul, I'm awed.*
> *Did I say once your words were cold?*
> *I take it back.*
> *I wrote and didn't feel you answering*
> *and I got scared.*
> *Then your reply*
> *wrote itself upon my world,*
> *and the letters came alive.*
> *How could I ever doubt that you were real?*
>
> *You seem to send me a series of new births*
> *timed for when I feel my tiredest,*
> *and this one is still happening,*
> *so I wanted you to know just how I feel,*

and most of all to thank you
for your reply, when I reached out,
caught between faith and doubt,
wondering if you were there at all
or just a manufactured hope,
dreamed up in the overworked factory
of a weary mind.

But after I finished my last poem
and stated my case as best I could,
flashing messages
that reached, I hoped,
from my world to yours,
I just felt spent.
Receiving no reply, I thought,
"My soul is remarkably hesitant,
or I didn't explain just what I meant,
or worse—my soul is so aloof
that my plight to it is meaningless;
it can't relate."
So part of me brooded
while a part said, "All right,
if my soul can't be trusted, I'd better know now,
and if I have to make it just on my own
I sure as hell had better learn how."

And then,
between one moment and the next, I saw
a path open up within my head.
It led straight up to the southeast corner
of the living room,
and there, transposed against the white bare wall
the image of a library hung visible,
with rows of books and a table,
not flat but three-dimensional
inside itself. That is, the vision
didn't spread out into the living room,
but the depth opened up
with its own space, so that I gasped.

I watched from here, and there
a double of myself leaned up against the rows
        of books,
nearly weeping with relief,
thinking, "Thank God, that I've come home."
And our thoughts, hers and mine, were one,
so that for a moment I was there
and here at once,
and both of us were jubilant.

That path did something.
I recognized it instantly
as something I'd been looking for,
a magic road of the psyche
that was mine alone,
as if a flower suddenly realized
the direction in which it was meant to grow;
a path not just of least resistance
but of power; as if in annals forgotten
each soul
carries future memories of roads
it must and will follow—
intimate passageways through the cosmos
that belong to itself alone;
and discovers its own true tone
that opens up clear avenues ahead
through cosmic woods that otherwise seem
frightening, and snaps back branches,
suddenly showing a bright clear moon.

But in any case, I knew this path
to be my own,
like a personal signal given me in some time
before memory,
So when I sent out my S.O.S.,
that signal came flashing from eternity,
searching times and places
till it discovered where I was,
and found me just when I thought
that I was lost.

I think
of the nerve ends of the universe,
crisscrossing in a cosmos
of interrelatedness
we can hardly understand.
Then I yell "Help!"
from one corner of a tiny world
hung between the centuries
that sparkle like a million golden cobwebs,
dangling alive and glorious
in some spectacular universal brain—
but that message goes out.
So however gigantic
the universe is,
my tiny plea set it jangling.
And even worlds apart from me
moved, sang, trembled
as my alarm
traveled outward, making contact,
touching the wild neurons
of some overall mind
who then sent help,
as maybe my brain sends
blood to my finger when I've pinched it,
knowing the direct path
through the body's myriad worlds.

But what a response!
for the library didn't vanish
but remains just out of sight,
surfacing now and then
just as clearly as before,
and my double sits at a table
reading a book that I've begun
to translate here.
Once, dry leaves rushing across the parking
        lot outside
were the sounds the rustling pages made
in the book next to her hand,

as they moved all at once
to her surprise, for there was
no wind there,
and here, I laughed.

But in whatever way truths exist,
I know that the books inside my head spring alive,
And that when I'm in that library, I've come home.

But in what sense?
I only know that the path led me there,
and that I'm meant to write those books
and bring them to life inside our world
by an intent
I recognize as ancient and yet new,
Not imposed but chosen,
yet chosen in response
to some natural incline of being
that wants to go one way, not another,
because it knows what's best for it and feels
promptings that line it up
with inside directions of the mind,
or soul.

After I wrote the poem, I kept sensing that "other self" in the library. Sometimes I'd see her sitting at the table. Sometimes she walked to the window that overlooked the grounds, and my consciousness would flicker back and forth so that I would be aware of her environment and mine as well. To some extent her knowledge of the library was imparted to me. Writing about this, I call my image "her," yet I also identified with this library self and certainly on occasion she seemed aware of me.

Through her I knew that the library windows looked out to different centuries. These exist all at once as the library grounds, and make up the environment. The books are written by people who go into the library from their own window of time and keep transcribing the classics, revising them, and creating them anew through their own experience. The books are then produced in a new time and place period. Each new version of any book changes the classic model of it.

I knew that the library was also the materialization of a certain level of the psyche, even as our world is. Only there, time is laid out like space is here. The windows of the library coincide with definite places in our space-time. In our world, these points of intersection may appear as natural objects, and these correlate with coordination points in the psyche. Moving toward these coordination points in your mind automatically lines up your consciousness to some extent with this other reality, and stablizes conditions enough to allow for more or less conscious entry and return.

I knew even then, for example, that the corner of the living room served as a reference point in that respect; but at the usual level of consciousness used by most people, the library entrance just wasn't there. Only a wall. Knocking the wall down wouldn't reveal the entry either, obviously, because it only existed at certain levels of consciousness. You turn your focus instead of a doorknob to find it. It only exists at certain states of the psyche, when inner and outer coordinates line up so that the two worlds merge.

I had the feeling that I'd actually been operating in the library for some time without being aware of it, and in the few days since it first appeared I'd become more conscious of my activities there and here as well. Several times I had vague glimpses of the library grounds, but without being able to interpret them clearly. For instance, *here*, time and space are more or less interdependent. *There*, the elements or time are laid out like space is here. *There*, time expands and the variations appear as probabilities: Instead of today turning into tomorrow, today's equivalent turns into the probabilities of itself—and you can travel to any of these in the same way that we travel from city to city.

I knew all this in a kind of bleed-through of knowledge from my double, but as I looked out of the library window I knew that I didn't see what she was seeing, only my version of it. Every time I looked out, I saw this world.

Yet I realized that with greater training, I could learn to see probabilities also. It was as if I were just beginning to use new senses there, and discovering a different kind of depth perception.

In the meantime *this* world kept changing, but so gradually that I was unaware of some developments until a certain level was reached and my physical senses began to register events in a different way. My sight must have been changing without my notice, for example, because on the fourth day following my first view of the library I was suddenly aware that my area of physical vision had expanded in some fashion.

We took a drive that afternoon and I found myself reading store window signs all at once: that is, I took in a larger visual area. Instead of looking at one store, I'd see several at once and be aware of all the details involved, such as the contents of the signs and displays; where before I'd have noticed these things one at a time. I wasn't making any effort to see better, and there was no strain involved. The world was just presenting itself to me in a new fashion.

Everything still seemed much more solid and better constructed and my body felt as if it fit into the environment in a snugger, somehow more satisfying way, as if it were in a better perspective. It also felt more substantial and in clearer focus. But the greatest difference I noticed that afternoon was in my responses to people. I didn't view them through my personal prejudices. As space somehow seemed wider, so a new kind of psychological space opened up. Until then I hadn't realized how often my encounters with others had represented an instant point of judgment; others judging me and me them; each bearing the full brunt of the other's critical attention.

Suddenly my psychological field of vision also seemed wider, more expansive, not cramped or threatened by others so that I could be more friendly toward them and more curious in a childlike fashion. I seemed to be viewing others from a different perspective, but also I seemed to be viewing a different perspective of them—in which they weren't cramped either, or afraid.

At the same time, I hadn't "given up" my old kind of judgments about people. I could make them when I wanted to, but when I did, I was aware that they actually limited my perception of any given person. I found myself thinking again that everyone was a classic model, yet each was also a fantastic eccentric. I saw a weird and beautiful give-and-take between the person and his or her model. Some people pulled against the model of themselves, almost defiantly, yet using it to create their own variation and original eccentricity. Others imagined the model in their minds as a kind of super-self or as some ideal that could never be achieved, and they tried to whip themselves into shape. Others painted themselves into reality like children going mad with paintbrushes, getting paint all over but having a ball.

I saw that each of us is a beloved eccentric not only because we have inner models of the self, but also the freedom to deviate from them, all of which makes the model living and creative in our time. I saw an old lady, for example; or I *would* have called her an old lady with my old sight. She wore cotton stockings, a brown and green boy-type sweater with stripes, a full maroon fall skirt; and a wide-brimmed young-girl-type hat, with a fake flower on it, over her straight gray hair. She was very thin and flat-breasted, and she dallied along, rocking gently back and forth on her heels as gracefully and unselfconsciously as a twelve-year-old alone on a country road.

She wasn't trying to "look young." Her thin neck was wrinkled, and the boyish sweater, full skirt, and floppy hat gave her the most incongruous appearance: Yet it was perfect, as was the freedom of her motions and the day-dreaming, strange agility of her gait. She was living in herself and in her own model at once, and qualities of male and female, youth and age met in her with such unity that I swore I'd never be able to think of them as opposites again.

I kept saying to Rob, "Look at that man," or "Look at that woman. Perfect!" till Rob was nearly as delighted as I was as I kept trying to describe my perceptions. It seemed that I was seeing people's validity as it existed apart from me and my beliefs, though I knew I created the reality in which that was possible. People's bodies fit more securely in the world as mine did, and even the cars driving past seemed to be built better.

But what did it all mean, I wondered, and how long would it last? So far I'd only "picked up" a few paragraphs of the book that I was supposed to be writing—or transcribing. And what about the whole idea of models? I was vaguely familiar with Plato's concepts about ideals. They sounded terribly rigid to me, assigning all originality to absolute models that we could only try to copy at best—and even then we'd be doomed to failure. I only knew that there was a great give-and-take, a playful elasticity between the models I sensed, and their many versions or eccentricities, as I'd taken to calling them.

And what about the title, *Psychic Politics*? Where did that fit in? I received a few hints the next day. As I sat at my table, once again I felt that "something was waiting for me" at the library. The following few paragraphs came instantly into my mind, and at the same time I sensed that my double was reading the same paragraphs from a book at *her* table. I wrote the material exactly as I "heard" it, and in the same order. I had the definite feeling though that this was like a test run; that the various paragraphs didn't necessarily go in the order given, but served as sample bits of material from different parts of the book so that I could have an idea of some of the areas to be covered.

From the Library
  1.   If you learned to remember and interpret the unofficial messages of dreams, the decoded data would produce a history of mankind far more accurate and extensive than any you have; an open-ended record that would not end at the present point of awareness, but contain projections of future probabilities and provide excellent models for further creative action. . . .
  2.   The kings, queens, presidents, and dictators of the world rise to prominence and power just as the ego emerges from the psyche; vital, energetic, and responsive. So

are the world's leaders as responsive to its people, even when this does not seem to be the case. A country's leaders ignore the unofficial messages of the psyche for the standardized picture of reality to the same extent as do its citizens.

3.   The organized structure of civilization cannot be discounted from the inner organizations of the psyche. If you do not know yourself, you will not know your world; exterior actions will seem incomprehensible, and your private acts seem to have no meaning. . . .

4.   Persons unacquainted with their own power will feel isolated and alone in the private and public world. They will turn the inner framework of the self upside down if necessary, to shake out the elements of power locked up inside and free themselves from repressions that exist within the mind. In the exterior world, this often results in the over-throw of the leader who was the living figurehead for that inner private oppression. . . .

5.   The private psyche has within itself models that clearly state the unique potentials possible for its own achievement. It is, itself, a version of such a model, freely choosing from the infinite variations of itself those probable actions best suited to its fulfillment. Its choice is spontane-ously correct; freely made, yet inevitable. . . .

Psychic Politics—or the politics of the psyche—I was beginning to see the connections: Already, because of my new inner experiences, my relationship with the world and other people was changing. As I read the paragraphs, I realized that the alterations of perception and visions of the library were all parts of the book too: Daily events and the library material would go hand in hand. But again, in what way?

As I sat wondering about it, I was aware of my double working at the library table, now and then glancing out that southeast window at the spacious grounds. My consciousness was in my body and in my double's simultaneously for a few minutes. It was delightful to look out at the fresh green trees and full foliage there, while the sky outside my living room windows was a misty blue through bare autumn branches. As I sat musing about this, the phone rang. I shook my head, probably grimaced, and picked up the phone.

A man's voice said: "Seth?"

I groaned mentally. "No, this is Jane," I answered.

"Atlantis. Delantis. Voom. Voom. Voom " the voice said, emphatically, excitedly, spacing the words and delivering them like bullets. Then, silence.

Talk about messages from strange worlds, I thought, while I scribbled down the "conversation." "What?" I asked.

"Listen. Panic. Panic. They say I'm crazy here. I'm Jed Dare, Bare. Where. Care."

"Uh-huh," I said.

"I sent you a book. About a hook. Baalbek and the end of the world. Symbols. Signs. Lines."

I vaguely remembered. One day the week before an envelope had come, with all the other mail; only this one contained about thirty pages of symbols. That was all. I couldn't make heads or tails of it. "I couldn't read it," I said.

"Well, read it. Now. Now. The fly and the golden molecule. Save the world." The voice paused. Then it thundered, "Get Seth. Forget death. I'm going to save the world."

"Look," I said. "You're on a pretty heavy trip. None of us, single-handed, is going to save the world. And when we think we are, usually it means we're worried about ourselves."

"I know. Know. My destiny is to save the world. I know. Go. Atlantis and the worlds blow away."

"Listen, you aren't relating well—" I was worried for him, but couldn't get a word in edgewise.

"Oh-ho, I am. Damn. Tune it at four. The magic hour. But as Seth. Then I'm going to save the world."

"Wait, wait a minute," I cried, but he hung up.

The next day came, though, so he must have felt pretty good about it. If he hadn't saved the world, I wouldn't be alive to write all of this down. At least not in his system of reality.

But I sat there, dismayed. A week had passed since my first library experience, and I'd enjoyed some of the most fulfilling, peaceful days of my life. Then that strange voice over the phone; another tortured cosmic superstar, out to save the world.

I resented the interruption, yet I knew the man had called for a reason, and maybe if I understood it then I could help others. But what did the call have to do with psychic politics? I really believe that all mental illness is emotional or psychic, an unbalanced mixture of psychological aspects, so that the person lacks a certain kind of psychological solidarity. There are inner explosions, psychic revolutions, as repressions look for a way out, pushing here and there, then emerging in an uprush of energy, throwing out all kinds of previously unofficial data that is often dramatically and symbolically represented.

Those who feel a desperate compulsion to save the world single-handed carry an impossible load of responsibility under which they are sure to break. Actually they're usually trying to save the world of the *self* against their own idea of evil or destruction or sense of unworthiness, which is then projected outward. Then they identify with the psyche's dramatic personifications and a super-self is born, a hero to fight the "inferior" self, in a drama seldom understood.

The visions of the psyche should make the world saner, wiser, more creative, kinder, more expansive. I thought of the book's title again, with the uneasy feeling that I wasn't *just* going to get material from my "inner library," but be presented with some exterior messages as well, and perhaps encounter some challenges I hadn't counted on.

Chapter 4

Rob and the Roman Captain. Models and Reincarnational Selves

So far my library experiences had been private, even though they were changing my view of the public world. I suppose that I hoped to get answers from the library; God knows I had enough questions. But I thought that perhaps I might just "tune in to" the library each day, mentally see the book that my "double" was reading, and then transcribe it here. I'd actually seen little of the book, but I knew it was there, and I imagined that I'd begin to see it more clearly. I didn't realize that the book copy itself would only be part of the affair.

Thus far, Rob had been on the outside looking in, but that state of affairs quickly changed. He became involved in a series of mental events that began quietly enough, but ended up by making us—again—revamp our ideas of personality. The first episode happened on October 27, 1974, only a few days after my own library experiences began.

This was the same afternoon that I saw the "old" lady in the wide-brimmed hat. We'd taken a drive, and I talked constantly, telling Rob how I was viewing the world. When we returned, Rob took a nap while I prepared supper. He lay down about 5:00 P.M. and amused himself by imagining the two of us on a vacation on a yacht in the Mediterranean. The following is an edited version of the notes Rob wrote immediately afterward, for the consciously imagined scenes were suddenly replaced by something else.

"I found myself seeing the bottom of the Mediterranean. I knew that the sea floor at that spot was four hundred feet down. There was no land anywhere, and I don't remember having any awareness of my physical body while this was happening. The vision was clear and in color, but it wasn't startling or super-real. I was studying the sea floor, noting the rounded, rather small rocks, some gullies, and the murky bluish-green color of the water. I saw sea creatures of some kind. They were round, about the size of dinner plates. They were half-spherical and either had protruding spines or were covered by indentations; from my view over them, I couldn't be sure.

"This view didn't last long; a few minutes, perhaps. The next thing I saw was myself—on board a Roman warship or galley. Somehow I knew the time to be early in the first century A.D. I was amidships, looking toward the stern of the craft. 'I' stood at the very rear of the ship, looking forward. I didn't like the 'I' I saw, and I didn't look like myself at all. I was a big man. My chest was wide and powerful, my arms and legs thick and sinewy. I wore one of those Roman-type uniforms where the arms and legs are mostly bare—with a short skirt, a belt, and a vest-type garment. This was leather, I believe, decorated with metal circular grommets. I don't remember any weapons.

"I knew that I was an officer in some sort of Roman regiment or legion. I wore a heavy metal helmet that swept down over my forehead. Beneath my helmet my face was red, very broad and strong, with a square chin. I looked splotchy. No room for much feeling or emotion here, at least of the gentler kinds, I'd say.

'For a moment I think I looked through the eyes of that man as he peered forward and saw twin rows of galley slaves, toiling at their oars. A narrow plank walk or catwalk separated the two banks of miserable human beings.

"In my first view of 'me,' from amidships, part of my lower body was obscured by something—a flap of canvas or cabin perhaps—I couldn't tell: The thing, whatever it was, was too close, as if it were too near the lens of a camera that was focused on more distant objects.

"Now for the third bit of 'seeing.' Off to my left as I lay on my cot in the studio (though I wasn't aware of the cot), I saw just the head of a younger man. It seemed to be floating in space, below my own position, which I assume was that of the Roman soldier on board the ship. This head wore a helmet similar to mine. At the same time I knew that its wearer was either a high-ranking noncommissioned officer, like a sergeant in our own armed forces, or at least an officer of a rank below mine, which was fairly high. The face had a long moustache but was otherwise clean-shaven. Its eyes were either closed or downcast. I knew the head was that of Tam Mossman, Jane's editor at Prentice-Hall.

"Actually this view of Tam, with the odd position of the head and the floating quality, was much more like other visions I've had. The other two earlier ones were much more like 'being there.' The one of Tam was more like a vision and as myself, the Roman soldier, 'I' knew I was seeing it.

"This was the end of the series of images and visions I saw. All three of the sightings had been quite short. I drifted off into more ordinary images, and soon fell asleep."

Rob told me about his experiences at suppertime. Were they valid glimpses into a past life existence, we wondered, or fictional pictures thrown up by the psyche whose real meaning was symbolic and not literal at all? In other words, was the psyche telling a story in images, to make a certain point, and were the seeming events only illustrations of an inner script we hadn't learned yet to decipher? Rob certainly felt that he was that Roman soldier, even while he didn't particularly like the man; and it was the Roman soldier who saw the "vision" of the other officer, who was Tam Mossman.

Rob is more open to reincarnational information than I am, though he is just as critical in examining it later. I'm afraid that I got put off by the kings, queens, christs, disciples, priests, and priestesses who seemed to parade through the psyches of my contemporaries; and by the reincarnational data given by many psychics. It seems that almost everyone has a distinguished reincarnational family tree, blooming with famous historic personages.

I've often thought that these purported past lives of fame and grandeur represent more heroic portions of the psyche, buried beneath prosaic life; I was willing to admit their value in reminding a contemporary personality of its own greater abilities and potentials. Beyond this, I usually thought that conventional reincarnational information only had a dim correlation with deeper aspects of reincarnation that were hidden beneath the psychic conventions.

Rob and I both accept Seth's contention that time is simultaneous, so past, present, and future lives would have to exist at once, even though we might experience them consecutively. We'd often thought that "reincarnational readings" might be fictional representations of actual existences, clothed in drama and fantasy. My reaction has been to throw my mental hands up in dismay, I'm afraid, and I rarely look for reincarnational information on my own or ask Seth for it. In fact, when Seth gave brief hints of his own "past lives" in *Seth Speaks,* I thought: Now what did he have to go and do that for? Is he telling stories to illustrate the fact of simultaneous existences, or is this to be taken as literal?

A year or so earlier Rob had some intriguing experiences with a "past" personality of his own. I described these in *Adventures in Consciousness: An Introduction to Aspect Psychology*, and I was more than willing to admit that some valid "other personality" showed itself through Rob, and related to a friend—Sue, who related herself, as a past contemporary. Rob was curious enough to follow through when any reincarnational data seemed to present itself, but none had for a year—until this Roman soldier episode.

Now I saw the affair in a different light than I would have earlier, though. I began to wonder: Were reincarnational personalities variations of models? Were they different but original versions of a psyche in various time and space contexts? I knew that my library windows looked out to other time periods, even though so far I hadn't been able to see them. Was Rob in his own way looking through the windows of the psyche, and seeing glimpses of one "eccentric" version of himself?

I felt that the Roman soldier experience was somehow connected with what the library was trying to tell me. I was delighted to have more material to work with on reincarnation—as long as it was Rob's, and I did hope that Seth or the library material would provide more insight into the entire affair. But "the affair" had barely begun. The next afternoon when Rob lay down to take a nap, he had the following experiences. Again, I'm quoting his notes.

"As I lay down, I felt a distinct rhythmic rocking motion. It began at once, as soon as I closed my eyes. I didn't see anything, though. The movement—from head to toe, not from side to side—somehow told me that I was lying flat on my back in a small boat, perhaps a rowboat. It was moored somewhere off a shore, and bobbed gently in the sea. The very pleasant rocking continued for some minutes, at an unvarying pace. I told myself that I could see what was going on, but nothing happened. Though this seemed to be a rowboat, there weren't any seats or crosspieces that would prevent one from lying down as I was."

Rob remembered this experience and wrote it down as soon as he got up from his nap. After the rocking-in-the-boat episode, however, he went into a rather disturbing experience, which he forgot entirely until the evening of the following day. He said that it was almost as if he didn't want to remember. Again, from Rob's notes:

"I realized that I was floating in seawater. I was face down. Briefly I felt the salty water in my mouth, as one would in such a position: At the same time I heard the water's soft gurgle, and felt its slap-slap against my head and face. It was quite warm and pleasant.

"My situation wasn't, though, for I also realized that my hands were tied behind my back. I felt this. This meant that my plight was deadly serious. I couldn't have accidentally fallen into the sea with my hands tied, I thought. I had been flung there, yet I had no memory of how I came to be so threatened. In fact, though the sensations of the water were definite enough, I felt no alarm or panic. After all, I knew that I lay safely on my cot, while exploring this reincarnational drama. I wasn't even sure if I was the Roman soldier of my October 27 experience, although I suspected that I was. I had no feeling of choking or drowning, but my awareness of whatever was going to happen ended right there.

"It seems no accident that I had trouble remembering this episode though. If I had (or am meeting) death in that fashion, I might not want to recall it."

The experience had been disturbing, but hardly terrifying, yet Rob felt that his first instinctive reaction had obviously been to blot the affair from memory. The episode triggered another one, however, that was more vivid—and its meaning was unmistakable. This one happened two days after the last; again, when Rob lay down for a nap.

"This seems to be episode #3 in a series of reincarnational dramas, or else it's an example of a remarkably consistent appearance of a certain probability or probable life of mine in the first century A.D. It appears to be the resolution of the life of the Roman captain. . . .

"This afternoon, once again, I saw a succession of images after I lay down on my cot for a nap. Throughout the vision I was seemingly a disembodied observer of my own fate in that life. First I saw a group of five or six raggedly dressed, barefooted natives on a beach of some North African country. I didn't know which one. The beach was wide and gently sloping, the countryside behind it barren. The beach itself was bordered by a steep cliff, perhaps twenty feet high, that ran about forty yards in back of the smooth sandy shore. The sky was cloudy.

"I knew the men were fishermen, though I saw no boats. The peculiar thing was the way these men fished. They stood on the shore and hauled a very long net into the shallow water. The net was perhaps forty feet wide. Each end of it was fastened to extra-long ropes that had been tied onto the four corners. These ropes were what the fishermen hauled on—a most peculiar arrangement, I thought in the vision. . . .

"My dead body, that of the Roman captain, was tangled in the net. I watched the fishermen roll it up in the wet sand, where it lay face up. Now the blotched complexion was pasty white. The body was a massive, very strong and compact one, though not young. The fishermen stripped its uniform off, for all of its pieces had value to these poor people. I lay naked on the beach. Then they rolled me back up the slope to the foot of the dirt and stone cliffs, scooped out a shallow grave, and pushed me into it. In a few minutes I was covered.

"There are additional elements in this series of visions that I haven't correlated. Once earlier, for instance, I saw a body—myself—in the water before beaching. A large tree trunk was involved, one so old that the bark was gone and I saw the smooth white-colored wood, roots and a few broken-off stumps of branches. Now my body was either lying on top of this tree trunk for a while or was somehow tangled up with it. I seem to have an ill-defined memory of both the tree trunk and by body caught in the net.

"At one time my body floated face down with the left arm dangling and the hand turned back, palm up. I showed this clearly in a sketch I drew, afterward. I drew myself lying face down astride the tree trunk."

Again we were intrigued—and curious. Were these home movies in the psyche's vast theater of the mind being shown to Rob's contemporary consciousness? Was the Roman captain another, alternate self, living out its life in a drama happening the same time as Rob's present existence, but on a different channel of being? If so, and if Rob could tune in to the soldier's life, then could the soldier tune in to Rob's existence? If Rob and the captain were both versions of another, multidimensional self, then was it aware of being each of them?

In *Adventures in Consciousness* I introduced what I call Aspect Psychology, theorizing the existence of a source self from which our present identities spring. I call us "focus personalities," because as far as we're concerned, our lives are focused in this physical reality. The Roman captain would be another focus personality, then, existing in another time and place while Rob lives in this "present" century. Reincarnational personalities would be different focuses taken by consciousness as it impinged into three-dimensional experience. They would be connected, however, through their common source self. Theoretically when any focus personality turned away from its usual orientation, altered the direction of awareness, it *could* glimpse those "other lives" in a sort of multidimensional bleed-through.

As we discussed Rob's latest experiences, though, there were several things that bothered us. For one thing, there seemed to be a contradiction, and a glaring one—at least at a certain level of understanding. In his "reincarnational encounters" with our friend Sue the previous year, Rob had pretty well established the existence of a personality called Nebene—who also was supposed to have lived in the same time-slot as the Roman captain. Rob decided to keep an open mind, though, and to encourage such visions in the future. At least we'd have more material to examine and correlate.

In the meantime, Rob mentioned his reincarnation episodes in my Expansion of Consciousness class. A sculptor and artist, whom I'll call Peter, was a regular student at the time. He's traveled extensively, and he had a few remarks to make about the cliffs and the fishermen Rob saw. In describing the cliffs, Rob said that they looked as if they'd crumble if anyone tried to climb them. Peter replied that the cliffs and beach were quite like those he saw on a trip to Spain. They were fifteen feet or so high, composed of soft dirt and small rock, and also set back from the beach as Rob indicated.

Rob felt that the cliffs in his vision were in North Africa, which would be just south of the area Peter described. But Peter also went on to say that the fishermen on the Spanish coast operated exactly the way the fishermen did in Rob's vision. They used long ropes to haul their nets to shore, while they stood on the beach. These were odd, unexpected "correlations"—but within our time period. Would even poor fishermen use the same methods now as those used some nineteen hundred years earlier? So we ended up with some more questions to file away and consider. We were collecting tiny chunks of the psyche's data, like pieces of a jigsaw puzzle, and we didn't know where they all fit in. But we weren't rejecting anything just because we didn't know its proper place, either. In a way, Rob was casting his mind out like his fishermen's nets, while he still stood firmly on *this* shore. Who knew what he'd come up with?

It was on a Monday afternoon that Rob saw the natives bury the body of the Roman soldier. That night we held a regular session in which Seth continued his own book dictation. Perhaps because I experiment with alterations of consciousness so consistently, I keep my various ventures rather separate, just for simplicity's sake. As far as I was concerned, Seth was still working on his book while I was working on mine. To Rob, the connections between the two were quite clear, so that night when Seth started a new section of his manuscript, Rob was more alert to the possible implications than I was.

For one thing, Seth's book wasn't divided into chapters. Seth said that the chapter form itself programmed our thinking in a linear fashion, and he was experimenting with a different, more intuitive organization that would automatically stimulate the reader to react in a new way. The section he began that night was called "How to Journey into the Unknown Reality—Tiny Steps and Giant Steps—Glimpses and Direct Encounters."

If I'd paid more attention, I might have wondered just what "glimpses and direct encounters" might include; and what they might have to do with psychic politics.

Chapter 5

Glimpses and Direct Encounters. The Fly and the Book

The next day as I sat at my desk, I saw myself in the library again, sitting with an open book before me. I looked like I do in a portrait Rob painted of me several years ago, and I was dressed the same way; in a green jumper with a white blouse. As I watched, that "other me" went to the library window, looked out, and returned to the library table. She began to read, only the words sprang into *my* mind, and I typed them down exactly as I got them, as quickly as I could.

From the Library

MODELS AND VARIATIONS

These classic models are everywhere mirrored in all universal systems, and in each they are the ideals from which

all varieties and versions of themselves constantly emerge.
They are, then, the source of all phenomenal life and represent the inner structure behind all forms. They do not produce copies of themselves, however, but new creative *eccentricities* which, in turn, alter the models.

They also appear as the biological working models
of the genes and chromosomes, and they can be affected and
changed at any time through mental experience. They are, in
fact, instantly responsive to mental and psychic events,
through the natural interchange between the psychological
model accepted by the focus personality, and the reflections
of that model through the entire body structure. The molecules themselves faithfully follow both their own inner model
structures and, in their organizational patterns, those psychic
models accepted by the psychological entity.

THE IDEAL, MOTION, AND CHANGE

In this vast interplay of creativity, the ideal is
constantly replenished and expanded through the auspices
of eccentricity; and eccentricity is constantly provided
with a model against which to assert its fresh versions.
A multidimensional thrust is therefore achieved, a give-
and-take between each model and its variations, which is
the basis in our world for all change and all seeming
permanence.

Within this elastic yet supportive framework there
is, then, an order in which all action occurs. Indeed, the
nature of the framework itself causes all action, for the
models themselves maintain their eternal integrity on the one
hand, yet constantly create their own variations. These tendencies are everywhere active, in biological structures and
psychological states, and are reflected outward into the behavior of nations and governments.

In this context, the terms 'revelation' and 'revolution' are pertinent. Each variation upon a model is a revelation which in turn brings about a revolution of a kind; a
change in a previous condition. The revolution makes sense,

however, only in terms of the model it represents or is acting against. The violent revolutions that often occur in the psyche within, or in the world without, are basically unnecessary. They represent an ignorance of the connections between models and their eccentricities; and the give-and-take between them.

Only when this natural motion of model into eccentricity, and eccentricity into new model is tampered with, do violences occur. Only when the essence of permanency is understood as containing its own motive power—out of which change itself springs—will violence cease. Then the motive power within any given model can be released, automatically thrusting out into new eccentricities that are characteristic of the model chosen.

The generations provide us biologically with an example of the interaction of models and their variations as these occur within serial time. The models transform themselves into biological versions, endowed with the basic structures necessary to physical life, and with all the eccentricities possible within a generalized earth model.

Cave man and Industrial man are both versions of a model of man that is, itself, constantly changed by its own eccentricities—and their subjective experience of reality is so different that the respective versions follow entirely divergent paths. Cave man did not turn into Industrial man. Nor is Industrial man a better version of an earlier model. Each chose eccentricities that involved specific orientations within the same time-space framework. Each use the contents of a given earth differently.

Cave man and Industrial man also utilized models of time differently, and therefore have their existence in divergent time systems that meet only at one point in a jointly experienced focus point—the historically accepted era of the cave men from which we think we emerged.

THE POWER BEHIND ECCENTRICITIES

The eternal, ever-changing model is the energy behind its own variations, though through their existence these replenish and reinstate the model. Lining the known self up with its model can be explained as a magic act or as a scientific one, according to your orientation and framework of belief. This recognition of the model by the known self is, at our level of existence, a further creative mutation. Instantly fuller powers are brought into play for effective action, in which the model and its creative version interact with new exuberance.

The known self or focus personality becomes aware of its own source, yet is struck anew by its own uniqueness as itself. The model or source self becomes more responsive, more aware of its own creation, and freshly delighted by the recognition given it by its offspring. A more flexible give-and-take results, in which the joys of mortality are triply experienced by the focus personality because of its comprehension of its own timelessness. The contrast brings a new dimension into experienced time. To some extent, the focus personality and its model or source self coincide; the focus personality is "magnetized," drawn to its model, which is then drawn to earthly experience. Coincidences then occur that line up inner and outer experience so that the focus personality can tune in to other versions of itself, bringing further knowledge and experience into normal living.

Suddenly the book and the library vanished. This was the most material I'd received from the library so far. It came in three separate segments, as given. As I wrote it, I was again struck by its classic nature and inevitability, and by the feeling that the material is true on its own whether or not it is ever accepted by anyone—and even if I rejected it. Seth always speaks to people, and emotionally directs himself to their needs. He interprets knowledge, or so it seems to me, cleverly and beautifully couching it in terms that will intrigue and challenge others. The library material, I feel, exists whether or not we understand or accept it. I am re-creating it and it is re-creating me at the same time; yet in other terms it's like a monument with writing on it, in some other dimension, there for those who want to read it even if generations pass it by.

As I sat there, though, I began to see the idea for this book more clearly. It would revolve around the idea that the focus personality rises out of the civilization of the psyche, taking its form and characteristics from models that exist within the mind as Aspects of our own greater identity. The book will probe the nature of those inner models and show how we choose from them the Aspects upon which we build the physically oriented self.

Once we become consciously aware of the models within the psyche, we have much greater freedom; either to creatively deviate from them or to conform to their mental contours, according to our purposes. Such awareness instantly opens up the effective use of power in our lives, for we're automatically encountering Aspects of our own greater being.

In a kind of politics raised to a higher degree, we govern the country of the known self, with the ego or focus personality rising as ruler. This focus personality can be a dictator, benign despot, president, high priest, religious figurehead, king or queen, according to the nature of our beliefs about the private and objective worlds.

As I thought about this, it became clearer and clearer that we interpret reality in very rigid terms, accepting experience that fits in with our beliefs, ignoring events that don't seem to make sense within that framework, and distorting much "unofficial" information so that it will conform to our concepts.

It's one thing to become intellectually aware of this, however, and another to meet such events firsthand. Each new excursion out of the official context is exciting; it's also an assault on the entire remaining framework of old beliefs. Several days after getting the library material, I was presented with an event that once again intrigued me and yet seemed to send me reeling, mentally at least, into areas that I'd successfully avoided before—because they didn't fit into my system of beliefs.

The episode was preceded by a briefer event of a different sort. I was sitting at my table again, looking out the bay windows at the intersection below. It was a Seth session night, but still early, so I turned around to look at the wall where the library usually appeared, wondering if my double image might be there.

Instantly I saw my double in the library. Then spirals of energy, silver-colored, suddenly surrounded her. There was a lurching in my stomach as the energy moved, circling my double's image until finally she disappeared and the spiraling energy took her place. I could feel myself drawn into the energy too; and for a moment at my table I felt uneasy. I conquered my momentary cowardice just as the energy began moving at an incredible speed. Then I was inside it—or I was whatever it was. It moved to the library window; then was instantly outside.

Everything was giant-sized, as if I were looking through binoculars. "I" was walking up giant stalks. At first I didn't know what they were or what I was, for that matter. The stalks were tall as redwood trees, and suddenly "I" realized that I was an insect of some kind. This was a grass blade. I thought I was a fly in a gigantic forest—a giant fly, because everything was so large and super-real, and I'm used to thinking of flies as small. But I was an ordinary fly, I realized, and this was what the world looked like! Oddly enough, this made me feel better. I didn't care what I was; as long as I was something. So I felt myself go up the grass blade. It's impossible to verbalize the sensations I had, but I remember being aware of the weight of my wings. They seemed very sturdy and reassuring.

By now I was rather proud of myself for coming to terms with these new conditions, and I decided that I might as well explore the environment as the fly. I flew off the grass blade, but this act brought about another flurry of confusion. I flew into the library again, out of it into my physical living room, and then out through the bay windows into the air above Water Street. I lost all sense of having any kind of form, and I can't remember what else happened. I have a dim memory of flying bodiless "somewhere." The next thing I knew I was back with my body at the table.

The episode had been fascinating, and the wild gigantic greenery still flickered in my mind. After that, I certainly didn't expect anything except a normal Seth session, although I did hope that Seth might explain what had happened. In the rest of the time before the session, I did a few chores, then Rob came out with his notebook and we talked, waiting for the session to begin.

First we discussed a letter we'd received that day from a Jungian psychologist. He asked if Seth might have anything to say about Carl Jung for a conference that was scheduled to honor the hundredth anniversary of the Swiss psychologist's birth. Seth had briefly mentioned Jung in his book, *Seth Speaks.* I thought that Jung's theories were far superior to Freud's. Otherwise he'd never "turned me on" particularly. Besides, I had the idea that Seth was going to dictate some readers' exercises in alteration of consciousness for *"Unknown" Reality*, so I didn't particularly want Rob to ask Seth about Jung that night.

Then, more or less out of the blue, I said, "I don't know about Jung. But suddenly I have the craziest idea that I've got a whole lot of information on William James."

"James?" Rob said. "What's he got to do with it?"

William James, the noted American psychologist and philosopher, had died in 1910. I paused, not wanting to take time out from a Seth session. Yet in my mind's eye I clearly saw a book. It was a small paperback; open, printed on grayish paper. The print was also very small and the book was off in the distance. I closed my eyes so I could see it better, and mentally found myself squinting.

I could hear Rob getting his papers ready, and I told him what was happening. He said, "Okay, go ahead," and as the book copy became clearer, I read it aloud. A few times I missed a sentence and had to go back to read what I'd missed. Somewhere along the way, the image of the book vanished and the words just came; quite quickly, so that Rob was kept busy taking notes.

The material was crystal clear and came very smoothly. I spoke in my own voice, using my own gestures, and felt that I was still reading from the book, even though I no longer saw it. It was a book by William James, written in first person, yet I felt the emotions James described as if they were mine; or as if I were James reading aloud from his book.

Chapter 6
The James Material and the Carl Jung Text

I started "reading" at the top of the first open page I saw, which was in the middle of James' book. Apparently I started in with the second part of a sentence which must have begun on the page just before:

". . . that when some people listen to music, they prefer lively pipers' tunes, where others by temperament need a somber melody that with its own brilliant but dark notes reflects the nostalgic desolation that the soul experiences as its own. Not that the jolly [man] is less sublime or more shallow because he listens to lighter, happier strains, but that the person of melancholy temperament must need feel the contrasts between dark and light, and in those read the travails fashioned within the soul. Those travails, dictated by religion's dreary bells, peal through such a temperament which takes upon itself the full weight of spiritual incongruities.

"There are those who seemingly cannot escape questioning in whatever ways the irreconcilable conflicts that arise whenever the soul dreams of God and then projects that dream into the living world of man's society. Those driven in such a manner find it impossible to dwell upon the joyous Christmas bells without hearing at the same time, and with utter anguish, the funeral toll; and [they] cannot watch a holiday parade without at least being symbolically aware of the final march, as with heavy head and lowered eyes bereaved relatives follow the death coach to the grave.

"All of my scientific investigations, all of my most rational stances and posturings were but a facade, in that they represented my attempts to rid myself of those particular nuances of soul, for I strove for a respectable framework in which I could behold myself and others with a like anguish of mind. In that, the dry intellect's weary probing brought me some fame, but no acclaim can be felt as joyful when the mind itself feels like a dry bed of kindling, forever searching to be fired but left instead piled elegantly in a fine hall; never lighted.

"It occurred to me that it might be far better to be of lowly mind, bearing an intellect that did not look for such a lofty home, that did not question so vehemently and so was fired by answers that might seem simplistic to me, and yet could light another, and warm the timbers of the inner home.

"So I wished at times for a peasant's mind, and romanticized the natural; seeing, for example, in a working man's faith the homey joys of the soul that I myself so missed. I abhorred flowery sentimental language, and I strove in my time for a quiet enough prose, yet I envied those who could so easily weep with joy at the sight of a rose, or find the morning so refreshing that it dissolved the nightmares that always existed, for me at least, between the dusk and the dawn."

One part of my mind was engrossed in what I was doing. Another part was quite free, so that I found myself simultaneously reading from the book, delivering the material, and mentally commenting on it. It was almost as if the book existed "somewhere" and that if you read it, you "became James" to some degree, so that his emotions and personality sprang alive. James used entirely different phraseology than Seth or I do. I felt a strong sense of integrity behind his words and personality, and his views were given from such a different viewpoint from mine that I was intrigued. I went on "reading" aloud.

"There are those, and I have written about them, who waken from years of desolation, who are indeed in their own minds at least, born again. All previous questions crumble, and yet the dust of their vestiges forms into a soul's living monument a faith—faith in God or man.

"Yet in rational terms how silly and sentimental are some such visions. I looked, therefore, beneath their form: for their form, it seemed to me, was no more than the bright images one sees when staring into an open fire. I recognized that the sudden element of faith was important: It could be faith in a stone. I examined those doctrines in which others couched such faith, and never did I find a form worthy of the faith, the confidence, or the hope it seemed to inspire.

"Therefore, faith's justification escaped me. At times I myself experienced what I would not publicly relate, as strong revelations. Momentarily I seemed to awaken to a great hope. A great hope seized hold of me, and yet when I examined my own vision I could not find anywhere within it a rational justification for the unreasoning, childish but exultant faith that so briefly showed. I was convinced that, like many others, I held my consciousness in a vice. The more my heart tried to escape it, the more my reason would protest. I was led to believe that the heart's knowledge is directly opposed to intellectual knowing. I was not a warm man; for although there is warmth in nostalgia, it is not heat-giving.

"My brother [Henry James, the novelist] played out his heart's warmth through fantasies; at least that is what I thought then. Basically I considered the novel a form given to gentlemen in which the indelible living pages of the heart were transformed into superficial tales for other men to read, and where the emotions were dealt with second-handedly.

Melancholy written in a passage has almost an ennobling character, but in the heart it is a black blot, as if an internal bottle of black ink forever flows out its shadows upon the soul.

"It is easy to smile upon a child in a child's body, and those artless gestures and babbling laughs have a charm difficult to describe: yet in a grown man would the same sounds strike the ear like senile jabber, so it is difficult for a man to be true to his native childishness. My intellect was my parent—a stern master indeed.

"I said that I was ahead of my time, that I dared speak out to my colleagues in the hallowed halls of universities. I have been praised because I uttered such words as 'ecstasy' or 'grace' or 'spiritualism' in the academic halls, yet I needed those institutions, for their dictates would not let me stray too far, after all, from the accepted knowledge of the times. I did not dare leave the structure of my own bookishness.

"I gave testimony to the emotions of faith, joy, optimism, and ecstasy, and spoke for them firmly—but always in such a way that they could not overtake me. I couched them in terms that would make them as acceptable as possible. I gave them the respectability of my name, while my manner and nature separated me from them sufficiently. I spoke of holy tremors, but when I did my words were firm, lettered, disciplined and controlled—so did the dreary workings of my own intellect dampen the half-kindled fires of my own soul—and so did I myself trample out with firm stamps the smallest kindlings that might have burned.

"I have since learned that the intellect and the emotions together heat the souls of men. The intellect with its questions, used properly, is like one stick rubbed against the soul: An ignition occurs; but only if the intellect's questions are addressed to the innermost soul and not to itself. When the intellect asks itself its own questions, there is but one dry stick, and no response. I sensed the fine unknowable fire of faith. I knew it existed. My life was like one lived in a gigantic dark cave in that respect, in that I could imagine the fire but I could not be warmed by it, and it always belonged to someone else.

"My melancholy was the one constant that represented my yearning, and so I could not desert it, nor it me. It provided its own shadow of warmth, and by its dreary light I at least had glimpses of a greater, less dependable but brighter vision. I saw it, however, not in the experience of those I respected, but in the faces of outcasts, and I feared its unpredictability.

"In my time, 'progress' was the shiny word, and the generation waited with dewy-eyed enthusiasm for technology, the new God, to set it free. So there was overwhelming enthusiasm and great optimism, yet by temperament I basically stood apart. My emotions were natural prey, I thought, to illogic, yet something within me yearned for old ancient gods. At the same time I denied them. I found, I suppose, the shadows in a weird way were reassuring, dating back to a psyche's past; and in all the new rambunctions and rejoicing, I felt the heavy shadows of inquisitions and ancient gods upon my soul.

"I sounded modern, and felt myself, in your terms, avant-garde. I was a man of my civilization. I looked forward, and saw technology as a bright and shining sword appears out of the mysteries of nature to cut asunder the embarrassing heavy illogic of the soul, and to spread before it a clear, understandable, rational world. I confronted the great incongruities that swept all peace from my days, however, for no matter how I tried, I felt the power of a faith that denied my reason, as I understood my reason.

"So I looked for faith in the ignorant and I found it—in them but not in me. My intellect agreed that faith existed and yet at the same time held me from it. Ironically I gave testimony, then, to a faith that I myself could not feel. There were those with a melancholy as deep as mine who rose above it in the flickering of an eye. All contradictions vanished. I marveled. There were those who gave up their illnesses, and I marveled. There were those whose fears dissolved overnight, and again I marveled, and I gave testimony in my books and lectures. Yet in the back of my mind I thought that their previous doubts and agonies must somehow have been psychological posturing—else how could they have so magically disappeared?

"There is nothing as frustrating as a man who clings to his own melancholy, so I despaired time and time again until my own despair became familiar. At times it was even boring. In all of this I stubbornly continued searching for instances of this irrational faith in others, and my sense of desolation existed in direct proportion to the heights of ecstasy that had been reported by others.

"Yet I slid into death like a pebble falling; dropping. For a while no wind disturbed those ripples. Then slowly my consciousness emerged again, and even my melancholy had its own mind. Symbolically I found myself still alive, resting quite like an insect above the still waters of my own desolation. In an image I still remember, I flew round and round, recognizing the peripheries of my soul. I lit upon the shore of myself, and then I took my own form, finding me naked and alive by the pool, dark and mysterious, that represented for me the motion and boundaries of my own psyche.

"In that vision the sun was shining and I was a young man. I dove into those waters of my own soul. There was a languorous, sensuous free sense of dropping into myself, of inner journeying, and the dark richly colored waters were somber but beautiful. I dove with ease, not having to hold my breath, and what had been the waters of my desolation parted for me, and I found myself at the bottom of a sea floor. I was quite aware of myself, yet here for a boy's delight there were caverns and castles, coral mansions, that I knew represented my own buried wishes. Over my early childhood fantasies there glimmered fairy princesses who moved with me from castle to castle, and all the childish delights I had long ignored were mine.

"When I surfaced it was—in my vision—twilight. There was a procession, a procession of the gods that went before my very eyes. I wondered and watched silently. Each god or goddess had a poet who went in company, and the poets sang that they give reason voice. They sang gibberish, yet as I listened the gibberish turned into a philosophic dialogue. The words struck at my soul. A strange mirror-image type of action followed, for when I spoke the poets' words backwards, to my intellect they made perfect sense.

"The divisions I had placed between the intellect and the emotions were my own. I had denied my intellect its gaudy colors and dressed it in a gray robe."

Finally I took a break and went to the bathroom. I'd been delivering the material steadily since it started. Once or twice I was aware of Seth, in the background someplace, acting like an overseer. Otherwise, I was completely engrossed in James's story, even though this was the time usually devoted to a Seth session.

At the same time, I grew increasingly uneasy. I'm always suspicious when some well-known deceased historical personage is supposed to have spoken to a medium or group of sitters in somebody's front parlor, and that goes for my parlor as well as anyone else's. It's not that I consider such communication impossible, only highly *improbable*—not that I doubt the survival of personality either—but I'm sure that the how's and wherefore's are quite different than we might suppose. As I delivered the material, then, I was aware of these feelings too, yet I was determined to continue. I'd promised myself to be freer with my abilities since I first saw the library, and not to block experiences because I didn't like current explanations for them. James's material impressed me. I thought his style of writing was delightful and beautifully balanced. Rob had been interested in James in the past, and I was sure that his interest must have something to do with the evening's events. Once I stopped delivering the material, though, my questions came to the forefront of my mind. "Yeah, Jane, here we go, William James; sure, Jane. Try for George Washington next, why don't you?" Even while I was thinking *that*, I saw the book again, only from the outside, clearer than before. I read the title: *The Varieties of Religious States.*

I'd read little of James, but Rob had read his *Varieties of Religious Experiences*; and of course I was aware of the similarity between the titles of the two books. But I *knew* that the book did exist somewhere, and that I was getting a part of it.

I could get the whole thing if I wanted to! "To hell with that," I thought, "who wants to write somebody else's book?" Even at the time I recognized the humor; because after all in a way I write Seth's books for him. Yet Seth I'm sure is somehow connected with my psyche; so it's sort of like being a part of the family. William James definitely did not fit that category.

I went back into the living room. Rob and I exchanged brief glances of amusement, astonishment, and perplexity. Just as we were ready to resume, I had the feeling that James was going to comment on Freud or Jung. This made me more uneasy than I had been, but I decided to continue. At once I started reading the book again.

"I tried, at least in my lifetime, to deal with the dimensions of the soul. I've learned far more about those inner contours since [death]. I admit I gave lip service to the emotions, so that the soul's dimensions seemed to gobble them; yet as Freud's views are understood, as he left them, I feel that he deepened man's melancholy, substituted the subconscious for Hell, and rearoused lingering demons of the soul that before had been [in] religion's realm.

"Religion at least offered some handy methods that would relieve the spirit's great anxiety, and Freud's couch lacked any of the true deep symbolism. His symbols dealt only with the surface-taught paraphernalia with which every infant is automatically equipped at birth, and through culture. They represent to me local instances having to do not with spiritual significances that ride within experience regardless of training, but instead with the results of schooling that is applied by parents from without. And as their theories stand, to me both Freud and Jung missed the grandeur of the soul, though Jung came far closer in his unending exuberance.

"The soul's triumphs and agonies are beyond the boundaries of sex, and if I portrayed the soul as neuter, not hinting of its true, rich complexity, still basically Freud and Jung each viewed reality through the mirror of their sex.

"We are temperamentally different, yet I have always preserved a distance, so that the great emotional encounters between Freud and Jung still strike me in an unpleasant fashion. I clung to my intellect—as much a failing, I admit, as clinging to one's sex in such an endeavor—yet Freud's and Jung's emotionalism could have been somewhat more tempered with a keen intellectual zest. To me, Freud's intellect was muddied. Jung's exuberance freed him to some degree, yet I found his symbolism cloying heavy.

"From my past this would necessarily follow, for Jung encountered his emotions in a way impossible for me. The breadth and depth of those emotions led him, I think, despite himself to sense the dimensions of the soul. I still feel that his symbolism gets in the way, however, and becomes a too-heady ingredient that can lead to psychic drunkenness, illuminating at the time, but lost in the morrow's soberness.

"I could not for the life of me, *in life*, imagine such constant complex playing of the emotions in grubby dally-ings, yet all the while I yearned for them. Jung played with the most primitive of emotions like a child with blocks or mudpies, yet in a peculiar alchemy, the emotions themselves led him into an understanding, easily and naturally, that was almost impossible for me."

The material seemed endless. I was beginning to wonder when it was going to stop, when suddenly it did. I decided to get a snack and suddenly I became aware of "someone" very emphatic, exuberant, saying "Yes, yes, yes," and I knew it was supposed to be Jung. Rob didn't look too happy when I told him. According to *his* notes at this point he "threw up his mental hands" and wondered if "we were to be entertained not only by one famous personality, but two." I wasn't happy about it either. What was going on?

I sensed my own resistance. Again I reminded myself that I'd blocked material in the past if I didn't want to handle the questions it entailed; and I was determined not to do it anymore. The question of communicating with the well-known dead was one of those questions I just hadn't wanted to grapple with. "Well, I *am* getting something on Jung," I said, somewhat defensively. Rob grinned at me; sort of.

I didn't see a book this time or anything at all, just

sensed this almost erratic personality, and in my own voice I spoke for ... Carl Jung or his equivalent. At least I'd be democratic, I thought, and give him equal time. The words just came; their source seemed less steady, though. They emerged in bursts of explosive rhythm, then became much weaker, then stronger again.

I spoke in my own voice. I didn't feel another personality present, either—it seemed more as if I was playing a record of a writer reading his own works.

Jung appeared much more energetic than James; almost adolescent in his energy and enthusiasm; yet in a strange way he seemed shallow in contrast to James's sobriety.

"Numbers have an emotional equivalent, in that their symbols originally arose from the libido that always identifies itself with the number 1, and feels all other numbers originating out of itself. The libido knows itself as God, and therefore all fractions fly out of the self structure of its own reality. The Father-God and the physical father alike ally themselves with the number 1, and see their magical transformation occurring out of a constant addition, arising from their own basic omnipotence.

"The son, symbolized by 2, feels the father and the number 1 as a threat from which it emerges and from which the son emerges triumphant, grateful and yet rebelling. The 3 is the female principle, which neither the father or son, or 1 or 2, can deny.

"The psyche forms a triangle of 1, 2, and 3, and centered within is the personality, held in focus and yet not in focus by the trine principle. I have been working with higher mathematics, but not remotely—instead, excitedly— computing the nature of symbols with the reality of numbers. The shadow in the male is the 3, and in the female is the 1, and the basic inner encounter of the female and male characteristics give rise to stabilizing and then calming forces.

"In dreams the numbers may appear as words, obviously—the number 1 as 'one,' or 4 as 'for'—but there are great as-yet-undiscovered correlations that exist between the emotions and the numerology of the soul. The number 4 signifies a secure framework in which the male and female principles are accepted. The number 5 can represent the birth of a new instability in the personality when it appears in dreams, for it represents an over-swelling of the male or female element, so that overall stability is again endangered.

"These numbers, held unconsciously, as I now believe, have cellular connections that determine bodily health, and serve as unconscious clues to specific diseases or healings. I am presently convinced, at least, that the predilection toward a specific 1 or 3 held unconsciously by a woman about to conceive will bring about conditions bearing on the sex of the child.

"Arrogance and dependency—two faces—also involve the 1 and 3, and the type of illness chosen will have to do with a minus quality; the 1, signifying maleness, unrecognized, might entail a stress disease even when all exterior conditions would seem against it."

Numerology is a subject in which I have little interest. I delivered the material—discussing what Jung "said" were some of his ideas since his death; but another part of me was bored. I thought, "If this guy's been dead for twenty years or whatever, it seems he could come up with better ideas than this." Yet my feelings didn't seem to impede the material I was delivering one whit.

"Prostate diseases I now believe to represent denied female tendencies. It seems quite clear to me at least now that a magical type incantation of numbers could be used as an unconscious healing process, even if the patient was not told the reason behind the exercise. I am also convinced that certain illnesses begin and end on certain dates for the same reason, though this is simply put, and that the power of astrology has far other roots than currently supposed.

"My excitement with some of these theories grows. I realize it is impossible to tell you what I am learning, but I have discovered the emotional validity of cells. The mind's symbols spring in part at least from this cellular atmosphere, which at birth is generally though not always clear.

"In a primitive emotional structure the cells

emerge in an intelligent medium, far different than anything I surmised before. I did not understand the immediate direct correlation between the self and the mass unconscious, or thoroughly comprehend the instant response with which they meet."

Once more, the material promised to be endless. It was nearing midnight. I decided to stop and immediately the material came to an end. I remember Rob's face, though, when we sat there just afterward; it looked worried. "I'm uneasy about all this," he said. "Really uneasy."

I said, "Let's go to bed. We'll figure it out tomorrow," but by the time I reached the bedroom, I was more troubled than I had been earlier. I was upset because Rob was. If *he* was upset, I thought, then maybe I really had something to worry about. Troubled, huddled up under the blankets I caught myself thinking, "Great, Jane. What have you gone and done now?" For a minute it seemed that all of my fears had come home to roost: I was just another batty lady conversing with the leagues of the honored dead.

No matter how I looked at it, I didn't believe that James or Jung was speaking to me or though me; yet Rob told me that the James material was really terrific. So what did it all mean? Did I just want to impress a group of psychologists? Well, that wouldn't work, I thought angrily, because I wasn't going to send them any of the material for the conference.

Yet . . . I could see that James book in my mind's eye and I knew that it was a fascinating manuscript. I thought, sitting up, that I could get the book and then present it as a creative device; call it an imaginative projection, or even, "An Imaginative Interview with William James." On that basis alone, it would be legitimate. I could never present it as, well, as anything else, I thought. And then I remembered how tempted I was in the beginning to just write about Seth's ideas as if they were mine in ordinary terms, so that I wouldn't have to grapple with the problems of doing otherwise. I kept seeing that "damned book" in my mind. It intrigued me; but then, books always do.

That night Rob and I both went to bed, troubled.

We had no idea what the implications of that James material were, and we certainly didn't realize that in a strange way it was a cornerstone, connecting Seth's book to mine, and mine to his. Seth's later explanation and further information from the library literally brought to light a new way of looking at the psyche's relationship with life and death.

Chapter 7

More from the Library. Seth Explains the James Material and Introduces "World Views"

The next day, Tuesday, I sat down to write at my table, but my mind was on that evening's "psychic class" when I wasn't trying to come up with an acceptable explanation for the James-Jung events of the night before. No sooner did I sit down, though, when I began getting material from "my library book." I took the material down directly on the typewriter:

From the Library

MODELS FOR CREATIVITY

The essence of man is not destroyed. Neither is it held in static form, preserved like a spiritual mummy in some

museum of souls. Instead, after death a man's or woman's
essence continues its experiences, though a different model
of existence is followed, a different frame of reference
chosen, and another version of psychological being is pursued.

The present model for physical life precludes any
easy mixing of the living and the dead, any casual encounters
between those in flesh and out of it as a common occurrence.
This was not always the case, for at one time the dead and
living mixed far more openly. Man's consciousness chose to
focus upon ever-increasing specifics in terms of time, however, and gradually closed out the reference points in which
such encounters could occur.

In the previous wider reference there was enough
leeway for corporal and noncorporal experiences to intersect
in space under certain conditions. The closer time reference
chosen closed this gap, requiring on the part of the dead a
specific focus they could not easily achieve in order to make
their presence felt.

The path of the living and dead become divergent.
Earlier, however, the dead continued to instruct—parents
returning to their children, and dead travelers returning to
their tribes, telling of their journeys. In this way, for mil-
lennia, knowledge was passed on through the centuries. Man's
consciousness was more flexible and accommodating, yet
while it operated in that manner, the possibilities for more
specific experience and more precise focus remained latent.
Man gradually altered the focus of his consciousness, perceiving as real only those phenomena that fell within a
particular range, bringing into actuality levels of physical
experience to which he had been blind earlier, and gradually
becoming opaque to other stimuli which he had once perceived clearly.

Encounters with the dead then became blurred,
occurring in dream states; which always represent other areas
of consciousness dimly perceived but not accepted as official
reality. When this happened, the dead became colored with
the symbolism of dreams also, for when symbols operate,
they are always signs of a reality not directly, but opaquely
perceived.

These ancient psychological pathways of consciousness still lie latent, however, operating as alternate possibilities and ruling certain neurological pathways that have been largely abandoned. Some persons have greater memory than others of such abandoned avenues of perception, and through the ages have used them to increase their own knowledge and to view physical life from a different perspective. Generally, however, these roads became bypaths, thickly cluttered with overgrown ancient memories and strewn with psychic statues, as it were, that once had meaning and served as guideposts between the living and dead.

These pathways are traveled in dream states, but there again they are paved with symbols. These serve as methods of communication and yet also operate as barriers, keeping apart various levels of reality. The dead and the living in your time speak opaquely then, through dreams and symbols, for the model for reality that you have chosen precludes the dead's more expansive view.

Even then, in dream states you come alive to your native consciousness, and in periods of revelation and inspiration you open those paths of the mind when it is safe enough to turn momentarily from the specific focus of waking life. That focus requires a finely tuned precision in time orientation; instant response that requires your attention.

The inner portion of the self, the psyche, however, follows that other model which serves as a supportive framework for the conscious life you know. The creative mind functions basically in accordance with this freer perception, seeking its associations outside the recognized time framework, ranging far wider in its travels and drawing for its purposes from the knowledge and experiences of the race as a whole—as it exists in and out of time. This data is then used with new creativity, further altering the physical model of existence.

The creative mind itself, then, rebels against too rigid a focus, and searches through the centuries while the body is still clothed in time. Yet it searches precisely because of the body's physical orientation, in order to illuminate the nature of its existence. In the world of the creative mind there is little difference between the living and the dead. Ideas are freely exchanged between them in a commerce that forms much of the world you know.

This commerce is continual, though couched in symbolic form that serves to veil the original encounters so that the necessary separation in focuses can still be maintained. Intent, emotional intensity, and personal characteristics dictate this commerce and open the lines of communication that exist, connecting mind and mind.

There is a constant give-and-take not only between the living and dead, but with the living and those portions of the psyche that exist in noncorporal form; between the "living" and the "dead" portions of the self, then. Yet symbolism remains as the language of this commerce. Its rich and varied structure allows it to handle the weight of greater theoretical structures that your focus necessarily precludes.

Attempts to make this commerce literal, to bring these encounters down to earth, fail miserably because denied the symbols, the range of that reality cannot be contained in the usual dimensions of your lives as you understand them, and contradictions instantly seem to occur. The realities don't mix smoothly: Rough edges show and the dead then appear as caricatures of themselves, less dimensional than you, while stripped of the multidimensionality of their own state.

If symbolism is understood to be a language, then it can be used by both the living and the dead, and seen as a structure in which such encounters can occur—but these are encounters of mind, as states of being move closer to each other with symbolism a bridge between.

Mankind views physical life as exteriorized and outside of the context of mind. Yet the universe is the three-dimensional projection of minds' activity. The phenomenal world springs into being in accordance with inner models. Infinite versions of these bridge the gap between the invisible and the visible, taking physical form and then returning to the inner models in which their overall vitality resides.

These models are themselves conscious, not operating as dead ideals but as every-changing structures, carrying within themselves as inviolate integrity which is not threatened but strengthened through change and eccentricity. So all men and women living exist as completely in the inner world as in the outer, and each smallest feature within physical reality has its inner counterpart from which it emerges. Within and without, there is constant change and fluctuation—yet always in response to the model which responds to its own eccentricities.

Therefore this book, not yet completed in your time, exists in a library that is a model for the libraries that you know; and yet in your terms this book is also an eccentricity, for it is not a copy but a new edition, completely recreated, while holding within itself the kernal of its own integrity.

The creation of this book is original in that it has not existed in this form before in your world, yet it is also written in response to its model; and the same applies to all creativity.

When the material stopped I read it over and saw that it was a partial explanation for the disturbing James material of the night before. Then another idea came to me. I started laughing, because it suddenly occurred to me that I'd tuned in to my library during the latest Seth session, but had picked up the wrong book—one that "belonged" to James instead of me. Maybe *Varieties of Religious States* was a model of a book James intended to write.

I still didn't connect any of this with the book that Seth was dictating, though, until we held our next regular session the following night. This session seemed to pin Seth's book and this one together, and it became apparent that my own experiences were giving me personal examples of Seth's theories and in the same order as he was delivering them in *"Unknown" Reality.*

In this particular session he began his first discussion of "world views," which was to be one of the cornerstones of his own manuscript. It would also serve to open up my experiences by providing me with a new framework in which to explore the reality of after-death perception. The

entire session ran twelve typewritten pages, but here I'm only
including those portions pertinent to the James material. The
session was part of book dictation and is directed to the
reader.

  "This section [of *"Unknown" Reality*] deals with
the various exercises that will hopefully provide you with
your own intimate glimpses into previously unknown realities.

  "I said that your normal focus of consciousness
can be compared to your home station. So far, exercises have
been described that will gently lead you away from concen-
tration upon this home base, even while its structure is
strengthened at the same time. You can also call this home
station or local program your world view, for from it you
perceive your reality. To some extent it represents your personal focus, through which you interpret most of your
experience. As I mentioned, when you begin to move away
from that particular organization, strange things may start to
happen. You may be filled with wonder, excitement, or perplexity. You may be delighted or appalled, according to
whether or not your new perceptions agree or disagree with
your established world view.

  "Instead of a regular session [last Monday night],
the framework of the session was used in a new kind of
exercise. It was meant as an example of what can happen
under the best of circumstances when someone leaves a
native world view and tunes in to another, quite different
from the original.

  "You always form your own experience. Ruburt
tuned in to the world view of a man known dead. He was not
directly in communication with William James. He was
aware, however, of the universe through William James's
world view. As you might tune in to a program on a television set, Ruburt tuned into the view of reality now held in
the mind of William James. Because that view necessarily
involved emotions, Ruburt felt some sense of emotional
contact—but only with the validity of the emotions. Each
person has such a world view, whether living or dead in your

terms, and that 'living picture' exists despite time or space. It *can* be perceived by others.

"Each world view exists at its own particular 'frequency,' and can only be tuned in to by those more or less within the same range. The frequencies themselves, however, have to be adjusted properly to be brought into focus, and those adjustments necessitate certain intents and sympathies. It is not possible to tune in to such a world view if you are basically at odds with it. You simply will not be able to make the proper adjustments.

"Ruburt has been working with alterations of consciousness and wondering about the basic validity of religion. He has been trying to reconcile intellectual and emotional knowledge. James was far from one of his favorite writers, yet Ruburt's interests, intent, and desire were close enough so that under certain conditions he could experience the world view held by James. The unknown reality is unknown only because you believe that it must be hidden. Once that belief is annihilated, then other quite as legitimate views of reality can appear to your consciousness, and worlds quite as valid as your own swim into view. To do this, you must have faith in yourself, and in the framework of your known reality. Otherwise you will be too afraid to abandon even briefly the habitual, organized view of the world that is your own. . . .

"Ruburt tuned in to William James's world view because their interests coincided. A letter from a Jungian psychologist helped serve as a stimulus. The psychologist asked me to comment about Jung. Ruburt felt little correspondence with Jung. In the back of his mind he wondered about James, mainly because he knew that Joseph [Rob] enjoyed one of James's books. . . .

"It is quite possible to tune in to the world view of any person, living or dead in your terms. The world view of any person, even one not yet born from your standpoint, exists nevertheless. Ruburt's experience simply serves as an example of what is possible. Quite rightly he did not interpret the event in conventional terms, and Joseph did not suppose that James himself was communicating in the way usually imagined. . . .

"James was not aware of the situation. For that matter, James himself is embarked upon other adventures. Ruburt picked up on James's world view, however, as in your terms, at least, it existed perhaps ten years ago. Then in his mind James playfully thought of a book that he would write were he 'living,' called *Varieties of Religious States*—an altered version of a book he wrote in life.

"He felt that the soul chooses states of emotion as you would choose, say, a state to live in. He felt that the chosen emotional state was then used as a framework through which to view experience. He began to see a conglomeration of what he loosely called religious states, each different and yet each serving to unify experience in the light of its particular 'natural features.' These natural features would appear as the ordinary temperaments and inclinations of the soul.

"Ruburt tuned in to that unwritten book. It carried the stamp of James's own emotional state at the 'time,' when he was viewing his earthly experience, in your terms, from the standpoint of one who had died, who could look back and see where he thought his ideas were valid and where they were not. At that point in his existence, there were changes. The plan for the book existed, and still exists. In Ruburt's 'present,' he was able to pick up this world view as expressed within James's immortal mind. To do this, Ruburt had to be free enough to accept the view of reality as perceived by someone else. . . . Ruburt allowed one portion of his consciousness to remain securely anchored in its own reality while letting another portion soak up, so to speak, a reality not its own. . . .

"Such creative 'architect's plans' are often picked up by others unknowingly, altered or changed, ending up as entirely new creative productions. Most writers do not examine their sources that closely. The same applies, of course, to any field of endeavor. Many quite modern and sophisticated developments have existed in what you think of now as past civilizations. The plans or models were picked up by inventors, scientists, and the like, and altered to their own specific directions, so that they emerged in your world not as copies, but as something new. . . ."

In the rest of the session Seth elaborated on the whole concept of the world view, particularly as it can be perceived through intuitions, automatic writing, and creative inspiration. He stressed that tuning in to world views could be extremely beneficial, adding to knowledge and also providing practical solutions to problems. More to the point of our immediate concerns, though, he cleared up some questions we were asking about historic personages popping up in numberless living rooms, communicating through a medium's trance state or through the Ouija board.

He said, for example: "Many people working with the Ouija board or automatic writing receive messages that seem, or purport, to come from historic personages. Often, however, the material is vastly inferior to that which could have been produced by the person in question during his or her earthly existence. Any comparison with the material received to the written books or accounts already existing would immediately show glaring discrepancies. Yet in many instances, the Ouija board operator or the automatic writer is to some extent or other tuning in to a world view, struggling to open roads of perception free enough to perceive an altered version of reality, but not equipped enough through training and temperament, perhaps, to express it. . . .

"The most legitimate instances of communication between the living and the dead occur in an intimate personal framework in which a dead parent makes contact with its offspring; a husband or wife freshly out of physical reality appears to his or her mate. But very seldom do historic personages make contact except with their own intimate circles."

Seth expanded on all these topics during that session, which is included in its proper place in *The "Unknown" Reality.* I've had some other experiences with world views since, as a result of following Seth's suggestions as he outlined them that night. At the time, though, Rob and I were really grateful for Seth's explanations since it cleared up issues that we'd wondered about off and on for years.

Seth didn't mention the Jung material and we forgot to ask him about it. I don't feel that I responded to

Jung as well as I did to James (in the context of the experience). In fact I think I was somewhat antagonistic. I kept wanting to say, "Come on, slow down a minute so I can get this straight." Or, "You *must* have more to say than that." I assume this was as much a world view as James's material was, but it was a much more emotional one. James's were somehow remembered emotions, while Jung seemed very anxious and eager. Perhaps I picked up only a part of Jung's world view—a strong emotional element—so vital that I responded emotionally too.

I was still intrigued by James's book though—it was so easy to "see," that I enjoyed the directness and simplicity of the method used. All I had to do was close my eyes, bring the book closer, and read it aloud so that Rob could copy it down. It's true that James's emotions did bleed through the words to some degree, as if the letters themselves spoke with a nostalgia or melancholy of their own. But Jung's emotional state seemed like a bouncing rubber ball, hard to follow.

After Seth's session, Rob and I just sat staring at each other. My own library material explained my James experience in one way, and Seth explained it from another angle. When Seth spoke—particularly about communication with the dead—he sounded amused and compassionate at once, while there was no emotion ever implied with my own library material as far as I could tell. It just seemed to "be there" with no personality attached, not caring whether or not I understood it, like a message on a blackboard.

Chapter 8
Unofficial Contents
of the Mind

I'd been writing down all my experiences, carrying on with my classes, and continuing with life's normal routines. By Sunday I was ready to go for a long-ride and get out into that clear autumn air and sunshine. Yet then, precisely when I felt so relaxed, I suddenly felt some new material from "the library book." I sat down at my table, listening to the leaves rustling everywhere outside, and began to write down the words that dropped so easily into my head. This particular material was quite important to relation to later concepts, yet I took it down half humming under my breath and with a sense of great inner play and exuberance.

From the Library

THE PHYSICAL UNIVERSE AS A TRIUMPH OF ECCENTRICITIES

Model Universes:

These models can be considered as entities with a propensity for pattern-forming; aware-energy, eccentricitized out of itself as it emerges from unrealization into realization, from undifferentiation into differentiation. The structures within our universe are eccentricities seen in that light; specific versions of an inner model. Time, space, matter—all of these specific references are eccentric variations that make our world uniquely itself, even while they rise out of a universal model that also makes all other versions and eccentricities possible.

Because we experience time, then it follows that time exists in as many other versions as possible in other universes. The electron's spin here is eccentric behavior, appearing here as model behavior only because it is the eccentricity we recognize as real. The private earthly sensate experience of each of us exists precisely because of the eccentricities manifested in our particular model of the universe.

These models can also be thought of as the intent that energy takes, the creative inner potential for form, the pattern for fulfillment inherent in energy itself as it sprawls out of itself constantly into differentiation. The eccentricities are the models' physical shapes, at least in our universe. They are the particular individualized waves or knots or "disturbances" appearing out of undifferentiation—consciousness congregating and coming forth in a pattern or model that is merely a suggestion through which its eccentricities can make themselves known.

Since everything actually happens at once, with an orderly abandon almost impossible to describe, then the models and their eccentricities are manifest and unmanifest "at the same time," and time itself is simply one version that infinity takes. The versions of the models affect and change the models themselves. The variations then form their own new patterns which, again, exist in the manifest and unmanifest alike.

We speak of matter and antimatter and of right- and left-handed universes, but all variations or degrees occur between these extremes, yet all are connected through the all-pervasive model of the universe which is manifest in each version. In other words, our world is one of reality's signatures, written indelibly in our experience and environment. But it is only one of many such signatures.

If we could see the features of our reality as eccentricities or variations of a model, then we could at least be on the lookout for other versions, even if we only considered the alternate patterns that sometimes show up in our world—the unofficial happenings, the latent bulges, psychological or physical, that ripple gently beneath usual experience but don't appear as definite features of mind or matter.

Such psychological or psychic "bulges" or unrecognized features, such as telepathy or clairvoyance or telekenesis all suggest other ways of dealing with space and time. In some other systems of reality these may represent normal psychological behavior. A completely different kind of model of the universe would be used under such circumstances; and literally experienced.

When the material stopped, I read it over and noticed that a change had taken place. Before, the copy had often referred to people at large as "you." Now the pronouns "us" and "we" were being used almost exclusively, as if my own consciousness was translating the book at the library end, or as if two lines of consciousness had somehow been merged.

There's little doubt that our idea of the universe changes as we become aware of some of the unofficial properties of the mind. Even our experience with the universe changes. In an odd way, we might move into another version of reality, while still sharing with others the same general mass contents of the world. Maybe we just use those contents differently.

I'd known that I could be aware of the actions of

people apart from me in space. I could no longer accept a model of the universe that limits perception to the interaction of the physical senses with space and time. So I'd been seeing reality in a different way. More "bulges" or features were apparent to me, yet I had no great interest in precognition. Certainly I made no effort to poke into people's lives psychically. This library material fascinated me, though. I began to wonder about the contents of our minds. How much unofficial knowledge did they hold, and in what form? Were there different ways of putting reality together—ways that were practical enough to make sense at the physical level?

Without making any decision to experiment, I did take advantage of a few opportunities that almost immediately presented themselves. Both involved telephone calls.

Now and then someone contacts me asking me to locate a missing person. Usually I concentrate on our books and don't get involved with such cases. For one thing, I don't like the idea of tracking anyone down for any reason, and if someone leaves home there is usually a good cause. But this particular day a mother called, very upset. Her teen-age daughter, whom I'll call Anna, had disappeared. Barbara—the mother—was particularly worried because Anna had only recently recovered from a major operation, and needed rest even though she was well enough to attend school. In the beginning of her call, Barbara was crying. I calmed her down by asking her to spell her name for me—twice. She sounded to be in her early fifties; embarrassed about calling me, ready to be belligerent and defensive if I objected—yet all the while feeling that she had no right to take up my time.

Mostly, though, she was angry at Anna, who'd stayed out defiantly until five in the morning the Friday night before her disappearance. Then, after a family argument, she'd been grounded for the weekend. Her mother weakened enough to let her out that Saturday afternoon, though, and Anna had never returned. She'd been gone over five days. I felt that Anna probably knew what she was doing, yet Barbara was terribly worried that the girl may have met with foul play.

I told Barbara to give me a minute, then I lit a cigarette and let my mind wander. Were Barbara's present activities in the contents of my mind, mixed in with a million other details? Would my conscious request to know her circumstances unravel the bits of information I wanted? Then smoothly, from nowhere in particular, came the name Larry. Barbara said that she didn't know the names of many of Anna's friends. Larry meant nothing to her, but she herself knew a Clary. I tried again. "An uncle Arnold is important to her," I said.

At first Barbara didn't say a thing. Then she said, slowly, "Why, yes. Anna lived with her Uncle Arnold when she was a little girl. In Mexico. But that was a long time ago."

I nodded, forgetting she couldn't see me. But at least I'd picked up some definite information. Then I got something else. "This sounds silly, but I'm getting a word, like Fresca."

"That was her favorite Spanish drink, in Mexico," Barbara said. "She loved it."

By then I felt more confident. "I get a strong connection with numbers," I said, and Barbara told me that Anna was having serious difficulties with her bookkeeping class because she'd fallen behind during her school absence.

Then the word "crockery" came to me. It made no sense to Barbara at all, so I followed it through mentally to myself. This led me from crockery to glass to the name Glassner—which I then said aloud. Barbara then told me that Anna's best friend was a girl whose last name was Glassen.

By this time I was convinced that my impressions were actually pertinent. Only then did I ask myself mentally where Anna was and when she would return. I told her mother that the girl was all right and had met with no crime or accident. She was thirty minutes or thirty miles away and would call when her anger faded. She'd be home safely in the very near future. I also gave a few more names, though at the time they meant nothing to Barbara.

She hung up, very relieved. I hung up—and started worrying.

Suppose, just suppose, the girl really had met with

a bad accident—or worse, suppose she was dead? Surely it would be easy for me to be correct about certain events and then block dire ones from my awareness. Suppose I'd built Barbara up, only to have the very hard facts of life knock her down again, confirming her worst fears? I sincerely wished that she hadn't called.

At the same time, I stared at the impressions I'd scribbled down as I was talking, and remembered the library material. How much of the contents of the world were in the contents of the "private" mind; hidden, nearly invisible, but present? Uncle Arnold was certainly a specific enough impression, and it applied directly to Anna. If I'd said Uncle Joe or Pete, even, I wouldn't have considered the impression anything special because the names are so common. Yet there was a song popular at the time, with the words "Uncle Arnold" prominent. I'd heard it often* Had I simply picked the words up out of my own experience, and did they just happen to fit Barbara's experience too? Did my knowing the song make the impression less valid?

I looked at my paper again. Crockery had led me to glass and finally to Glassner—and I knew a man by the name of Gassner. Anna's best friend was Glassen. Again, did the close similarity of names make the impression less valid? Or did I unwittingly seek out associations in my own life that would be pertinent to Anna's? Were the contents of my own mind organized in a different fashion, shifted, so that the precise data emerged? Were all details ignored except the ones that related to Anna?

I was getting excited because certain correlations suddenly sprang into my awareness between that performance and the writing of poetry. I feel accelerated when I'm caught up in inspiration, just as I often do when I'm giving impressions. It's as if the particular poetic concept charges your entire mind, searching its contents, coming up finally with the specific words or phrases that are artistically pertinent—heaving aside literally millions of other possible phrases for the one precise, apt one.

*Later I realized that the song was "Uncle Albert"—but my seeming mistake was precisely what led me to the correct impression.

Did the same kind of process happen when I gave myself the task of finding out information about Anna? If so, what a more creative way of dealing with the universe; and of dealing with facts! While I was thinking of all of this, though, I kept telling myself that Anna hadn't returned yet.

I'd no sooner recovered from that call when the phone rang again. The voice that spoke had about as much energy as one of the limp gray leaves that hung, dismal and alone, just outside the window, except that the leaves began to move quicker and quicker in the autumn wind while the boy's voice got slower and more hesitant. I'll call him Len. He was calling from Oregon.

"I've read two of your books . . . I just called . . . I hate to put you on the spot, but could I talk with you a minute? I'm just beat," he said, in a half-whisper.

"What's the hassle?"

"The world," he said, weak. "It's too heavy. I think of suicide all the time."

My cat, Willy, was on my lap. I shoved him off, thinking that *he* never contemplated suicide.

"So if you'd just let me write to you—"

"Okay," I said. "But my mail keeps piling up and up, so it might be a while before you get an answer. Listen, though." And I went into the whole thing, explaining that we create our own reality; that hassles just don't tumble down upon us, that we aren't victims; that we have to give to life as well as take from it. Then I told him about *The Nature of Personal Reality*, stressing the fact that Seth had written it particularly to help people help themselves out of their difficulties.

"I believe it all when it applies to somebody else," he said. "But I can't make anything work for me. Anyhow, I haven't read the book yet. A friend of mine has it. But if I can't make the book work, can I write you a long letter?"

I said yes, told him I'd send him some energy, and suggested that if he'd feel around inside himself, he'd feel his own energy source. He said, weakly, that he'd try. So when the call was over, I closed my eyes and requested that the inexhaustible energy of the universe would flow through me out to him. Instantly I felt and mentally saw a "road" go out sideways to the west. It was straight, suspended in the air, going through everything, reaching out until it found the boy. As it did, a delicious relaxation spread across my own shoulders.

I smiled: the road had gone so unerringly to its destination. Was this another way of using the contents of the mind and the world? Of course, physically I couldn't prove that anything had happened at all. But in the important inward order of events, exchanges had taken place that presupposed a different model of the universe than the one usually held.

As usual, there were so many questions. Did that energy actually behave as I experienced it? Did it travel through everything that was in its way, ignore the curvature of earth itself, heading for its destination? Or was all of this my interpretation? But as always, there were other more emotional questions. Why should a kid get so tired? Why shouldn't life itself be enough to content any of us and fill us with wonder? Why did so many people feel drained and powerless? Why did my cat, Willy, run outdoors, finding the same backyard a new source of excitement each day—why was he so filled to his bristly brim with vitality while so many human beings sagged in their spiritual beds, pulling desolation over their heads like a cover?

I could tell from the phone call that Barbara and Anna didn't get along at all, for example. They each pulled against each other, as if Barbara expected Anna to be a "model daughter" and found it impossible to relate to the person Anna was. I had to admit I was confused. All I really wanted was more material from the library—at least so I thought. I'd been so engrossed with my new ideas about models and eccentricities that I'd forgotten the way the term "model" was usually used.

As I sat thinking about this, the following material came to me; obviously a mixture of library material and my own level of consciousness. The two blended in together so smoothly that it was difficult to find the seams; yet I knew that they were there, invisibly connecting and yet separating various subtle alterations of thought patterns. That is, I recognized that I was getting an answer to one of my questions. The pronouns "we" and "us" were being used again which meant that my normal orientation was involved. Yet there was that sense of "the other," also, that subjective thrill of awareness as if my consciousness had its toes in a different ocean and was wading outward in new currents.

From the Library

MODELS AND ALTERNATE ECCENTRICITIES

"Our linear time concepts lead us to our ideas of straight-ahead progression and to a certain mental singularity in which it seems that the self is a single entity with no place to go but straight ahead, or it will fall behind; with no direction but up or it will fall down; and with nothing to do but "progress" toward perfection, or disintegrate. The adage "Know thyself" presupposes a model of the self that is stationary. For knowing the self at any given time actually changes the self into a new knowing self, which must again be known and thus changed.

The word "model" unfortunately often suggests a perfection beyond which change is unnecessary or even disastrous. Again, our time concepts blind our vision. For the model of the psyche is endlessly various, characterized by infinite eccentricities each within the other in a kind of sprawling spontaneous order. Our usual ideas of order, however, automatically suggest order in time, consecutive and almost mechanical progression. We can even find creativity messy or chaotic if it does not follow our ideas of what order is.

Yet true order uses our time but is not bound by it. True order straddles our reality and appears in it as the manifestation of phenomena in time, so we suppose that order must follow time. We imagine that we must progress "a step at a time" toward a given goal that exists ahead of us, and we plan our lives accordingly.

The psyche itself is so richly various that it

presents us with endless banks of potentials and alternate models, each geared, however, in some indefinable way to our most intimate being—ours and no other. We are the ones who insist upon stripping down the luxuriant model to what we apparently think of as a more efficient time-version that fits our limited ideas of personhood. Then we end up with such appalling concepts as "the model parent" or the "model child." We use the model to enclose, not free, our individuality; to trap and not liberate our eccentricities, to regiment rather than express our deepest abilities.

We seem to think that there is a contradiction between having a model for reference, and deviating from it. We need to develop a loving recognition of our eccentricities.

Again I read the material over as soon as it stopped, and the connections between it and the day's events became clear. I thought, "of course," because the energy I sent to the boy and my impressions about Anna both happened outside of our usual ideas of progression and time. The energy seemed to go from Elmira to Oregon instantly, as if no time or space were involved at all; and the facts about Anna just appeared, without any physical digging.

In *Adventures in Consciousness,* I used the term "living area" to denote our physical life line from birth to death. It's on that "line" that normal progression happens and sense data connects with space and time directly. The information about Anna didn't originate on my own living area though—it was as if my consciousness stood on tiptoe and pulled in that data from somewhere else—and the energy I sent to the boy wouldn't appear in his living area in usual observable terms either. That is, it wouldn't land plop in his hands like a magic red apple that he could show to others. Instead, this was some kind of sideways "progression" or development, an extra dimension of activity that affected the living area but didn't "happen" in usual physical terms.

Then I thought of Seth's latest material on world views. We share certain mass information with our contemporaries, so our individual world views must merge at some point. When I wanted to know Anna's circumstances, did I shift the contents of my mind so that they became organized according to Anna's world view, rather than following mine? Did I let Anna's associations rather than mine deal with shared world contents as they appeared in the contents of the mind?

The following day, Monday, October 28, I had a very odd experience involving the use of energy that made me wonder even more about the nature of time, experience, and the nature of reality itself.

I was writing up my notes of the day before when the phone rang. The call was from a man who said he was internationally known as a member of a profession deeply involved with world economics and security. I knew nothing about him or his work and less about his particular speciality. Yet as we talked, I began to get impressions about his professional activities. I didn't say a thing about these at first, but then they came so strongly that I thought it best not to ignore them. Feeling rather silly, because I wasn't acquainted with the phraseology, I told the man what I was getting. He asked me to keep his identity a secret and not to reveal the information I gave him. For that matter, he only told me that it all applied, but without telling me how.

He was actually calling about a friend I'll call Perry, who was in very poor spirits, and after we spoke awhile I promised to send the young man energy to help him. We hung up. I sat quietly for a few moments, then thought of Perry. Instantly I felt and mentally saw another "path" go out shining through space. Then so quickly that I gasped, the path came back, rolling backward like a rug, unrolling inside my head with Perry in a fetus position—falling softly on the floor of my skull.

All of this was in miniature. I thought "Perry feels that his head is a prison," when his image flopped inside my mind. I "saw" him looking wildly about. Immediately I made large open windows all around my skull (which now looked like a glass globe) so that he could look out. He stood up and went to the windows, so I made bright paths that extended outside, telling him mentally that he had many choices and alternate directions to follow. The path he liked was the one that went directly out the front of my head. I lined the road with stately green trees and extended the perspective so that it went out into the distance. Perry walked a short way when a giant figure of a man blocked his path; his huge legs were all I saw. Perry dived through the giant's open legs, flying free in an even greater distance that appeared to accommodate him. I knew that the giant represented Perry's distorted hero worship of the man who called me on the phone, and realized that Perry had finally freed himself of that imprisoning figure.

The entire experience startled me, though. It was the first of its kind. When Perry's image slid into my mind, I "knew" that I should act quickly to help him. Any action involved didn't happen in our usual system of recognized events, however. Was the entire episode a symbolized representation? Why had the "road of energy" brought Perry *into* my mind, for me to deal with, rather than just helping him at his end?

The next day my secretive caller phoned to tell me that Perry had attempted suicide by taking pills, but had received care in time and was now out of danger. Perry's suicide attempt and my experience happened at the same time—yet I hadn't interpreted the events that way when they occurred. Perhaps I should have supposed as much because Perry was in a fetus position at first. The events as I *did* interpret them were real enough so that I took immediate action: But if I really did help Perry, it was at a different level of activity, in a kind of reality with different rules, using another model of the universe that permitted such events.

Though I didn't know it, I was to have more experiences shortly that happened . . . in some "unplace" else . . . yet connected to the world we know.

Chapter 9
The Ape and the Silver Guide

While all of this was going on, I was exhilarated by the autumn itself, yet as the middle of November came I grew slightly disquieted. I hadn't actually been in the library in several weeks, though the "book material" seemed available enough. Maybe, I thought, the initial experiences were only meant to put me in touch with a different level of consciousness: maybe I'd never go into the library again.

Beside this, I'd been troubled with some annoying health difficulties for several years. There had been some definite improvements since my first visit to the library, but I was anxious to clear up the entire condition. Seth had been of great help, but he told me that I made my own reality just as everyone else did, and it was up to me to alter any conditions that bothered me. My overall health was excellent:

but my body was stiff so that I had difficulty getting about. Worse, I understood what I was doing, and while I was bothered by the symptoms I also realized that they provided me with quiet; cutting down distractions while allowing me to do just what I wanted to do—write at my desk. I might complain, yet suppose I was as physically flexible as anyone else—would I have the discipline to just sit in my room and do my work?

I'd discovered just about everything I needed to know about my condition through working with my beliefs as Seth suggests in *The Nature of Personal Reality*—and I knew that I clung to the symptoms because they still served a purpose.

All of this was on my mind that evening of November 18, 1974. It was 7:30. I looked over to the southeast corner of the living room where the library was. It appeared, but this time the books were gone. My body was lying flat on a long low table of some sort. Then as I watched, my body, there, kept sitting up and down so fast that in my chair at the desk I almost got dizzy. In here someplace I closed my eyes, to "see better." I also realized that I was forming the other images in some way not immediately known. As soon as I closed my eyes, I saw a man come into the room, pull up a chair beside the other me, and sit down. He took my hand. I knew that he was a doctor.

The strangest part of this experience was the fact that I only saw this man's face clearly. I kept staring at it. His whole face was like a dull silver, with something like a muted silver halo about his head. The "halo" wasn't perfectly round, however, and didn't glow. His hair was white and bushy; quite normal-looking. It was the contrast between the mundane look of the hair and the dull silver face that struck me so forcibly. At the same time my "own" body, at my desk, began to feel very warm and relaxed.

I opened my eyes, wrote down what I was seeing, then closed my eyes again. This time a man lay on the table. He was strong-looking, remarkably muscular, and he was in the same position as my double had been a few moments earlier. I knew that he was another version of me, or vice versa. I didn't see his face, though: it didn't seem important. Suddenly I felt the strength and agility of his muscles—from the inside. Then he stood up and walked around, exercising various portions of his body.

Again, I opened my eyes and wrote down what I saw. I've learned that it's easy to forget the details of such "inner sightings," so I've trained myself to put myself "on hold" at one level of consciousness while I record my experiences at another level. I wrote down the entire episode with the man at once, for example, yet I didn't remember until later that he had first appeared in a pyramid of light.

These images were startlingly clear and vivid. The next time I closed my eyes I saw a man's leg, in detail, again with attention to the muscles as if to impress me with muscular agility. The leg kept changing positions, then vanished. It was instantly replaced by a picture of a man and women lying close together on sand, just at the edge of an ocean. The woman was blond, with a fuller shape than I have, yet I knew that we were the same person, and suddenly my consciousness was in her body rather than in "my own" at the desk. "I" sprang up easily, and walked along the beach with the man beside me, taking the greatest delight in the swift easy motion of my legs and laughing as I wiggled "my" toes in the sand. Then the man and I ran hand in hand for a swim in the ocean.

At this point I became worried that I'd get so engrossed in the experience that I couldn't record it properly. I forced myself to open my eyes, and had difficulty holding them open, much less writing. I just managed to scribble down the last scene when I saw the man again, so once more I closed my eyes to "see better." This time I saw a close-up. The man had a marvelous build and seemed filled with vitality. As he performed several gymnastic exercises in the sand, at the table I felt the same muscular motions.

Briefly my consciousness came alive inside his body, and then the physical sensations were even stronger and more definite. As I flashed back to my own body, I got another very close look at his face and blond hair. There was no mistake—this was Ruburt—as he appears in a portrait that

Rob had painted of him several years ago. Ruburt is supposed
to designate another part of my psyche, and Seth always calls
me by that name. Again, I flashed into his body, feeling it
from the inside. This astonished me, that I could be so comfortable inside a male figure. I also realized that Ruburt was
not as passive as he seems in Rob's portrait, though he certainly wasn't aggressive in conventional male terms either.

Then I sensed an unpleasantness. The woman
vanished. The man stood up and threw a dark wavy spidery
shape from him against a wall that had sprung up from nowhere. Immediately I realized that this represented the
negative aspects of my own self-image. The spidery shape
raged as if alive, flew out into the air, and from it a small
dark Indian emerged, with bent-up legs. Instantly he turned
into a baby. The woman reappeared and picked up the
infant. As the baby, I bit the woman in the chest. At once I
connected this with the phrase "biting the breast that feeds
you" or some such. The episode was so unpleasant that I
opened my eyes, wrote the whole thing down, and wondered
whether or not I wanted to continue.

This was a completely different kind of experience
for me; but it was happening in the area of the library. It was
obvious that some kind of therapeutic intent was involved, so
I decided to go along with it.

I closed my eyes again. Instantly the man and
woman were there. They stood on either side of the long
table and looked down lovingly on the baby. Then my
consciousness was inside the infant. I was being pushed in a
baby carriage through the library—which was suddenly there
in its usual form, replete with bookshelves—and as we approached one of the shelves, I reached out with chubby baby
hands and picked up one of the books.

The next moment "I" was a huge male ape, sitting
at the library table. At the same time I was also watching
him. He had the strangest human-animal eyes, wise and
compassionate, and he was supremely certain of his own
existence as it straddled the animal and human world. So
quickly that I almost got dizzy at my desk again, my consciousness spun out of his body and leapt into the baby

which suddenly appeared in the ape-man's lap. With great deftness, the ape-man cuddled the infant, holding it against his hairy chest. As the baby I felt a vast sense of comfort and security. This lasted a few moments when the ape-man changed into an ape-woman who then held me in her arms. I was aware of a great creature animal-like mother love, beyond anything I've ever imagined. Then, at my desk, the thought came to me: "Of course! The ape mother is so strong you couldn't hurt her if you tried. She's stronger than hate or anger, and her love contains such understanding, that no child's rage could possibly upset her."

The sense of creature support was impossible to describe and as I felt it my body at the desk grew even more relaxed. Yet, almost paradoxically, I felt energetic at the same time. Then the entire affair just vanished. I opened my eyes, finished writing my notes, and sat there, staring at the now-ordinary room.

I have to admit that I was pleased with myself. In the past I wouldn't have allowed such an experience, or the moment it became unpleasant I'd have cut it short. That is, in a definite defined state of trance, I would allow myself a good deal of freedom—after all, a trance is a trance; it's not supposed to be normal consciousness. But mixing "hallucinary images" with usual consciousness was something else again; a phenomenon I'd only experimented with in isolated brief instances. These images had been as real as ordinary people, yet transposed into the "imaginary space" of the library, and my own awareness has zipped back and forth so quickly at times that afterward I had trouble remembering who or what I was when.

As I finished my notes, details kept coming to mind that I'd forgotten, and just then Rob came into the room. He'd been working in his back studio. "It's session time," he said. Then, quizzically, "Why so quiet? What have you been up to?"

I looked at the clock. It was 9:00 P.M., so the entire affair had lasted an hour and a half. Grinning, I showed my notes to Rob. He asked me if I wanted to call off the regular Seth session, but I shrugged and said that we might as well "go the works." Actually I was curious to see if Seth would have anything to say about my "silver guide," as I called the man with the dull silver face—and the ape-man. We had a glass of wine and a snack and began the session a little later than usual, at 9:40. I was still rather groggy from the whole thing, but Seth came through at once, as emphatic and vigorous as ever. As you'll see, he explained my experiences beautifully.

This was a personal session, containing no book dictation for The "Unknown" Reality, and I'm only giving the highlights of Seth's explanation here, reserving the right to withhold some other, intensely private material. I should mention first, though, that my grandfather was an Indian with French-Canadian blood, since this applies to the session. Also, a week earlier a doctor had appeared in a dream and assured me that my physical condition was improving. Seth refers to this "dream doctor." This session is particularly valuable because Seth explains how the psyche can communicate with conscious levels when permission is granted.

From the Session for November 8, 1974

"The ape on one level represented the animal instincts feared by Ruburt's mother and grandfather as well, so Ruburt also learned to look upon them [the instincts] askance. These instincts are the earthly doors of the soul's energy. Who closes them does so at some peril."

Seth went on to describe the ways in which my mother and grandfather had both tried to deny their creature instincts. He spoke of my love for my grandfather, and my partial early identification with him. Speaking of my grandfather, Seth said: "He gambled compulsively in an attempt to hide his sexual wants. He did not trust the body, his or anyone else's. . . . He abhorred liquor because he was aware of the tales saying that it was the Indian's downfall . . . and he repressed his feelings to counteract the Indian 'image' of being uncivilized. He was an outsider: a short, small, dark-skinned man. . . .

"He felt himself a pygmy because of his size and because, as part-Indian, he was looked down upon. To some extent, Ruburt identified with him. He was, after all, the father of Ruburt's mother, and to some degree Ruburt saw him as the greater source out of which his mother came.

"The ape emotionally represented the instincts in their true light, as dependable, supportive, and as the basis for earthly existence. Ruburt, then [in tonight's episode], experienced the strength of the earthly source. This means that he is to trust his instincts. At the same time, the ape male and ape female represent the sexual quality of the earth, male and female being simply other versions of each other. In still other terms, Ruburt now experienced the yearned-for mother love that was warm in its animal female understanding, supportive and strong enough to easily bear a child's small ragings and momentary hatreds. . . .

"At one point Ruburt saw the ape, still male, and a portion of himself, sitting at the library table—for *in your position* it is the animal instincts themselves that propel you to search for answers. The ape was at home in the library, and his face was compassionate. Identification with the instinct brings compassion, and that compassion and wonder spark the creative abilities. Ruburt's idea was still one of controlling those instincts and his 'animal' abilities. On yet another level, because the ape was in the library, Ruburt was symbolically seeing the force of his own physical nature, quite at home with itself and at home in the psychic library of the mind. . . .

"The ape also acted as an animal medicine man-woman, symbolically acting out a part that once could very well have been performed in fact."

(Here Seth refers to his contention, in *The Nature of Personal Reality*, that animals once had a different relationship with humans; in their way they acted as physicians, teaching animal use of herbs and a certain "acting out" of symptoms.)

"Ruburt has been reading about shamans. Their connections with animals are little understood. In his own way, however, Ruburt began a shaman's journey for himself, letting the psyche's images come alive, and making the inner workings of the mind more obvious.

"The episodes served to connect him in trust with his own deepest instincts, and he saw that these were loving. The ape could not have appeared, however, until the blond man forcibly threw out the elements of that negative image. He dashed it against the wall. The pygmy Indian with bent legs emerged, signifying the identification with Ruburt's grandfather.... He identified with him as a child, seeking protection from his mother in someone who seemed to love him more. The negative image, dashed then, gave forth the symbolized image that he had been using in his mind. Following this, he turned into a baby, because the identification began early.... This was not entirely a negative identification by any means....

"The silver figure is the other end, the other pole of the ape—the spiritual guide, if Ruburt will forgive the term, as the ape was the animal guide, for both are related and both were compassionate. The 'spiritual guide' was the doctor Ruburt heard in his sleep—and immediately questioned—and he is quite valid. He is not just a symbol, either, but represents a quite real psychic construct, alive in your terms but in a different reality, and connected in a way with Ruburt's physical being—with the source of the flesh that physically composes him.

"It is not just the soul, but the soul of the body that you must learn to trust, for the soul in the body represents the corporal meeting of the physical and nonphysical selves in the most practical of terms. Ruburt is not relying upon 'his own' resources alone, but upon those great dimensions of energy that connect the soul and body—the silver guide and the ape."

I felt a new delightful corporal certainty because of the evening's earlier experiences; and added to this was a psychic satisfaction with Seth's explanations. Unknown to me then, I was to have other experiences with the ape or animal medicine man—and in connection with the library. As we went into bed I wondered: what kind of a library was this anyway? Obviously there was a lot more in it than book material. Like symbols that came alive. As it happens, I didn't know the half of it.

After the session was finished, Rob mentioned a few rather important questions he had about some recent reincarnational experiences of his own. Suddenly I felt Seth "back again" with the answers but it was late and Rob was tired himself, so we decided to call it a night. *Somebody* had an awful lot of energy, I thought; and we trailed off to bed.

The following day, Tuesday, I felt exuberant and refreshed and my consciousness seemed crystal clear. As I sat at my desk, a few paragraphs came from the library book. I wrote them down at once:

From the Library

The focus personality rises into prominence from the rich infinite reality of the psyche or source self which constantly supports it. The focus personality cannot drown in its own source, or be annihilated or dissolved within it, because it is the face of the psyche turned toward the earth. Drawing from the psyche's greater knowledge reinforces the focus personality's ability to deal with the world's contents, increases creativity, and automatically reveals the self to itself—and thereby reveals the true meaning of the world's contents.

These are then understood to be the physical manifestation of the contents of the mind. This knowledge alone gives the focus personality additional power, as it learns that it can mix and match these merged contents, bringing into physical reality greater variety and deeper meanings which then enrich the mental and physical landscapes.

This material came very swiftly and easily, but by the time I'd finished writing it, I knew that my perceptions of myself and the room were altering. I scribbled down what I was perceiving, though again in this instance it was sometimes difficult to make myself bother with the effort of writing. I'm quoting these notes exactly as I wrote them to preserve the sense of immediacy.

"I'm looking at the corner intersection, yet I feel other 'me's' sitting at other corners in different times and places; I mean, I feel them emotionally. In this moment at least I know that . . . the me I identify with is only one me in one location or position in a larger field of reality. But all the other me's form an inner network almost like our concept of planets but in an inner cosmos, with inner structures or 'nerves' connecting us, like a multidimensional *body*, only that isn't exactly what I mean. I'm in one position within it, only the position itself involves a whole reality of experience.

"The totality straddles all of the me's, and theoretically these me's can meet consciously in a kind of inner space travel. There *is* some 'universal' communication between all of these me's. The greater psyche is the medium in which these me's exist, as we say that space is the medium in which matter exists. Yet the various me's *are* the psyche, made of it, inside it just as space is inside objects. The psyche wrinkles, knots, focuses energy, pushes it up so that it forms waves or particles in mental space in the same way that matter is 'knotted' in space. The me's are eccentricities—each with its own version of reality, forming it along with the others and then perceiving the world contents.

"These me's represent features or structures of a multidimensional self, and are a part of it in the same way that my hands are a part of me—poor analogy, though, because these me's are completely independent in their environments.

"I can feel the communication between all of these me's—but can't really get a hold of it. Again, though, in a kind of inner space travel you can move through the reaches of the psyche to these other systems of reality, each with its own me. But the doorways are within the psyche itself, and each me will use whatever symbolism is available at its end as a sort of mental vehicle.

"Since the same psyche is involved, I can have some inner recognition of these other realities—in which these other me's exist. This recognition shows me that the contents of *this* world can be altered at least slightly if I want; I can view them with the cast of another me. But all these me's exist in one psyche at one time, and 'I' can die in one part of that psyche and come to life again in another section—like a light blinking off and on in different places.

"I'm a one-world version of myself—of my greater self—one of many entirely different but related me's, each focusing in a unique reality and using different eccentricities. There are groupings that we don't understand. Each psyche or source self has portions that correlate with the same portions in other source selves—hence our shared experience in this and other realities."

While I was perceiving in this fashion, I seemed to be going so fast psychically that my mental properties could never keep up, and what I wrote is a pathetically weak and diluted description of the emotional and intellectual experience itself. My thoughts seemed to drop off finally, where I couldn't follow them after a while. In a sudden vision, I saw *our* life as a single cell structure, with Seth's existence like an organ in comparison. Then I saw him as a wandering messenger, traveling from one part of my inner psyche to another, from "me" to "me," as an astronaut might go from star to star. It seemed that my me's grew and divided psychically as cells do physically; only developing further, becoming more aware of their own existence and of greater structures.

In some kind of inner dizzying experience I can't describe I felt that what is unconscious activity from our focus was once conscious focus—the degree possible to us "at the time." We climb ahead, the previous conscious activity taken for granted, then forgotten like hills in the distance that we've already traveled. I could ... feel this, and I knew that we travel through the consciousness of ourselves. Part of us is still buried in activities "we" now consider unconscious, and in activities we aren't aware of. The vision again, is almost impossible to describe but I felt our me's group and regroup, even while each retains its identity. And I thought that the self I'll be tomorrow is unconscious now, yet the me-ness climbs above these operating unconsciousnesses, rising each day in its new-old, future-past identity.

As the vision faded, I tried to see if I could glimpse the books in the library. Mentally I saw one in its place on the shelf, and suddenly I *did* get dizzy because as I looked, the book vibrated and I felt it turning into all of its different versions at the same time. Then it came to me that earlier, I'd tuned in to *my* version of the book, but if you tried to see its greater multidimensional reality, then the book changes so quickly that you can't keep track. Or at least, I couldn't. If you could alter your focus in lightning fashion, each version would be distinct.

But I was in a daze—a delightful one—and decided to let things rest where they were. I got up to do some house chores, and began to see where "psychic politics" fit into my latest experiences. I'd wondered considerably about the book's title, but now it occurred to me that I was heading toward a new politics of the self, and finding a different kind of self-government—and a larger world of the self than I'd ever known.

Chapter 10

The Boy with the Hole in His Chest. A Young Celibate, and the Book of the Gods

A few days later I was chatting with a friend, Greta, on the telephone, and she asked me how this book was progressing. "Great," I said.

"That's to be expected," she said with a laugh. "Marlo Williams says it's all that help you get from the devil."

"Marlo Williams? Wow, that's a bit much," I said.

"Wow's right," Greta said. "I asked him if he'd read any of your books, and he said, 'No, because they were written by the devil.' So I said, 'Maybe it's just her subconscious or something, did you ever think of that?'—just to see what he'd say. And he said—you won't believe this—he said, 'That's what I mean—the devil.'"

Greta paused, waiting for me to savor the full

implications of the remark, but I was appalled, mostly because Marlo Williams was an editor on a newspaper in a nearby town. It made me uneasy to think that anyone in such a position went around believing in the devil.

"He's getting worse," Greta said. "That fundamentalist religion he's joined sees the devil's work all over. Only what's this about the subconscious being the devil too? That doesn't give people much leeway."

"It sure as the devil doesn't," I laughed. But I was concerned, and I remembered the phone call later that day when I read my mail. There was a letter from a young man I'll call Joe. He was writing from India where he was following a well-known guru, and trying to escape the "codified, stagnant life of New York City."

He was finished, he said, with the lust for money and prestige that he found in our American society, and he was fed up with the male-wage-earner role. He'd given it all up to search for truth. In line with his guru's teachings, Joe meditated several hours a day, to "purify" himself. He was desperately trying to cut sex out of his life, he continued. There was only one hitch. Whenever he meditated he developed terrible headaches and was beset by "terribly lustful thoughts." The harder he tried to forget them and the more stubbornly—and desperately—he tried to meditate, the more persistent the headaches and fantasies became. He wanted to know how he could rid himself of these "debasing sexual feelings."

Joe's particular guru didn't believe in the devil, but the natural needs and desires of the body were seen as impediments to spiritual growth. At nineteen, when everything in Joe's biological and spiritual makeup yearned to rush outward into the reality of flesh, to mix exuberantly with the soul and body of earth, he was stubbornly holding back. He was accepting a model of the self that had little to do with his own being; a limited model that denied him strong elements of his own nature.

I could see through *that*, yet I'd repressed many spontaneous elements of my own nature to discipline my "writing self." Our concepts of selfhood have been so limiting that one way or another each of us suffers from them, I thought. Contrasted with our usual self-images, how much more expansive were these new ideas of models and eccentricities as mutually supportive and cooperative. I remembered my experience with all the "me's," and caught a glimmer of that vision. In contrast to our usual concepts, I sensed again that each of us carries within the psyche our own greater model—a multidimensional one, sprawling forth in the personality with a thousand seeds or eccentricities, each part of the model, versions of it, each bringing forth new alternate models, just as each seed potentially can grow a new tree, based on the old but different and unique. And then, I wondered, per usual, why we limited ourselves; and how we could escape our own self-labels.

You'd think that the young would burst through any limitations, just through sheer exuberance. Perhaps many of them do. Yet that same day a young man from Maine visited asking to attend class; and he was about as exuberant as a wet dishrag. He was soggy and drowning in the murky mess of his own ideas about himself. Yet he had a great sense of humor. He was a big strapping lad, really, with red hair and a smile like a holiday banner—that showed, though, just about as often as Christmas lights. I'll call him Gordon.

He was so tall that it was really hard not to see him, yet he scrunched down, bent over, and did everything he could to make himself invisible. His eyes were always downcast, and he acted as if he'd explode in panic if you dared try to meet his glance. He was twenty years old that day, and worried about leaving his teens behind. He'd been traveling around the country, "trying to be anonymous." Whenever people got to know him, he moved on, as if he had some dark evil secret to hide, or as if people would chase him down the streets if they understood his feelings about himself and the world.

Gordon hung around for a few months, getting himself a job at McDonald's. Once when he saw an acquaintance enter the place, Gordon hid in the back room. Later he said that he couldn't bear to be caught in his uniform. And, of course, he worked in the back usually anyhow, and sometimes at night as a cleanup man. We used to burst out laughing, just imagining him serving Big Macs to the public, smiling the television-brilliant "let us nourish you" grin featured by the McDonald's people in the TV ads.

One night he visited us, almost on the sly, and drank some wine and suddenly talked—and talked and talked; and grinned his own unique way. But all his funny stories were at his own expense. He said that after he'd been in one place for a while, he thought of getting a fake moustache and paste-on eyebrows and a wig, so he wouldn't be known, and no one could yell out "hello" as he walked down the street. At the same time, he yearned for contact; and hated himself for wanting it. His humor was extraordinary, but if you caught him at it, he was ready to dive for the door.

That night though, he told us his secret, and showed us the sign of his inferiority: Opening his shirt he pointed to his chest, which was concave, so that it seemed to have a hole in it near the heart area. The doctor told him that it wasn't dangerous, but it kept him from getting the proper amount of air into his lungs. To us, his chest just looked slightly odd. But to Gordon, there was a definite hole in his chest, the sign of iniquity.

When he left, I thought of him and about the editor who believed that the subconscious held "the devil," and about the nineteen-year-old who was trying to cleanse himself of sex and love and emotion because they didn't fit into his ideas of what was good or pure or right. It seemed clear to me that our self-images are intimately interwound with our religious beliefs, and often based on models that don't fit; models that are bloodless—and connected with gods who created earth almost as an afterthought, and have been embarrassed about it ever since, never ceasing to complain about their own creations.

And I thought of Plato. He set up a whole cosmology over two thousand years ago. What an accomplishment! Yet one in which man was only a shadow of his soul's worth—a universe in which the race was pitted against perfect models in whose light its members would always appear inferior and blighted. What a bloodless elegance to lay upon the flesh, and how Plato used it to keep each man and woman in proper place!

The models I sensed were far different, like great suggestive creative patterns to be used; each alive and mobile as divine amoebas, each variation eternal in one sense—its imprint never erased—and yet on the other hand, always splashing forth eccentricities and new versions of its own existence.

It's precisely the eccentricities, I saw, that brought the models to life in our world. If this isn't understood, then models are turned into rigid tombs stifling all change and variety; molds into which all creativity becomes pre-determined and rigid. Plato froze one version of a model and closed his eyes to everything else. But those "ideal" models of his exist not outside of us, but in the intimate world of the private psyche, written in our own ideas and genes, inter-acting with us as we do with them.

For me, in a strange fashion, those models exist in my library—my versions of them, at least; concepts that would rise from the joint fountain of intuition and reason. I saw them as models alive through their own eccen-tricities—models that we could glimpse ourselves by altering the focus of our consciousness—models that could unite inner and outer reality and show us our own psychological solidity.

For inner and outer worlds merge in our experi-ence, in each of us privately, in the natural world in which we exist, and in the cultural world of our religions, sciences, politics, and arts. We've been suffering from a lack of depth perception, never seeing that subjective and objective experi-ence were just two versions each of the other, split only in our perception.

The gods in the psyche and the gods outside are one, but we've been forced to think of them separately. The exterior world of politics and law represents the inner politics of the self as it organizes and governs itself in relationship to physical existence. The model and its eccentricities are the seemingly double faces of the same thing—our creativity and its individualistic flow from which all of our private and joint creations spring.

Most likely I discovered "my library" as a natural result of my own eccentric wanderings through the inner and outer cosmos; discovered it amid tangled doctrines and overhanging threats; found it like a child—the magic spot in the middle of the strange forest. It's in the center of my psyche, of course, and because it is, it also exists in the cosmos. I've been searching for alternate models for reality, without knowing it, for my entire lifetime—for an alternate philosophy that would work better for me and for the world; another world picture, a fonder birth of concepts that would spawn fresh creativity. I still have to learn what I'm doing—how to get and interpret the books in the library—but it's a lovely venture, and I have the time.

It's not just that we *have* greater selves, but that we *are* greater selves. Perhaps we wanted to discover ourselves only a little at a time, exploring our own psychic territory section by section. Seth may well represent part of my own unknown territory, and if so, then each person has his or her "Seth" level or its equivalent. Maybe Seth "built" my library. Maybe he exists apart from me only in my understanding, or maybe we are each eccentricities of a model, operating at different levels of reality.

Maybe I'm climbing through Seth's psyche. Maybe I'm only the small portion of my earth consciousness that's met my own greater identity. Maybe the psyche or source self is eternal and immortal psychologically as well as in terms of time, so that from here we might bask in the light of its being but be unable to see or feel it all at once.

What we need is a whole new myth of man and his beginnings, one that leapfrogs local gods and places God inside his creatures, within creation. We need a god as blessed or flawed as its creations, a whole new cosmology giving birth to a God that is male and female, Jew, Arab, American, Chinese, Indian; that is within each individual alike; that is not parochial and not man's alone; a god that is within stones and stars; a god-goddess big enough to be personified as a Buddha, Christ, Isis, Athena, Muhammad—animal god, insect god, tree god; each seen as a local symbol standing for an unexplainable reality that is too super-real to fit our definitions.

We need a new myth, imaginative and creative enough to leap above our puny facts. What boldness, to create a new race of the gods, glorifying individuality, seeing each as a unique personification—not sterile righteous lords sending down condemnations and handing out impossible edicts, but gods saying "Life is good. That's why we're alive, and alive in you!" We need father, mother, grandfather, grandmother gods, niece and nephew gods, who understand human relationships because they are alive in us and we in them—lesbian and homosexual gods, aunt and uncle gods—boisterous joyful divine families, mating among themselves and with us, singing of the beauty of the lovebed, appreciating the moments formed like solitary jewels from the vast necklace of infinity. . . .

The Book of the Gods—I'd like to write that, and *The Book of the Universe,* in which people-gods or god-people rise from nonphysical to physical life because they want to; because they dreamed in their solitary godhoods of green grasses and soft flesh and yearned to be born as men and women; flinging their godness into bodies joyfully, recklessly, come what may. And maybe, in between lives, they wander on the shores of inner rivers, planning their "future" lives with great excitement, creating them as a writer does his book, plotting crises and achievements, challenges and glories—then, once on earth again, changing the stories, making surprise endings, each character alive, remaking the plot; with each life forming a new dimension of actuality, providing greater knowledge of honor and love, and a new marriage of the soul with the seasons.

For if the gods didn't love the evenings and the dawns, why would their creatures?

A new myth—would it be true or false? What difference? Were Plato's ideas true? For generations we lived as if they were, and we found ourselves dwarfed by perfect models of ourselves to which no human being could conform. True or false? Our creativity is bolder than such concepts. Let us use it to fling new gods into the universe, and new histories of their births back through the centuries—gods that are ourselves in flesh; us yet not us; gods that can speak to us and gods who listen instead of preaching all the time; gods we can speak to and feel snugly within us, couched alike in our consciousness and molecules.

Since we really can't know what the universe is, as it exists apart from our experience of it, then most of our fondest theories are really myths and stories that we pretend are real. So why not construct myths we like for a change—gods that have better things to do than sacrificing sons, gods that are likable at least? What glorious epics we could create, and what a legacy to give our children. *The Book of the Gods*—I can see it in my mind, giving strength and creativity and joy to generations—perhaps if not in this world then in another, in some system of reality where myths are understood as the offsprings of the psyche; as the soul's playthings; as the games the people-gods and god-people play together as they try to find a common language.

Our gods have been so cruel and rigid and un-yielding that we've retaliated. We're killing them off. We got so frightened of them that we've set up nongods to take their places; gods as tired of consciousness as it seems we've become; gods who just want to sleep in oblivion; who haven't the energy for divine sex, much less physical, yet gods who still cry, "Repent. Come clean of your bodies. Give them up."

So I say, "Down with those gods by whatever name. Hello to gods that create life because they love it; and earth because of its beauty. The earth gods."

So for myself I'm imagining some part of a great infinite God breaking off from itself into a much smaller offshoot; forming a quite capable little god who wanted to be a woman; and considering the nature of physical reality, wanted to write books and love a man just like my husband who paints pictures. And this god said, "I'll make myself into a Jane"; and so he or she or it, did; and we became one, indivisible, and now we sit musing over the whole affair—a beloved cosmic accomplishment.

This is a minor enough god if you're thinking in terms of an absolute deity, but a god nevertheless; a chip off the old block, the part of the Big Boy or Big Girl that wanted to travel into earth life. And this private god is quite equipped to handle things at this end; put the body parcel of the molecules together just right, get the seed package born and grow it up—god and person emerging together, so that infinity and time alike are woven into our genes; mortality and immortality each combining here to form the selves we know.

I wish I could tell the news to that editor.

Chapter 11
Time and Time Structures. The Shape of Time

Tom Willow (I'll call him) is a scientist from a well-known research institute. He visited us that last weekend of November 1974. In an informal session that lasted from 2:00 on a Sunday afternoon until 12:30 that night, he asked me questions—and I answered them while I was in an altered state of consciousness.

It's rather difficult to describe the state, simply because it's so familiar and I take it so for granted. I feel accelerated, poised, yet passive at the same time. There's no resistance of any kind. So far, I've used this state whenever I deal with scientists on my own; rather than working through Seth. I take to this particular focus "like a duck to water." It's great fun and even a kind of sport to me. Finding out what's happening to electrons, say, is something I really enjoy. I admit that I feel much more free then than I do when I have people's emotions to deal with. I'd rather "find" a lost electron than a lost person any day, for example: I don't have to worry about whether or not the electron really wants to be found or not. I don't even know if electrons really can get lost, for that matter. But anyhow electrons don't cry, so I don't have their emotions to deal with.

Tom Willow placed his recorder on the table and we went to it, taking time out only for a supper of scrambled eggs. I made quick sketches of electrons to explain their behavior; always a great exuberant game to me, since I haven't any idea of the subject in my usual operating consciousness. In college I flunked General Science twice and never got to Biology or Chemistry, much less Physics. I wrote poetry about the frog's state of consciousness, though, while our science teacher dissected the carcass, and I kept wondering what amoebas were "thinking of" when I was supposed to be doing whatever it was you were supposed to be doing with amoebas—now I've forgotten—in General Science.

Yet when I switch my focus of consciousness, the microscopic world comes quite alive, and I feel challenged as I try to match my perceptions to a scientist's vocabulary. Tom Willow is one of those scientists who are very curious about the properties of the mind, and he'd visited us once before. We knew we worked well together. I didn't have to worry about skepticism on his part, though I was quite aware that his visit was unofficial. Which was A-OK with me.

Among other topics, I told Tom what I was getting on the structure and behavior of electrons; time and gravity; the interior makeup of the earth; and the purposes and inner structures of pyramids. Later Tom had transcripts made of our prolonged recorded conversation and wrote me a letter saying that "Part of the information is well known to specialists and is well established. Another part is new data, but is plausible and does not contradict what is already known. A third part is new and contradicts the scientific picture of reality; in some cases, however, the scientific picture is not accepted universally and is currently being disputed. All in all, this is just the right combination of old and new information that can be used best, in working with serious scientists looking for good ideas."

As a result of the material I gave Tom, I found myself suddenly obsessed with time. Instead of writing, I'd sit and try to "lean into" the minutes, or strain against them to see what happened. I drew endless diagrams trying to see if time fit into space, or space fit into time. I'd say to Rob, "I should be working on my book, but I've gotten into this time thing lately instead."

I honestly didn't realize that this obsession with time was connected with this book or with psychic politics. It was just a month since my first super-real view of the world and the beginning of this manuscript. I was beginning to see, by hindsight, that my ordinary encounters—phone calls, guests, and even dreams—seemed organized in the strangest fashion. Looking back at the month, I saw that each week or so had a theme that presented itself either in book dictation from the library, or in more ordinary experience. Then everything else seemed to revolve around the theme, including the Seth sessions. Yet while I was involved in a particular subject, I never realized what was going on. Often, I'd think that I was dealing with another topic instead.

So while I felt guilty about "taking time out" to do what I really wanted to do—study the nature of time—I was working on one of the inner thematic frameworks of the book without realizing it.

In the meantime, I was copyreading *Adventures in Consciousness* and trying to catch up with the mail. So much had happened to me in a month that the thirty days seemed to contain a different kind of time, folded in between the usual minutes. I felt as if I could get all the book material from the library at once by tuning in to this special dimension. Yet the book material seemed to wait until certain other experiences happened in our normal time.

I knew that I'd had various emotional reactions to time at different periods in my life. When I was a child, I didn't want to grow up and I did want to, according to my view of the adult world on any given day. Oddly enough, I feel more free in time than I ever did when I was in my twenties; and now, in my forties, my experience with time is far more enjoyable than it was only a few years ago. Up until then I was almost desperately aware of life's vulnerability, obsessed with the thought that each day the young grew older, and driven by the frustrating realization that there was nothing I could do about this at all.

The younger I was, the more terrified I was of growing older. I knocked myself out to produce my books, hassled by the knowledge of time's relentless passing. But now new feelings are coming to me, and emotional certainties. Somehow we project ourselves ahead in time through our own desires. I had two books coming out that year. Presently I'm writing this one. Seth has finished *"Unknown" Reality* since I began this manuscript, and has already begun another. So I've staked out the future and I'm already in it to some degree just as I'm in the past. My focus is now, but the future is already imprinted. My psychic footprints are there, waiting for me. This adds some kind of personal exploration to the concept of time. To some extent, the future loses its "scary" quality, yet still maintains its flexibility and mystery.

The day in which I write this page becomes merged with the past years I've been speaking of, and with future years when it will be read by others. So I'm rather surprised, I guess, to feel my experience with time changing. The days go by swiftly, today folding into tomorrow without an observable wrinkle. Yet the insides of the days, or their contents, seem fuller or wider. The days have more room in them than before.

We're so used to thinking about time in certain fashions, though, that new feelings about it are oddly disturbing and exciting at once. Shortly after Tom's visit, for example, on Thanksgiving Eve, I saw myself in the library, turning to another page of "the book" that dealt with time. Then, instead of seeing more library copy, I suddenly found myself wondering about the nature of time in a different fashion, almost as if viewing it from another perspective.

Maybe, I thought, objects are time structures first

and space structures secondly: That is, space may solidify into objects only because it's impregnated with time, and time may actually provide space with its "thickness." Similarly, past and future may represent the thickness of the present.

We can walk around a table and see it from all sides. We can even look up or down at it if we want. But we can't view all of the dimensions of an event in the same way. It's as if we can only see one corner of an event at once. And even though the table is an object, we can walk around it only in any given now. We can't circle it as it was yesterday or as it will be tomorrow, even though the same space is involved. Time and space may be aspects of something else, or segments of a greater whole that we perceive separately.

I go into the library from this time and space, yet its space seems to exist outside of ours, even though I can pinpoint where the two coincide. Even then our space predominates, with the library space superimposed upon it, or opening up somehow within it. I don't take my physical body there either, though I do have a counterpart one there. I've noticed that I can have what amounts to an hour's experience in the library, while only ten minutes of our time has passed. So it seems to me that potential events have to get "solid" in space and time for us to perceive them here.

Time separates objects. It must hold them together too, and be connected with gravity. More than space is between the chair and couch in my living room, otherwise all the other arrangements of those two objects in the past and future could fight for the same space arrangement—at the same time. So it came to me clearly that the space between objects depends on time as well as space arrangements. This must apply to the smallest of particles also. So what keeps cells together must be a force involving time and gravity as well as one connecting the spatial grouping of the atoms and molecules. Time and gravity, working together, must somehow form all of our space arrangements, holding particles in the proper "now," keeping them from flying apart or gluing together. Objects must be space-frozen in time, or rather thickened in time and held together through gravity.

If gravity unites events in time and space, then events not yet here are too far apart in time and space to be solid. They are invisible events, in the same way that there are invisible particles. These must come together in a certain way before we perceive any event, psychological or "objective." A psychological event must still connect with the object of the physical body. We may well be the nucleus of all the events that we perceive.

I thought of this unknown force as causing space *and* time, resulting in objects that were events thickened by time as well as space, having a point of integrity or prime reality or focus that we call the present. So if you changed one ingredient, would you alter time or events in any way?

Usually, of course, we just perceive events in the present. Years ago I tried my hand at making predictions, with some considerable success. I wasn't trying to find out "what was going to happen" per se. I was trying to prove to myself that we could, on occasion, "foresee" the future. Once I'd satisfied myself on this point, I lost all interest. Now suddenly I found myself intrigued with precognition again, from a different viewpoint. Did the fact of precognition alter the events . . . and if so, how? What happened to time itself when we tried to yank out events before they were "ready"?

More than this, the contents of the mind fascinated me. I was learning that the mind held far more knowledge than we usually use. How could we get hold of it? Later that year I did much more work along these lines that I'll publish one day, hopefully, under the title *The Psychic Contents of the Mind*. The work I did this particular week was intriguing though, precisely because it raised so many questions; and because the impressions of precognized events were so close— and so far— from the mark. Later I learned some fascinating things about the mind's processes as it correctly "looks into the future." But the "distorted" impressions put me in touch with time, and with my own mind in a particularly challenging fashion, and made me ask exciting questions that wouldn't have occurred to me otherwise.

This particular day I just decided to scribble down the first few words or phrases that came into my mind, and

then to check them against the day's events to see in what
way they might apply. I specifically decided not to question
what I wrote, or try to make it more specific. This is what I
wrote:

    1.   something in a wooden framework, flat, I
think, like a carton that glass might come in. Not large. My
science kit?

    2.   about apartment house. News. Lend-lease.

    3.   lung

    4.   Greek magnate

    I'd better add a word about the first impression.
Some time earlier I'd joined a science club that sent kits
every three months. I knew that one was due this month or
the next. By then I'd already decided to forget the whole
thing, though. So far I'd received two kits. I'd joined
originally because I thought that perhaps some knowledge of
basic science might help me form better psychic questions
and familiarize me with simple scientific experiments. We live
in a technological society and take advantage of, say, electricity all the time. Yet if my use of even a simple light bulb
depended upon my technical knowledge of its operation, I'd
be in the dark. So I joined the club.
    At once I was disillusioned. The ads said that even
a twelve-year-old boy could put the kits together. Nothing
was said about a twelve-year-old girl— yet with an English
major in college, I had difficulty making sense of the instructions. More, my steel filings didn't line up on the little
magnet the way the book said they would. In a strange way,
the gadgets seemed to separate me from knowledge, rather
than bring me closer. And I became stubborn, discovering
that the whole idea of predictable experiments went against
the grain. It was the *un*predictable I was after; and the direct
knowledge or experience of reality—if I could get it.
    In any case, I wrote my impressions down at
10:30 A.M. stared at them disapprovingly because they

seemed so indefinite, and went back to my writing. At 11:30, the delivery man came with a package—my science kit. The box was fat, not flat, but it was marked "fragile" (which could have suggested glass), and it did contain a light bulb.

Rob had answered the door, and he opened the kit. It was packed with old newspapers, and just on impulse I suppose, Rob started smoothing out the crumbled paper and reading it aloud. At first I didn't pay any attention. Then I yelled, "Hey, let me see that!" Both sides of the newspaper page were devoted to real estate ads, with large displays mentioning apartments, town houses, and homes for sale and rent. There were three large pictures of wooden frame houses with picture windows and wide expanses of glass.

Subconsciously I could have known when the science kit was due, but that's just what I was after—trying to discover the contents of the mind. And, I thought, the kit *had* arrived today, not yesterday or tomorrow. The newspaper packings *did* just happen to be completely devoted to real estate, as per my second impression. Still, the science kit package hadn't been of wood as I'd indicated, and it wasn't flat either. Had I somehow tranferred the data about the houses (wooden frameworks) from the newspaper page onto the package itself?

"Who knows?" I thought, and went back to my writing. Then, fifteen minutes later, at 11:50, the phone rang. The unexpected call was about "Gordon," the young man mentioned earlier, who wanted to be so anonymous. I took the call without thinking too much about it. Then I glanced at my impressions. The word "lung" seemed to jump up at me. Ever since Gordon had showed us his concave chest, I'd thought of him as "the boy with the hole in his chest." Now I was certain that the word "lung" was my subconscious symbol for him. Just the same I wondered irritably why I hadn't just written the boy's name down if that was so: Why use a symbol to begin with? Besides, I reasoned, you could say that anything was a symbol for anything, by hindsight, if you wanted. At the same time I "knew" that "lung" stood for Gordon.

At two that afternoon—another phone call, from a

young woman I'll call Sally. Sally, I knew, had begun working at a lunchroom some weeks earlier. She phoned to tell me that a mutual friend had been surprised to find her in the lunchroom, and asked why I hadn't told her that she was working there. I thought this was hilarious, and asked Sally if she wanted me to send out announcements about her new employment. Again, I hung up without making any particular connections between the call and my impressions, but I glanced at my pad anyway. And shook my head. Sally worked for a man called George the Greek. He was referred to by that name regularly. My impression read, "Greek magnate." A small businessman running a Greek lunchroom is hardly a Greek magnate. Yet certainly the impression applied. But why the exaggeration?

In regard to impressions 1 and 2, the science kit already existed in space and time when I made my notes. The kit must have been in the post office or in a truck on the way here. In usual terms, I had no way of knowing this, of course, much less of knowing what the package was stuffed with. Impression 1 definitely referred to the package—the science kit—but again, the details weren't right. In breaking the data down, had I confused the glass wooden structures shown on the newspaper with the package itself? It was almost as if I saw the object (the kit) out of shape by trying to perceive it ahead of time.

This idea struck me vividly. Just maybe, I thought, space and time together *do* form the shape of objects, and under certain conditions, at least, we tune in to a level where the object isn't fully shaped "yet." The mentally perceived shape of the kit, long and thin rather than its actual fat and square, might be legitimate, at one level. Maybe the kit *was* long and thin, and got fatter and squarer as it approached me in time. Whether or not I was right in this particular instance, I was certain that time helped shape objects as much as space does.

Was the shape of the kit dependent upon its placement in time, and perceiving it "ahead of time" did I tune in to a sort of pre-shape? And what about "Greek magnate?" Again there was an exaggeration, only of quality rather than shape in usual terms. Sally's boss was important to her. Did that importance magnify him to a magnate in her eyes? I had more questions than I could handle. Mostly, though, I wondered how much time had to do with shaping objects and adding to their solidity. I was certain that time added shape to space.

But time—all different kinds of time—seemed to swirl about me that week. Time and timelessness. Yet in the past month, my super-real view of the world had begun to blur at the edges. I'm not sure when it withdrew or when I withdrew from it. I was left with my memory of its existence. Yet if the world was no longer super-real, neither was it the world I had known before. Its greater dimensions surrounded it invisibly, emerging now and then, suddenly, so that one object would attain full brilliance, reminding me by contrast of the magnificence of the whole.

The ape man-ape mother image returned unexpectedly too. Once when I was feeding the pigeons outside the kitchen window, I stopped, vividly sensing my "earth self," filled with the certainty that my own emotions were warm and reliable, with their own compassion and wisdom. I felt the rhythms of my body as secure and dependable—anything but unpredictable as sometimes I used to see them—and I was struck by the sureness and ancient knowledge that somehow resided within my flesh.

I hadn't had any prolonged experiences in my library, though, and I wondered: Would the library itself gradually vanish? The birds fluttered around the roof. I closed the window. But soon my thoughts would flutter about a lot quicker than those pigeons, because a few nights later Seth introduced a new concept that—once again—made us reorganize our mental worlds.

I never did put that science kit together. Finally I gave it away, with the two others, to a friend who had a twelve-year-old boy. Oh, well, I thought; you can't win them all.

Chapter 12

The Jamaican Woman, "Counterparts," and Four-Fronted Selves

While I went around trying to poke mental fingers into the "pie" of time, and thought that I wasn't working on this book, Rob had another psychic upsurge—some more reincarnational experiences. As usual it seemed that real life was messier, more exuberant, more rambunctious than any theories meant to explain it. That is, experience itself kept running ahead of us, escaping the theories, and at the same time initiating new concepts which in turn would become stepping-stones for further subjective events.

We were delighted with Rob's recent reincarnational episodes, for example, even if we had many questions. With these new experiences, though, we were now faced with an embarrassment of riches. Yet there was no doubt of Rob's emotional involvement in these latest episodes; each one vital and brilliant in its own way; each one finding him aware of another self, as alive as the self he recognizes.

The "Jamaican woman" took Rob by surprise, for example, yet he knew that his own existence now was intimately connected with hers. I'm quoting a portion of his notes here, though the entire episode appears in *The "Unknown" Reality*.

"While typing the 716th Seth session tonight I found myself thinking, 'You've always been quite interested in the Caribbean area and its islands, and you know perfectly well why.' Then, in my mind's eye I saw a tall, heavily built black woman in ragged clothes, carrying a basket or bundle on her head. I knew that this was me in another incarnation—or so I thought. This may be jumping to conclusions on very flimsy evidence. All I have is the feeling to go by, and the fact that I got the chills, or a thrilling sensation, as I realized what was happening.

"I took the session page out of the typewriter and wrote the above sentence, then sat with closed eyes. Immediately I was subjectively flooded with a host of images, so jumbled that I couldn't separate them. Something about a burning village square in the mountain country of Jamaica. I felt like crying. I opened my eyes and began to type. I saw the typewriter through a haze, so I closed my eyes again.

"I saw—I was—a big black woman running for her life down a hilly dirty street. Someone—a man—was chasing her with a firearm. Slap, slap, slap, went the big bare feet, dirty and calloused. She was terrified. Fire. I thought of my own 'death.' I opened my eyes, staring wildly at the wall of my studio for a moment.

"What was that I wrote not long ago—about learning to go along with unpleasant reincarnational experiences? Not so easy, after all. I dared to close my eyes again. Ah, relief. 'I'—the woman,—darted around a corner of a mud-type hut or shack. Into a doorway, a room. The walls were a foot thick. She was saved. The footsteps of the pursuer pounded past, down the hilly street. My head fell forward in blessed ease. A moment ago I'd felt like yelling. I really might have. At the same time I'd thought that this would terrify Jane, who was working in the front room. All through this, I listened to her typewriter going.

"I'll try to sketch the head of the woman. No name yet. My right hand rests in my lap, covered with my left, as I sit with closed eyes. I feel my right hand as bigger than mine; black, with short wide nails, light-colored against the black skin. She—I'm—illiterate. A rough life. I can almost write this, and see things with my eyes wide open at the same time. I'm half-frightened again. I lay hiding now on a scrubby mountainside, looking down at a bay of blue water (like a postcard scene). Something about a ship. A cane field—sugar—I hear a man beating his way through it. Calling. But they may not be looking for me. I get a name, but refuse to accept it.

"Now it's as if I'm getting so many images that I can't sort them out. I find myself thinking that half of them aren't legitimate, but made up of things I've read and seen about the Caribbean. Those things never gave me the chills, though. The woman has a heavy mouth, turned down, and some sort of scar on her cheek. I get something about a small boat, a handmade craft of reeds, very crude—I'm in it now. No sail. Now there was a small thin black man who was running with me, but he veered off to the left on the hilly street, so he got away too. There's something about a ship's cannon at the top of the hill, in the village, and an uprising or fight, involving troops. As best I can tell, the time period is within the early 1800s.

"After the woman ducked into the mud hut, she left again as soon as her pursuer passed. He'd soon return, looking into the buildings. She ran down a narrow street . . . that led her to the cane field. I 'saw' something in a well, dangling down on a string. But that's a terrible place to try to hide anything. That's the first place anyone would look. Yet whatever it was that was hidden was found in no time at all—and that's how all of this started. I'm getting that she survived all of this and lived to an old age. 'I' died of pneumonia and it was very peaceful, like opening a door and walking through, or rather *going* through. Someone was waiting for me. And I've still got the chills in my belly and legs as I write this.

"The name I got and rejected as so unbelievably corny was Miranda. That would mean nothing to that woman; it was a spelled name, and English besides. No, it was Maumee—Maw-mee—like a cry, like a native sound, a sound that had a black history from Africa and meant something to her bones, that spoke of ancient heritages, that was as natural to her as eating or sleeping, that fit her, what she was, and meant that *everybody knew who she was*."

This was the end of the main episode, though there were later ones, and some odd connections with experiences of some of my students. These are being included in Rob's notes for *The "Unknown" Reality* ... in connection with Seth's sessions on counterparts. As it was, Rob's Jamaican woman led us into another long discussion of reincarnation. These few paragraphs give an indication of our views at the time. Rob wrote them shortly after his experience.

"In a strange way, I think that the intellect can be helped to understand reincarnation by the very facts of emotional experience. The intellect can easily verify that the supposed emotions involving a reincarnational episode are real. They do have a basis, an origin. The question is the *source* of those emotions. The intellect finds itself in the position of evaluating experiences—emotional ones—not of its own province. If the intellect isn't closed to all ideas not native to the society of its growth, then it can learn much.

"It surely doesn't have to go around, waving its figurative arms wildly, saying, 'I was such and such in the first century A.D., and I was so and so in 1750,' and, given simultaneous time, 'I was a crew member on a rocket ship to Mars in the twenty-second century.' But the open intellect will surely find its very processes modified to some degree, however slight, by the very fact of its openness. It can at least accept reincarnation in symbolic form, or even as a sample of the psyche's innate creativity.

"So I take all of my own ideas on reincarnation with a large dose of caution, while not shutting any of them out. The strong, almost violent emotions I felt yesterday "in

Jamaica" were real. So were those in what I call my Roman series of a few weeks ago. . . . Yet I'm sure the whole notion of reincarnation (simultaneous or linear) is distorted to begin with. But distorted from what? That's the rub."

Those last three sentences are important, and surely Rob's questions helped trigger Seth's material on "counterparts." Yet he didn't introduce the concept in the session following Rob's experience, but in the one after that. In the first session he merely had one small comment, following book dictation. He said: "Reincarnationally, now [your experience] was quite legitimate, harking back to what I told you about the release of your own abilities. You helped that woman. Your present sense of security and relative detachment gave her strength. She knew she would survive, because she was aware of your knowledge. I will say more about it, but for now this is the end of the session."

At the end of the session I definitely felt that something was in the wind: I sensed the introduction of new and controversial material.

Still not using the term "counterparts," Seth "dropped the bomb" in his next class session. Rob had been telling the students about the Jamaican woman, when Seth came through, smiling and very active. He said, "You can live more than one life in one time. You are neurologically turned in to one particular field of actuality that you recognize. In your terms and in your terms *only,* the neurological messages from other existences exist within you as ghost images— messages to which you do not respond in physical terms. But they are present. They are indeed like ghost images within the cells, for the cells recognize more in this case than you do. . . .

"If you could think of a multidimensional body, existing at one time in different realities, and appearing differently within those realities, then you could get a glimpse of what is involved."

For the rest of the evening, class was in a mild uproar as we tried to answer the seemingly endless questions that such a concept involved. As usual, I thought this was a brilliant theory, but practically—well, how would it work? What did it do to our ideas of selfhood and identity? The politics of the psyche was a new kind of politics, indeed.

All of this was going on the same week that the physicist came, when I was so obsessed with time, so my mind was on those events rather than on Rob's Jamaican woman. Seth's contention that we can live more than one life in the same time period, caught me by surprise even though I'd had hints of this in a session immediately previous. I was intrigued as usual. Yet I found myself thinking, "I wish he hadn't said that," because in a way it was bound to be controversial.

When Seth introduced the concept formally in the 721st session, as a part of *"Unknown" Reality*, though, then Rob and I wondered why the idea had ever seemed strange. Seth explained it so simply that overnight, counterparts became such a part of our mental existence that it seemed we'd been familiar with the concept for our entire lives.

I'm including a very small excerpt from that session, leaving the further refinements and explanations for Seth's own book. The theory was definitely introduced, however, in response to Rob's questions about the Jamaican woman episode. It's useless to wonder when Seth would have brought up the subject if Rob hadn't had that experience just then. Seth's own book develops the concept further, and it's a pivot point for his explanation of personality.

Seth mentioned Rob's series of reincarnational episodes, tying them into some other material in the chapter. Then he continued: "You live more than one life at a time. You do not experience your century simply from one separate vantage point, and the individuals alive in any given century have far deeper connections than you realize. You do not experience your space-time world, then, from one but from many viewpoints.

"You do not understand how consciousness is distributed in that regard. . . . The people living within any given century are related in terms of consciousness and identity. This is true biologically and spiritually. . . . [In some of his reincarnational episodes] Joseph [Rob] was picking up on lives that 'he' lived in the same time scheme. In this way and in your terms, he was beginning to recognize the familyship that exists between individuals who share your earth at any given time.

"Each identity has free will and chooses its environment as a physical stance in space and time. Those involved in a given century are working on particular problems and challenges. Various races do not simply 'happen,' and diverse cultures do not just appear. The greater self 'divides' itself, materializing in flesh as several individuals, with entirely different backgrounds, yet each embarked upon the same kind of creative challenge.

"Each will choose his or her own framework according to the intents of the consciousness of which each of you is an independent part. In such a fashion are the challenges and opportunities inherent in a given time worked out.

"You are counterparts of yourselves, but as Ruburt would say, living 'eccentric' counterparts, each with your own abilities. So Joseph 'was' Nebene [as described in *Adventures in Consciousness*], a scholarly man, not adventurous, obsessed with copying ancient truths, and afraid that creativity was error; authoritative and demanding.... At the same time, in the same world and in the same century, he was an aggressive, adventurous, relatively insensitive Roman officer who would have little understanding of manuscripts or records, yet who also followed authority without question....

"In your terms, Joseph is now a man who questions authority ... who rips apart the very structures to which he 'once' gave such service. In greater terms, these experiences all occur at once. The black woman followed nothing but her own instincts ... and bowed only to the authority of her own emotions, and those emotions automatically put her in conflict with the politics of the times.

"Joseph's focus of identity is his own. He was not Nebene [the scholar] or the Roman officer or the woman. Yet they are versions of what he is, and he is a version of what they 'were,' and at certain levels, each is aware of the others. There is constant interaction. The Roman soldier dreams of the woman, and of Joseph. There is a reminiscence that appears even in the knowledge of the cells, and a certain correspondence. . . .

"The Roman soldier and Nebene and the woman went their own ways after death. They contributed to the world as it existed in those terms, and then followed their own lines of development, elsewhere, in other realities. So each of you exists in many times and places, and versions of yourselves exist in the world and time that you recognize."

Simply put, Seth is saying that we have what we think of as reincarnational existences in other times than our own; and that in the present world as we know it we also have other lives—called counterparts. I immediately connected this with my models and eccentricities. And I thought, "So that's it. People alive on the earth during a given century would be connected, like the leaves of a plant." Seth even mentioned species of consciousness—and again I thought, "Of course," imagining a time-species; all of us alive at one time, spreading through the century, covering it "end to end."

In Aspect Psychology, as introduced in *Adventures in Consciousness,* I'd envisioned the source self as spreading out through time, showing itself as separate focus personalities that we usually thought of as reincarnational selves. But now I saw that the source self (or psyche) actually spread out, peopling any given century as well. Groups of source selves would then ripple outward, giving us a basis for brotherhood that has far-reaching implications on all levels. Seth carries this concept well beyond the general statements quoted here. He also defined the concept in some class sessions, as he answered students' questions.

The connections between counterparts and the politics of the self are obvious. The private psyche would have invisible affiliations with its contemporaries. Operationally, counterparts would act like a private family of selves; inner versions of our family, national, and species relationships. Any given source self might have several focus personalities (or counterparts) alive on earth at once, each born into different racial, economic, cultural, or religious situations, so that life was experienced from a variety of standpoints as different elements of one time period were explored. Each counterpart would also contribute to the historic life of the century, in our terms of time.

Yet I kept wondering: Who keeps track? As usual, hints of an answer came when I was looking the other way, when I thought that I wasn't doing much at all.

For about two weeks, I'd had trouble getting into the library. It was there but not there. I tried to take it for granted that I was working at other than conscious levels; I kept up with the sessions and classes, but I felt a letdown.

At the same time, while I worried because I didn't feel inspired, I knew that I'd been very active in the dream state. But I thought, "Big deal—I want to be inspired in the waking state." And I managed to keep the two kinds of experience apart, even though I knew they were connected. Yet it was the nighttime activity that showed me, finally, what I'd been up to. *Then* it was obvious that I'd been dealing with the politics of the psyche in the most intimate manner.

In the meantime, though, for about a month I seemed to be getting some kind of material in the sleep state, usually following a Seth session. This had happened often in the past, but I was becoming more and more aware of what was going on. Words just kept going through my head, sentence after sentence, not in Seth's voice at all. This "voice" was mental, more like my own—like thinking, only "I" was thinking my own thoughts, or sometimes dreaming, while this was happening. The words were intrusive to that extent, and almost mechanical in their steadiness.

I responded in various ways: by trying to waken enough to write the material down (it was definitely "book" copy); by trying to comprehend what was being said; by switching from "my" thoughts or dreams to this other level, or by saying, finally, "Come on, quit it now. I just want to go into a normal sleep." But the words just marched on at their own pace, whether or not I could follow them. I could stop them by really trying, but couldn't slow them down.

Sometimes I just got frustrated, wondering if the material was really for Seth's *"Unknown" Reality*—and I had my signals crossed. Then I'd get confused, thinking that asleep I couldn't write the words down or record them, and where were they going, for heaven's sake?

  The material didn't seem to come from the library either. I took it for granted that I was programming myself in some way—but who was the self who was doing the programming? Sometimes I'd begin asking questions of the material itself and I'd get my own thought processes mixed up with the material. The material itself just went right on, "straight as an arrow"—my thoughts didn't seem to make any difference to it at all. Nor would the material answer my questions. It just kept on coming. So I'd take my questions back; learning that they didn't belong with the material. It was as if they were the wrong color and didn't fit. I thought of the material as coming in strands above my normal thinking level, and more and more I could differentiate between the two strands.

  Occasionally the material would just stop in mid-sentence, and I'd be annoyed, thinking that "I" would never stop writing in the middle of a sentence unless the roof fell in or something. Then the words would suddenly start in again as if they hadn't stopped; and though I couldn't be sure, I think they began again right where they'd left off.

  On a few other instances I picked up the material before it was ready, or so it seemed. Still asleep, yet in this funny state of consciousness, I'd get really annoyed thinking that the copy wasn't final, and that I didn't want it until it was. Even asleep, I insisted on good copy. I was particularly struck, though, by the fact that the material seemed unresponsive to my questions. It was as if I were equipped with a special set of mental earphones that picked up this certain station: So the material couldn't answer me any more than a record could.

  I still felt that the information was being transmitted directly into my mind, while at the same time the words seemed to march in from the right and go out the left side of my head, like notes on some musical graph several "lines" above the level of my own thoughts. My own thoughts were never disturbed in any way, as if the two sets of lines didn't meet but were independent. The only exception was willful tampering on my part, when I definitely made an effort to ask questions of the material itself: Then my thoughts bumped into these other words, with no marked effect except—again—that it was obvious the two didn't mix.

I had the image of my mind as a graph of some kind, with my thoughts always at one level, and this material at another. But did those intrusive words mix with my own thoughts at another level, one that I hadn't found yet? And were there still other seemingly independent lines that were psychologically invisible? Did my mind contain some kind of scale, with consciousness going up and down? And was I simply doing mental "finger" exercises?

Anyway, after the material on counterparts, I kept wondering who kept track of all those "selves," but I never connected the counterpart concept with the nighttime experiences. A few nights afterward, though, while I was asleep (euphemistically speaking) I found myself listening to that material again, and I thought, "Hey, I bet I can get some of this down if I do it just right." I'm not sure how I straddled the levels of consciousness, but I woke myself up and turned on the light. No one ever grabbed for a pen quicker than I did.

The oddest sensation followed. The completed copy began to . . . fall down to my level, crumble slightly, tumble in fragments, no longer as smooth and perfect as it had been, changing into concepts and images as if altering itself for my regular level of thought.

Complete or not, I had it. I felt triumphant even while I could write down only a small portion of the material. It vanished completely by the time I scribbled down the following:

FOUR-FRONTED SELVES

There can be, for example, four counterparts alive in one time period. These would form a psychic "block," and any one of the four personalities could pick up information from this joint pool (of identity). Each such person would be distinct yet each would be an added dimension of the others, so that on other levels the four (in this case) form an alliance and become a four-fronted self, forming a composite self bridging the given century.

Each of the four is equal, yet the overall psychic construction formed by their alliance is greater than the sum of the four parts. This alliance is a working one and once it's constructed, it always exists though it doesn't exist necessarily in our terms of continuity. It possesses a different kind of life (the four-fronted self), a life that "happens" whenever one of the counterparts tunes in to its greater framework. But the four-fronted self's own sense of continuity is not broken up and it exists outside of our space-time framework, while its counterparts exist in it. The conditions of existence are entirely different for the four-fronted self as a psychic construct.

I knew that I'd lost much of the material, and that the four-fronted self had been used as an example. It could be ten-fronted or a hundred-fronted, for all I knew. I did feel excited, though, because I felt that I was just beginning to unveil an original concept that would help us see ourselves in a far clearer light. (Even though, at this point, I was confused.)

This reminded me that just before the recent Seth sessions, I'd been getting glimpses of the material Seth was going to deliver, only in images and concepts that were not yet clear. It seemed as if I could either have a session in which Seth would deliver the information in completed form, or try to get it myself—in which case it would be fragmented. I chose the sessions. I had the same feeling with the "sleep material." By the time I got it my way, the polished quality had vanished, though I did get the essence.

The idea of one self seemed to be exploding into a group of numberless separate selves, a concept most difficult to follow. The next afternoon, however, I sat at my table, thinking, and I began to get the feeling of this . . . separate oneness. I wrote this page of notes, all the more evocative to me now, because as I type this final manuscript we've already moved away from the apartment room that I saw with such clarity.

"I'm listening to a symphony, its tones and notes emerging from the radio beside me. It's snowing lightly, and even with my head turned, I'm aware of the sleetlike snow-flakes falling past the wide bay windows. The traffic sounds merge with the music as the cars go shooting past on the slate-gray road, not yet snow-whitened. I look at my room with its small bright lamp lit on the room-divider bookcase; and at the few knickknacks—the bronze bird, copper five-and-dime Buddha, and the big, dull-gray wax frog. Each sits in its own spot, splendid in its own form, existing in its own eternity within the moment. Above, the six philo-dendron plants climb to the ceiling; an inside forest; green heart-shaped leaves rising out of space. And the green rug lies like a flat forest floor. The green couch rises like a languid furniture animal, breathing in long green sighs. And as always, the rooms seems significant and ways I don't fathom, as any place does when I catch it right. And what does it mean?

"To me, rooms represent the private consciousness with all of its beloved paraphanalia, its knickknacks or inner symbols materialized; a triumph of focus as if we're born and instantly form all this about us. We're in the midst of a symphony of objects, caught in one long passage and held, so that my bronze bird and copper Buddha and wax frog are held for so long—and then one day they'll collapse into crumbles of sound, their shapes disappearing into silence. But even then, the symphony can be played again, and the sepa-rate notes spring alive, alive as before, even though the original composers or musicians are gone. Yet in life and in this room the listeners contribute, the notes and objects themselves change and add to the composition in ways that we don't understand.

"So, privately, there seems something eternal about this room and its arrangement and me in it. And in the same way, the larger room of the world this afternoon is like an original version of an eternal symphony, forever happening yet never the same. Now the music on the radio rises to a crescendo and dies out, like objects coming fully into focus, bursting, and then retreating only to take a different shape and surge into another composition. When you sing a note, you let it go. And right now I feel like letting myself go in the same way."

I sat there, then, and felt other me's in other places looking around at the objects that surrounded *them* and wondering. And before I went to bed that night, I wrote the following poem.

Listening

I've put the glass of my mind
so close to the cosmic wall
that I've become addicted to the strange sounds
and eternal rattlings,
as if
a multitudinous mouse
went scurrying—
Is that all I'm hearing?

But listen.
My mind has a special hearing aid, appended,
like a new organ, uniquely fitted
to my occupation,
sifting, sifting sounds into patterns
or patterns into sounds;
an inner hearing
that magnifies without wires;
special equipment I've manufactured myself,
unknowing as a fish unknowing
forms its fins.
Or did it come built-in,
so long ago that I've forgotten?

> *If you say,*
> *"Mouse, what are you doing*
> *in my mental closet?"*
> *then all is suddenly quiet,*
> *so I've learned to wait*
> *for the cosmic rattlings,*
> *and I've even learned to put out bait,*
> *invisible but adequate.*

So I kept listening and I got an earful. I also tried to take my mind by surprise, to spy out my psyche at odd moments. It became clearer and clearer to me that all of our activities are based on our ideas about ourselves and the reaches of our psychological reality. Counterparts particularly intrigued me, though. Did the concept provide a biological, and psychic basis for the brotherhood of man? Seth said, for example, that many white people had black counterparts; and vice versa.

Most of all, though, I was beginning to see how little we knew about ourselves. What information did our minds contain of which we were largely unaware? And how could you find out, if you didn't really know what you were looking for? So occasionally, again, I began to jot down a few impressions at the beginning of the day, to see if these would correlate with current events. I wasn't concerned with public, but private reality. So my predictions were meant to apply to my own daily life.

When I wrote them down, they were usually disconnected. On December 6 that year (1974) I jotted down the following:

1. Minn.
2. Alaska
3. boy in trouble ... Carl? (I don't know any boy named Carl)
4. siq .. aquer

When the mail came, one letter seemed to apply to all of the impressions but Alaska. The letter was from an irate college boy I'll call Peter. He wrote from *Carl*eton College, Northfield, *Minn.*, and from his letter he was definitely in trouble, involved in a conflict of beliefs. He told me that he'd begun by considering me a "pure and productive medium" until he'd read Seth's *The Nature of Personal Reality*; then he'd sensed "stagnation," and could tell that I was repeating themes, "but in a more ego-directed and progressively useless way." From his letter it was only too clear that he considered the ego "bad," to be done in at all costs.

I looked up the last impression, number 4, in the dictionary. When I'd jotted it down, I wasn't sure of the meaning at all, and I had the idea that "non" should precede it, although I didn't write that down. The definition of *non sequitur* was: "An inference that does not follow from the premises ... Any fallacy resulting from a simple conversion of a universal affirmative proposition." The phrase was a perfect description of his attitude toward my latest work.

The second impression, Alaska, didn't seem to apply at all. Then I looked at the address again. The letter came from Northfield, Minn. Was Alaska my version of north fields?

Who knows? Yet the impressions convinced me, again that some future events are held in the mind, maybe in fragmented fashion; accessible if we want to find them and decipher our own symbols—and if we know what to look for. These simple "predictions" are just a few of the early ones I tried. Later I collected much more data that I still have to evaluate.

During the entire week or so, it seemed to me that I was working on three different subjects—the dream material that kept coming, time, and the contents of the mind. I'd made a few sketches, showing a "mind graph," and indicating the different levels at which I seemed to receive information. Then I got wondering: Did, say, knowledge of future events come in mixed with our ordinary think g hidden in usual associations that needed only to be re-sorte ?

And then the three subjects came into focus, and I saw what I'd been working on all the while. The soul or psyche has its own kind of "thickness," and that thickness includes not only time as the focus personality experiences it, but also events that are "out of time" to the focus personality. I'd been exploring the thickness of the psyche. Did my predictions, modest as they were, arrive into my usual thought patterns when requested in the same way that the sleep material came into my regular consciousness when I made a concerted attempt to get it? When this happened, the dream copy dropped down into my thought-slot, so to speak, in fragmented fashion, broken up into bits of concepts and images. When I was jotting down predictions, did I just bring in pieces and bits in the same way and for the same reason?

These questions led me back to the thoughts about time I'd had earlier that week: There's something invisible that gives objects their solidity and maintains their shape so that all the atoms don't collapse or fly apart; and the same kind of invisible value separates objects in time, so that events don't come together all at once to our perception or fly apart away from us. This is an inside-outside value that results in the correlation of subjective and objective experience. Acting inside matter, it builds up the solidarity of objects, and inside the mind it builds up separate solid events that exist apart from each other subjectively, as objects exist apart in space.

Sometimes, under certain conditions, we short-circuit this value or use it differently, perceiving events out of their usual sequence, and I suspect that this precognition also . . . alters the events in some fashion: we perceive them out of shape as it were, just as if they weren't "ready yet" and hadn't attained their proper condition. The connections between space, time, and gravity help us pinpoint objects and experience, and if the three elements don't correlate in just the proper fashion, then we don't accept an event as real: It lacks a certain stability or rightness and remains on the periphery of our attention. But outside of the normally recognized context, events might appear quite differently. Most likely there are bleed-throughs that we block out; ghost images, as it were, of future and past events alike. The past moment might linger in the background of the present one and the future might also overlap before the so-called picture changes and the present moment is clear.

Neurologically, we'd only accept the clear focus.

Perhaps if we were aware of the overlapping, we'd lose experience of the present, or maybe we'd learn a finer kind of inner discrimination. It might be fun sometime to try to hold over the "past" instant (the thought or image or whatever) and try simultaneously to anticipate the next instant. What would happen to the stability of objects? Would they appear longer, for example? Thinner? Thicker? Would they seem to move?

I don't have good depth perception. Does this somehow help me in altering my consciousness? Was I slightly out of focus with physical reality in that fashion, not as locked-in to the obvious? Originally I was left-handed too, so the two conditions might be related. Yet many of my states of altered consciousness involve vision changes, so that the world attains a clarity as far above normal depth perception as my normal sight without glasses.

Weird. After writing the above, I took my glasses off. The world lost much depth and color but gained a certain quaintness, became more "atmospheric," perhaps more mysterious. My hearing is super-acute, though. By my standards, half of the rest of the people would need hearing aids. My vision of the world may be as legitimate as any person's with normal sight. Objects may not have any one proper size or shape at all: They may simply appear in such-and-such a fashion according to our perceptions. If we see them out of shape, we may be tuning in to their other quite-as-legitimate variations.

Luckily, as I write all this, my chair and typewriter remain normal. And I put my glasses back on.

Chapter 13
The Exploding Psyche and Strands of Consciousness

Here I go again, being facetious, but I got another call from Christ just as I finished the last chapter. Not just any ole gal from Elmira can have God the Son call her up for a chat, so I should have counted myself lucky, I suppose, and if you're going to get a person-to-person phone call from Christ, what better time than the Christmas holidays? It was December 18, and believe it or not, I was signing Christmas cards when the call came. At first I had no idea that it was a member of the Big Boy's family; much less his favorite Son.

Actually, the voice was young and male and initially identified itself as Ed. Christmas music was playing on the radio. I turned it off and asked, "Ed who?" Silence. "Ed who?" I asked again.

"Are you afraid?" he asked, mysteriously.

This time I paused.

"Nervous?" he persisted.

"Just curious," I answered, sighing. "Should I know who you are or something? Have you called before?"

"Yes. I'm Christ," he said.

"Oh, of course, *that* Ed," I said. "I remember."

How could I forget? He'd called about a year previously, a nice-enough-sounding young man, in no way different from anyone else except that he was 99 percent divine. "Uh, you're still Christ?" I asked.

"You think I'm crazy," he said—sanely enough, I thought. He'd been sane enough to lie his way out of a mental institution the year before by telling the psychologists what they wanted to hear, and by pretending not to be Christ until he was safely outside. I suppose that with a secret like that, you have to tell someone though, so here he was, calling me again.

"You *do* think I'm crazy, thinking I'm Christ, don't you?" he asked, as if he was very disappointed with my level of understanding.

"I think that in those terms, every individual is Christ," I said. "I told you that before. If you use Christian terminology, then the Christ spirit *is* in you. And in every one else, too."

"That's not enough," he said.

"For me it is," I said.

"I'm Christ, and I'm going to fulfill the prophecies," he said, more excitedly now.

"That didn't work out too well once before," I said mildly. "I'd think it over if I were you."

"Now you're challenging me," he said.

"No. I never bother challenging anyone," I answered.

"Well, then, what do you think of it?" he asked, adding somewhat bitterly, "I wish you'd open your mind. I can't read your mind if you won't let me."

Thank God, I thought.

What I said was: "Look, Ed. Each of us receives revelationary material from the inner self or the universe or God, whatever name you want to use. It comes in dreams or flashes of insight or visions—any method suited to the individual. And we each interpret the information in our own way, too. You can live like Christ in the inner world and try to be Christlike in the outer one, but if you start shouting out to people that you *are* Christ—in conventional terms— you're going to get into trouble."

"I'm not shouting," he nearly shouted. "And I know enough not to tell other people. I really do."

"Okay," I said, feeling better.

"And while I'm pretty sure that I *am* Christ, there's a possibility that I'm really somebody else. I think he'll make himself known around Christmas. I mean, I might know for sure one way or the other," he said.

"Well, it's good to leave yourself some leeway."

"You have a young voice. I'm twenty-three," he ventured.

"I'm a lot older than that," I said.

"I know, I've read all of your books."

"Well," I said. "Just keep your Christhood to yourself, will you? Are you working, by the way?"

"Of *course* I'm working. It was a silly question. I'm working, to get the message across."

Again I said, "Ed, don't try to force a literal Christhood on yourself or the world. It just won't work."

"You're challenging me again," he chided, gently this time. "But I love you. Merry Christmas," he said.

"Merry Christmas," I said. We hung up.

In some way he gave me a present. I hoped I gave him one too. Christ or not, he sounded like a nice boy, and if he had to be somebody beside himself, then Christ was a better choice than Hitler, I supposed. Besides, I "knew" that he was in the process of changing: He was less sure now of his literal Christhood, and I meant every word I said to him. I also knew from talking to him previously that his message wasn't a violent one. It was himself, no one else, he was thinking of sacrificing. I hoped he'd give that idea up, too.

Yet I was disturbed, because those who think themselves possessed by the gods too often carry messages of rage and destruction rather than love. And why? The gods of the nations have the souls of generals, it seems, and righteousness far too often wears the face of wrath. Even in the psyche, religion and politics seem to mix uneasily.

That night, Rob and I watched part of a war movie on television, and Rob said that maybe the race was literally insane. He started talking about the pitch of emotional intensity connected with mass violence—the brilliant focus of awareness—life knowing itself as it teetered on the edge of destruction. We spoke about all of this for a while. I kept trying to defend us, the race, while secretly, bitterly, agreeing whenever Rob mentioned our cruelties.

The answers have to lie in a different context, yet I seem driven to find them—the answers to everything: life, private existence, the psyche's secret reasons. This strikes me as foolish at the same time, because no one person can discover all that—one small individual amid a blaze of being. Yet I keep trying. I wish sometimes that I could just rest in the world the way most people understand it to be, content with appearances. Then I think that maybe when you reach a certain point, your mind makes questions the way your body makes cells, and the questions go ahead of you in some fashion and you work your way thought over thought, on a tiny trapeze over the webwork of the usual world. Unknowingly you inch your way outward, like a spider, toward wherever it is that the questions reach. But when you get there and find the answers that the questions hooked on to, then the junction just brings up more questions, and there you go again, leaving behind you, unknowingly, tiny threads for people behind you to follow, and growing out into the inner cosmos in a kind of natural locomotion of the mind. Maybe.

Seth is beginning to leave more and more familiar concepts behind, and to change others or use them differently so that they no longer mean what they did. And a part of me is doing the same thing in this book, while another part sits here musing about it.

Now and then I have the suspicion that the further along you go, the more alone you might become because the people behind get tired too and want to stop along the way, and often they're tempted to call their stopping point the truth. In a way it is, of of course, because I suspect also that at our level at least, the truth is just the way reality appears at any given time.

Somehow, you have to climb above all those places to get out of our particular atmosphere and see anything clearly at all. So I suppose that the stranger things get, the closer I'm coming to a clear spot; where I can look back at all of the concepts of reality and see what they have in common. This would be something like just looking down at the earth, seeing all the different countries that exist, each quite valid, at the same time. Maybe there will be others at this clear spot when I get there, to pull out a handy hallucinary chair and offer me some beer and crackers while they explain what it's all about.

I'm not sure exactly what my concept of the psyche was when I began this book, but as our experiences continued, it seemed obvious that the psyche was not a single, but lofty entity: Instead it was more explosive and vital, shooting fragments of itself out in all directions while still—somehow—retaining individuality. The idea of counterparts gave a new kind of mobility to the psyche, but at least the concept of reincarnation set the stage.

Early that December, though, Rob had an experience that was quite unsettling in its implications; one that further disturbed our previous ideas about the psyche's separateness and integrity. The episode concerned Rob's father, who had died in 1971. Again, Rob was typing up a Seth session when he found himself in a slight alteration of consciousness, in which certain information came into his mind. He had no visual data this time, and just wrote down the material as it came to him. This is a copy of his notes at that time:

"In our terms my father is still resting. He is nonphysical, between experiences. He hasn't chosen as yet to do anything or go 'anywhere.' He knows, however, that he is preparing himself. I'm getting my familiar chills as I write this; but I don't see any visions. I know that my father has his next adventure all mapped out, and he knows what it is even though, in our terms, he hasn't consciously made that choice.

"The choice involves a small girl—I think her name is Miriam—in a small New York state town. It's not a long trip, something like hitching a psychic ride. My father plans to travel with the little girl, experiencing a touch of her life; her consciousness. He won't be invading her personality. She's a very normal little person, but with better-than-average intelligence. She won't feel a thing.

"After that, there's a long interval in what would be a past century in our terms. Miriam has been involved in several of these, and my father is thinking about this and wondering which one he wants to try on for size, you might say. He leans toward the thirteenth century in France—a small town near the Mediterranean Sea. He sees himself in a small boat. Miriam lives in the village: Per . . . sec. My father wants to work things out with the Miriam personality. Miriam, of course, was also my mother.

"Her psyche and my father's strike sparks when they touch; the fit is not too good, but both sides want to resolve certain problems. One of these is occupying *portions* of the same body at the same time—something like the male and female characteristics that we say each person contains. In that [French] life, Miriam grows up to be a rather grasping, good-looking woman. She is the stronger of the two, and throws my father off, embarking on a probable course of action at age thirteen that makes this possible.

"My father is thrown free, to his dismay. At the same time, a young man in the village dies. I'm not sure here—if I am of *any* of this—but my father whirls about in a nonphysical state, desperately looking for a place to land or fasten upon. He tries the youth's body, to no avail. So my father begins a new life in France, starting from scratch and being born again.

"Now my father is attracted to the New York Miriam in the same way. He wants to see, to explore what the earlier attraction was, if he can. Then he'll be content to go his own way. Miriam is just as curious psychically as my father is, and was. He now thinks it perfectly logical to live that past life; he isn't clear, but has hints and glimmers that all lives are simultaneous, and that he is hopping between them, alighting here and there.

"He understands that this is something like turning oneself inside out: all that's been hidden inside is known, and available. In France, my father was left without physical form, and chose to end that existence. (After which he was reborn.) That's right: A strong personality will sometimes divest itself of unwanted portions of its own psyche. However, these parts may orbit the psyche like satellites, and can be re-entered or reactivated at any time in our terms. This accounts sometimes for the way a personality will change its goals and behavior during its life-span, to the puzzlement of observers.

"My father was really a kind man, almost an apologetically softhearted one, in that thirteenth-century life, what he had of it. He had several earlier lives that were very severe, involving the military and monastic disciplines. Now my father waits, gathering his emotions slowly. He is somewhat loath to leave his present state—it is a very peaceful one—but he knows that beyond the door he looks at lie many things that now he can barely sense.

"Occasionally he looks at our world through very puzzled eyes. He sees foliage as heat images. He doesn't see Jane or me, but instead perceives half-formed focuses of energy that he really doesn't understand, although the *ideas* of Jane and me make some sense to him. He sees my mother [also deceased] better, and confuses her with the thirteenth-century Miriam and the New York State Miriam; for his life with my mother was also an attempt to reach certain goals. He feels he did not succeed here. He doesn't 'see' my mother but knows she is no longer physical. He does realize that she'll soon be born again, and that this time the Miriam part of her will choose to go its own way.

"That part of the psychic challenge has been resolved as best it can; those parts will not meet again in those terms. My father's altered sense of time can make the growth of a blade of grass take a second or a century, depending on how he 'feels.'

"This is the end of the material concerning my father. I was very upset after I wrote it. I don't know why. I think that I felt it contained so many distortions that it probably wasn't very reliable. I suppose I didn't trust my reception of it, since this is the first time I received material in just this fashion, and I sensed that I probably needed practice. On the other hand, I sought to accomplish something that I might have inhibited had I known what to expect. I also thought that the material contained some ideas that I regarded as psychic tampering—almost unhealthy, perhaps."

We *were* disturbed by the material; Rob particularly. It was precisely the kind of "information" most easy to dismiss as imaginative fantasy presenting itself as fact, yet there's something terribly arrogant in our taking it for granted that such offbeat data *must* be distorted because it doesn't agree with our previous ideas. To inhibit such experiences, as many people do, means that we constantly monitor one level of our consciousness with another so that our prejudiced perception rules the day.

The general idea that Rob's dead father was still resting was quite acceptable. But beyond that, there was the indication that personhood wasn't nearly as clear-cut as we supposed, almost as if it could disperse itself in so many unknown ways as to disappear as the kind of personality unit we recognize.

Memories from future and past seemed to be involved, and an interweaving of selves very difficult to follow. Yet who should know more about the psyche's experiences than the psyche itself? And why should we doubt the implications of Rob's material simply because it was so subjective? We also took it for granted that Rob's father's consciousness itself might be confused; granting that was the source of the material, communicated through Rob's mind. But maybe cellular knowledge and the psyche are so connected that somehow the child keeps track of the parent even after death; that the cellular consciousness itself follows its own offshoots in all directions.

If we're doing anything, Rob and I, it's exploring unofficial reality, studying and encouraging those events that are usually ignored; certainly this was one of those events. The next morning, I sat reading over Rob's notes. I was struck again by this seeming interweaving of selves, or of one self identity with others, as if one self could disperse itself, say, like a million raindrops, each itself and separate, falling in numberless backyards or environments, while carrying a sense of the entire identity at the same time.

And suddenly I sensed the self dispersed through unknown universes while still being itself; winding dizzily through labyrinths of psychological and corporal intensities, each one forming a life in its own context. Is the entire psyche like a multidimensional jigsaw puzzle, each part independent, with not one but a thousand proper places, each automatically forming a new version of the overall picture; leaping in and out of time systems as easily as a child jumps hopscotch squares? If so, how doubly precious are our private moments and our experience of psychological per-manencey! This is strong stuff for us, used as we are to holding our sense of identity firmly, defiantly, and applying its tests against the rest of creation.

Maybe, I thought, the focus personality is just one psychological window through which the psyche views reality; except that its mere looking creates a three-dimensionally-tuned consciousness that is you and me. My experiences in the library make me wonder what I'm doing at other levels of reality when I'm not aware of my activities there.

As I sat thinking, I could feel inner connections come into focus, though I couldn't quite get hold of them. Smoothly, just behind usual consciousness, a few speckled stones of comprehension were rolling down the slopes of my mind. *Then,* with my next question, I was on to something. I could feel myself beginning to understand something new—or something old in a new way.

Do we have numberless strands of consciousness, I wondered, as Rob's experience seems to imply? And theoretically, anyway, could we follow any of them into another kind of reality; even into another kind of psychological structure than the one we take for granted? In some strange fashion, are we composed of such other strands of consciousness ourselves, winding through the invisible nerve ends of the universe?

Do I follow my "I" by concentrating on my own strand of consciousness, which is made up of other interweaving ones, each following its own? Those others might be completely aware of me ... I might ride their strands, and my personality might be part of another strand that is more complicated in those terms than mine.

Again: dizzying concepts in which any God would be within the texture of the strands themselves; the principle behind and within the organization; the very standard of individuality maintaining itself amid unending diversity. I would be me precisely because in those terms I was also part of "others," though their kind of personhood might be incomprehensible from my viewpoint. And my workroom, I thought, with its homey paraphernalia, would be private and mine precisely because it was part of an unknown cosmos that weaved into and out of it constantly.

It was a Tuesday morning. I should have been making notes for my class that evening, but I became engrossed in the idea of these strands of consciousness and their implications. I saw them as forming focus personalities at certain points or psychological intersections. For example, is Seth me at a level of consciousness that is habitual to him but not to the me I know? If so, Seth would have his own strand of consciousness of which I would be a part—even as Seth might be a strand in a still greater kind of consciousness. This idea could be applied to the molecules that compose our bodies, too. To the atoms and molecules that form my flesh, do I seem like a different kind of Seth? Does my consciousness wind in and out of Seth's?

I was sensing different strands of reality, separate yet united. The strands might pool outward several times in a century, forming the counterparts. The whole idea evokes a dance of being in which our slightest aspect has a chance to develop, assisting in a million different constructions, yet retaining its own sense of direction, forming endless combinations, giving life to others as it receives it—part of an infinite chain of being.

This gives rise to other imaginings: Does the psyche change size—does it expand and contract? Strands of consciousness! The universe, or God, would be sending them out constantly. Our selves would represent our private paths of awareness—the way "Being" is scooped into our kind of existence, the way the cosmos makes itself. And if we could separate our own strands of consciousness, what would we find?

As I wrote and questioned, somewhere along the line I went into an accelerated state of consciousness. I'll quote my own notes as I scribbled them down at the time, so that the immediacy is retained. (Part of the experience reminded me of another, involving a piece of paper, that had taken place a few years earlier. See *Adventures in Consciousness* and *Dialogues of The Soul and Mortal Self in Time*.)

"I've gone into an altered state, as if some part of me is going incredibly fast. At the same time I've grown very warm; the back of my neck particularly, and although I'm excited, my eyes want to close. Must keep them open, to get this down. So this is another strand of consciousness that I'm following; another strand of 'me-ness' that really operates all the while. Maybe one that relates to a completely different reality? Yet I'm woven in it, and by changing focus I ride alongside it or follow it like a spider wandering the far threads of a gigantic web.

"I'm mentally dizzy. Psychologically, the feeling is pleasant, like the one I felt physically when I was a child and went spinning around in a circle; yet I don't feel disoriented. The room remains steady, and the sun has just come out. But I feel that the world is what you see when you whirl mentally at a certain rate—and if you move faster, or slower, then time and objects and space break up like the pieces of a jigsaw puzzle, assembling in new ways. These strands of consciousness each have their own speeds. Maybe I'm me only when my strand vibrates in a certain way; and when it vibrates at a different rate I'm another version of me, that's no copy but itself. Maybe me is just one note in an entire symphony of me's, some in scales so alien that I'd never recognize my me-ness at all.

"Again, as I sit here a symphony *is* playing on the radio. A few minutes ago my gaze turned toward the window. A piece of newspaper was blowing across the parking lot, and suddenly I felt its texture in a way impossible to describe: soft, limp, floppy. The wind caught its edges. It tipped sideways, leapt; shot ahead and was caught in the high bristly bushes. Held. Its motions seemed synchronized with the music playing on the radio. Soft notes—and the paper lay still, waiting. The music rose and the paper lifted, gently, and then fell as the notes died away.

"My hands felt that way, too; limp, passive, floppy—and my body, so that a part of me lay up against the bushes and the paper that was me curved around the prickers, not resisting but softly falling around them. The music boomed out. A flock of pigeons came to the roof. They pecked at the birdfeed in rhythm to the music so that paper, birds, and me were all caught in the same motion, responding. Another crescendo now. Yes, the birds all flew away together. Was this all my organization? What does it matter whether or not I transposed that order upon those events? It's real. Perhaps it's the real way things work.

"So I'm between just following this version of the moment, or writing down what I feel; or following other thoughts about strands of consciousness that come to me. It seems that this moment gives me hints about how consciousness itself works.

"As I write all of this down, noon has arrived. The music just gave way to the news, which somewhat annoys me. Yet what does it do to my strand of consciousness? They're talking about food prices going up, and I think: Well, we can always go on a budget again. A good, satisfying feeling. Then, ignoring the radio, I go back to my earlier thoughts, turn off the radio and the stream of consciousness that was connected with it.

"And it occurs to me that I choose from strands of consciousness all the time, and that my choices bring me certain experiences. This certainly involves probabilities. Our thoughts serve as focus points. To some extent, the thoughts are self-perpetuating and we habitually choose one kind over another.

"We really alter our consciousness constantly then, through our choices. For example, just before one of the latest Seth sessions I knew I could get certain material at one level on my own—but it would take some time and work—or I could get it from Seth much more quickly and in finished form. But in more mundane matters, the same applies. I know, for instance, that I accept some experiences that are 'negative' and these are also self-perpetuating. Can I locate a different strand of consciousness that concentrates differently on those matters?

"This reminds me. Earlier today a student called. He broke his leg last week. Since then he's worked on his beliefs constantly, and he saw how he consistently formed negative mental pictures, like mental snapshots, all adding up to his misadventure. Yet had he . . . chosen another group of thoughts, another strand of consciousness, his experience would have changed too.

"As I finished typing the last page, I was swept up with the paper again. That is, I glanced at it, saw that the same thing was happening again, felt my own swift identification with the paper, and decided to go along with it. Now the sense of texture is very strong—a sense—feeling, not an intellectual idea—so that my body feels the paper's experiences . . . as real as the way I'd normally feel, say, wet or dry. I feel the pressure of wind against the bush, pressing it; a miniature ecstasy of motion. Oh, the birds come again. My right hand prickles: Is this the paper against the prickers? A rush in my stomach as the pigeons sweep by again. And everything is connected. It's as if the birds fly through my stomach. The fantastic shapes the paper takes, each unique to the paper and to me; to us! Each shape puts us in a different relationship with everything else. Now the paper throws its head back, lies open, full of ecstasy with the wind. . . .

"Some minutes later, Rob comes into the room. I look when he leaves, but the paper is gone. I scribble down

the thoughts I have, very quickly; not put well. We make
organizations as focuses for our consciousness; recognize certain events as significant and ignore others. In our usual state,
the kinds of events I've just experienced with the paper aren't
followed. They're beneath our attention. As I write this,
there are three strands of consciousness that I'm trying to
follow simultaneously; four, when you remember that I'm
trying to write this all down at the same time. The birds and
the traffic are synchronized, moving together, and I can jump
in that with them. I have to get ready for tonight's class, and
a part of me wants to follow that direction. Another part of
me is aware of making a decision between the other two,
while analyzing them. But I know that if you follow other
sequences, you'll end up with different events. Is the paper a
kind of strand of consciousness always available, and could I
choose to spend a whole day experiencing reality that way?
Could someone experience a whole lifetime, concentrating on
the inner events that are usually psychologically invisible?

"Rob came back. I tried to talk to him, but my
speech was slurred and slow, although I knew I could click it
back to normal speed by changing my focus. I'm still aware
of the three separate strands of consciousness. In each, my
awareness is filled differently, or the same contents of the
world are experienced differently. The paper has drifted back
into my vision. We merge, while I'm still aware of myself,
merging. I feel the paper plop. I am the paper flopping on the
ground, but the paper isn't me sitting at the table. Or if it is, I
don't know it. Time is meaningless in usual terms, but each
smallest motion represents surprising change and variations
and everything still moves in rhythm. There are subtle
alterations of perception happening constantly, and temperature changes as the paper stirs; too damp to rustle.
Unbelievable in a way, though these notes show so little.
Unbelievable it's 3 P.M. I thought it was just past noon."

The experience wasn't profound in conventional
terms. It brought no great visions or "shattering" illu-
minations. Yet it *was* subjectively profound, precisely
because it was otherwise involved with mundane subjects—

the paper, music, traffic—and because it offered intriguing insights into the inner, usually hidden, other organizations that are nestled within any known given moment.

As usual, I didn't see then where these experiences were leading. But I wondered: When we send out our attention, do we project strands of energy that intersect with a person or object and strike a response—a corresponding strand of energy that causes a constant interplay beneath usual perception? I've taken it for granted that the piece of paper didn't have any awareness of me, my scrutiny, identification, or appreciation. But suppose it did? Suppose my attention caused ripples to which it responded?

So for a few moments, I sensed this interplay within matter—constant motion, strands of energy meeting, consciousness itself merging and forming invisible constructions as varied and valid as physical ones; even forming identities which themselves formed all kinds of combinations.

Dimly I saw how these applied to the personality. The prime Aspects operate like psychic sparks, their lively nature providing for an endless number of potential new beginnings. Like psychological atoms, they maintain a certain form within the psyche, orbiting the focus personality while still changing constantly; altering positions within the psyche in response to psychological activity, maintaining the stability of the focus personality—not only in its relationship with the exterior world but maintaining its psychological inner stance as well.

In our terms, the focus personality is the director. I had the choice of focusing on any of the three strands of consciousness earlier, for example. None of them were thrust upon me. In the same way, the judgments of the focus personality dominate in usual life and direct body activity. The arm muscles don't question the individual's intent to move them. They don't ask figuratively: "Now, does this arm really need to be lifted?" The focus personality makes the judgments which are then carried out. It's also the focus personality, with its beliefs, that rules the politics of the psyche as it's directed toward daily life. Only when those politics are detrimental to the entire fabric of the personality are inner steps taken, and pressure applied from within.

Most of all, I was left with the idea that the counterparts are eccentric versions of the source self, activated in the same time period. This would provide the actualization of a million varieties of experience possible for the psyche at any given earth period; as if one living psychological plant sent out its roots well beneath the ground of usual conscious activity; populating the planet with its psychic seeds.

I suspect that all the questions we ask about the exterior universe can be asked even more legitimately of the interior one, for in larger terms I see each as a counterpart of the other. The quarks and charmed particles postulated by the physicists will have their psychic or psychological versions, from which all matter and its "inner components" emerge. So any such psychological experimentation or investigation will most likely involve the "discovery" of smaller and smaller units of the self, each free-wheeling, each dependent yet independent, each perceiving a different kind of experience which is nevertheless connected with all other experience.

The physicists found that the sense world was a thing apart from the reality behind or within it—that objects, regardless of their operational stability and permanence, are actually masses of invisible, quickly moving atoms. We may be in for a far greater surprise: It's most possible that the self we recognize is also the result of our psychological perception of reality; as operational as an object and just as deceptive in appearance. The self instead may be a unit of identity, one of many, a psychic unit that rides strands of consciousness, composed of miniature and giant selves also—and part of a psychological universe we haven't even begun to explore.

We've discovered that the earth isn't flat; that we won't fall off its edges, and our experience as a species has changed as a result. Maybe we'll soon find out that the self isn't "flat" either, and that death is as real and yet as deceptive as the horizon; that we don't fall out of life either. Disorienting, sure, but challenging. We may discover a new kind of personhood that is truly multidimensional, and for the first time really find dimensions in which the soul exists, connected to the flesh but also separate—the invisible atoms of the self orbiting our known selfhood, forming psychological connections and mental worlds presently beyond our conception.

But once we hit on this idea; once we start reading the clues, then what a metaphysical chase! Most of our present ideas will be as passé as the "world is flat" concept of the past. Freed from our psychological blindness, who knows what interior frontiers we might explore, or what psychological universes will be presented to our view?

Chapter 14

Back to the Library. Climbing up the Steps of the Psyche, and the Girl Who Tried to Love Everybody

The holidays came and vanished, like all the ones that had gone before. That Christmas of 1974 was to be the last one we spent at our Water Street apartments, although we didn't know then. Rob was very busy, producing the diagrams for *Adventures in Consciousness* and the ink drawings for *Dialogues of the Soul and Mortal Self in Time*. We told ourselves that we were going to move when he was finished; but we'd talked about moving before. Still, the thought that we *might* colored that Christmas.

I worked on some new poetry, but during the holidays the library seemed distant, and it was difficult to recapture the feelings of certitude and high confidence I'd had earlier. The library seemed to hide its books and I became restless and annoyed.

I was in just such a mood when the following events suddenly roused me. It was early evening as I sat at my table, staring out at the bare trees. I must have closed my eyes for a moment when a group of very vivid mental images sprang into my mind. First, I saw my body curled around something, like meat on a spit, but without the fire. The image was projected out into the room just outside the area where I usually saw the library.

Then, with no transition, I saw my body stretched out in space, lengthwise: it reached past me into unimaginable distances, then elastically disappeared first way to my right, then way to my left. Each time it went through the apartment house walls, out into space, and returned again. My physical head was turning so fast to keep track that I got dizzy as I watched my body go back and forth before my mental eyes. This kept up for several minutes.

A quick series of lesser-felt images followed. A door opened into a drafty stone room: I was a child, shoved in there and told to play with "the other children". This faded, and my own body felt as if it were curling up into a ball. Mentally, I saw it go rolling across our living room floor. Then it turned into a serpent and began climbing a tree in a jungle. As all of this happened, I felt super-relaxed, warm, and flexible.

I started to write my notes about this the following afternoon when I realized that some library material was ready for me. I didn't see the library or its books, but the following material came smoothly into my head, each word plump and vivid as a piece of fruit dropped into a basket.

From the Library
The psyche is awareized energy, in a state of constant creativity; a psychic pattern multidimensionally expressed; each point within it changing in relationship to all other points, and thus altering the entire pattern or model.

Each self is immersed in the psyche, yet immersed in its own individuality simultaneously, experiencing reality in time and out of it at once. We create events naturally, in the same way that earth produces trees, grain, mountains, and seas. In earth experience, the earth itself is "given"; that is, it appears to be self-producing and self-sufficient within the framework of the universe. So, in the same way, the self is "given": The alliance of psyche and body produces mental events and experiences that also appear to be self-sufficient and self-producing within the framework of the psychological world. Yet everything is interrelated.

There is an inner landscape of the mind that produces thoughts, dreams, experiences, and events, and this correlates with the exterior landscape. It's extremely difficult to map this interior land because we confuse the brain's activity for the power behind the brain, and because we do not consider the interior landscape as real as the exterior one. We're also so immersed in the interior world that we take its natural elements for granted. Dreams, thoughts, and all mental experiences compose the natural phenomena of the inner reality. We travel through the psyche as we travel through time and across the face of the earth. When we encounter events, they will appear differently according to our position within the psyche.

Many dream events are versions of waking ones—not distorted at all, just the dream version, as the physical event is the waking version. While we accept the waking experience as the real one, it is no more or less real than the dream event.

Here, the material just stopped. I glanced at the clock. It was 2:30 P.M. I was still looking at the clock when I saw my double sitting in the library, at the table, reading. My consciousness leapt into that form, as I tried quickly to read from the same book she was reading. Instantly the letters of the words became shiny and turned into small brilliant squares. These opened up into pictures that represented peepholes into other worlds. At least, that was my understanding at the time.

Anyhow, I decided that it was now or never: after not being in the library in some while, I was certainly going to take advantage of my opportunity. So I tried to dive headlong into one of the miniature windows—my image had turned miniature too. In some way, I got stuck, couldn't go one way or the other, and I was thrown gently back into the library.

The next instant I was back in my body at the desk, while my double remained in the library. She perched on the tabletop, legs crossed; wearing the green jumper and black stockings that I wore in Rob's old portrait of me. Mentally I asked her if she had anything to say. She jumped off the library table, leapt into the living room, came behind me, and blended into my body. Then she emerged, blended with me again, reemerged, and went back into the library. Again I spoke to her mentally, asking her how much more material I'd get from the library. She laughed, and leapt back to the library table.

The next series of events happened so quickly that it was difficult to keep track. She jumped down from the table, and as she did, my consciousness was tranferred to her image. As this happened, she began to spin quicker and quicker, changing into a shape resembling an umbrella rack. She (I) had four sides, or four selves coming out of the rod part of this umbrella form.

While this was going on, I "knew" that there would be at least three books in this particular Aspect Psychology series; this manuscript being the second one and *Adventures in Consciousness* the first. Then I saw a wall of books in four parts, like an inverted pyramid, reaching upward indefinitely. The entire structure was wide at the top and I was at the narrow bottom, looking upward. I knew that I was supposed to fly to the opening beyond. Somehow, I was swept upward, passing all the books in their swirls of color. At the top, I faced the opening and a sky far above. Here I became frightened, feeling like a bird being thrown from the nest. I flew, arms outstretched, through the opening. Just as I felt panicky a tree branch appeared, with a globe growing from the end of it, like fruit. I clung to it, resting.

I'd closed my eyes, bewildered at the height. When I opened them, I was back at my desk in the living room. My double stood in the library. This time I asked her for some help with the physical stiffness that had been bothering me.

Almost at once, mentally, I saw a small fairylike figure with a wand. She came into my body, going from one area to another. I saw and felt "her" inside my head, for example: her wand turned into a dustcloth and the circle inside my skull was vigorously dusted (of mental cobwebs, no doubt). In any case, I felt the whole thing, and it seemed then that there were many windows that had been dusty, all around the circumference of my skull. They became brilliant and shiny. Then the little figure went down my backbone, like a miniature maid about to do the household chores. I felt her sweep the shoulder area ambitiously, as you might a landing; then down the stairs of the vertebrae, step by step, the wand turning into a broom or mop—whatever utensil was needed. After this, she vanished.

The radio was on all this time, playing rock music at low volume. It was a bright January afternoon, with sun coming through the window. I just thought about lowering the blinds when a mental movement "caught my eye." I turned, really startled this time, and closed my eyes to "see better." To my mental vision, a very large ape stood by the coffee table. The motion I'd sensed had been his leap from the library. The next instant, part of my consciousness was within his body. He made a complicated series of vigorous movements. I felt them from inside him; but my physical body also seemed to fill with flexible delight so that I felt as if I were moving more easily than a ballet dancer. The ape danced all around the room, leapt on the coffee table, then flopped full length out on the floor, in a playing-dead pose. I left his body, turning into a tiny image of myself. The ape reached out and picked me up. For a moment I was frightened, but he tucked me in a small flap of fur on his chest, like a sleeping bag, where I felt very snug and secure.

It was here, when I supposed the experiences to be over, that the strangest and most vivid episode began. Once again (in my mind's eye) the library became an upside-down pyramid. It existed as always at the southeast corner of the living room; the inner wall. Again my consciousness had its own image. In it I stood once more at the bottom of the inverted pyramid that reached upward, seemingly into eternity. Other selves—other me's—were climbing the sides of the pyramid, using the book sides as you would ledges, each ascending toward the wide opening at the center top. The whole affair was like a cavern. The sunlight shone down brilliantly from the opening far above, and fell down to where I stood, directly focused on me. Yet I noticed that the sun's rays also touched each of the other figures.

I'm not sure what happened next, but suddenly I was flying at top speed way up to the top of the canyon, to the distant sky. Hands came down and held me. At this point I was in the space beyond the cavern, lying flat in the sky. Hands passed my prone body on to other hands. I forget what happened again, and "came to" to find myself a baby wrapped in a blanket. Apparently in the meantime I'd been carried higher in space. I looked around. A woman was seated in the clouds. She was holding me tenderly. Although she had a halo I knew that she wasn't a representation of the Virgin, but that in some way I couldn't understand, she was my mother in . . . heroic terms. She handed me to a man seated beside her—my father in these same incomprehensible terms.

The man held me gently in the same fashion, then returned me to the woman's arms. I knew that they were "divine" or at least that their existence was in a far vaster context than ours; and I felt that I had originally come from the same "place." Dimly, though, some small part of my consciousness even then echoed upward with its questions: "Gods in the sky? Representations of the psyche's knowledge, symbolized?" Questions or not, I was supremely comfortable, secure, and loved. For a moment I wanted to stay right where I was.

Suddenly, however, the baby with my consciousness inside, whirled away through space; a very small infant with the blanket fluttering. The folds of the blanket formed patterns in space in a way I've now forgotten. I fell a very long way, then was swept back up again to where the woman was. Here my consciousness separated. Part of it became a portion of the veil about the woman's head. The baby and its portion of my consciousness rolled out of the folds in the veil—but the baby and the folds became one, and inside the

folds I fluttered down through space again. The folds
(composed of my consciousness) were like banners or
parchments, only alive. They fell to earth, came into my
physical body where they flowed into my muscles—or turned
into my muscles, I'm not sure which. As they took their
muscle-form, love from the woman rushed through them.

I opened my eyes, half dizzy and certainly astonished, to see the living room. This wasn't a dry intellectual
mental experience; I hope I've made that clear. I *felt* myself
falling through space; *sans* wings or any kind of known
vehicle. There's no doubt that I was quite frightened on
several occasions, but I also knew that I could transfer my
consciousness back to my physical environment. That knowledge always makes me more daring, of course, than I would
be otherwise. At one point I was intellectually embarrassed
to find the woman and man in the sky, replete with halos,
and myself an infant, however loved, however ... super-
naturally supported. At the same time, I made no attempt to
deny the emotional validity of the episode. I didn't think
that I was in an objective sky, say, so many miles above our
atmosphere though that's the way the experience presented
itself. I *was* quite willing to admit that the journey as I
experienced it stood for one just as unknowable in usual
terms, and just as divorced from the usual world.

This episode was quite different from more conventional out-of-body trips in which I often use definite
methods of leaving my body, and usually have another
"double" nonphysical body to travel in. Then I can often
check out my experiences later, say in another part of the
world, to see if they correlate with actual physical events. In
these, I don't change into other forms as a rule, although I
may have no form at all.

The "ape in the living room" was something like
the episode mentioned earlier in this book, and I interpreted
the ape as the "animal medicine man" acting in a therapeutic
situation. Still, such figures appearing in "my space" were
more intrusive and surprising than my strangest activities in
spaces that I didn't consider mine to begin with.

In other words, "gods in the sky" were easier to

take than an ape suddenly appearing in the living room and
making itself at home—even if it wasn't three-dimensional—
precisely because the ape was so between and betwixt accepted realities. If it had been physical, I could have shouted:
"Hey, there's an ape in the living room," and taken whatever
steps seemed appropriate. Had the ape only presented itself
as a mental reality seen in my mind *but not projected out
into* the space of the living room, then I probably would have
allowed it (the ape) fuller freedom in the episode. But the
combination of mentally perceived ape on the physical table
stopped me. What kind of a weird creature of the psyche was
this? Moreover, at times the ape and I were one. Since then
I've had more such experiences. They can be labeled hallucinations, but such a label tells us nothing about their
creative behavior or their relationship with the realities of the
psyche.

I had many questions, however. Some were at least
partially answered as you'll see later in this book. In the
meantime, the focus of my experience was shifting.

An unexpected visitor, and some new library
material, were each in their ways forerunners, presenting
clues as to the next few months' events.

The visitor, showed up the following Sunday, a
cozy, domestic day, at least until 6:00 P.M. I'd just washed
my hair. It hung wet and loose down my shoulders. Everything was just about ready for dinner. I was getting the cube
steaks out of the refrigerator and Rob was setting the table,
when we heard the Tibetan doorbells ring. Rob went into the
hall to answer the door. From the kitchen I heard his voice
and a young woman's. I paused, considering. No doubt about
it: A stranger was at the door. Would Rob invite her in or
not? I decided to leave it up to him.

I heard him laugh; his great surprised chuckle, then
he yelled, "Hon," and footsteps came into the living room.
"No," I thought, "I don't believe it." My hair was a mess; I'd
wanted a quiet supper and later I'd planned to just relax and
watch television. "No. You're kidding," I called back. But as
I came out into the other room there stood Rob with a
young woman in her early twenties. She looked embarrassed

but determined. Rob said, grinning, "She came all the way from Georgia just to see you."

All the way from Georgia? For a minute, at least, I didn't care if she'd come all the way from the moon.

But there she was, and presented with her, I found myself grinning too. "Give me a second," I said, and I turned the stove off and told Rob to get out some wine. We sat at the table by the bay windows. She was a lovely girl, but nervous now that she was inside; almost wan, pale, slender. She had long fingers. Her nails, painted a bright pink, were beautifully manicured. They looked incongruous though, in comparison to her air of heavy earnestness. That is, her fingers looked happy, but her face didn't. I'll call her Margery.

"I've read all your books, and so have my friends," she said. "We have a group. We live together. I'm sorry to invade your world, but . . ." She broke off, and looked to be near tears. By now I liked her: she wasn't a stranger anymore. There would be a reason for her visit; a reason why Rob let her in.

"When did you leave Georgia?" Rob asked.

"Yesterday morning, around nine," she said.

I groaned: "Suppose Rob had turned you away at the door?"

"Then I'd have just gone back home," she said. And in a rush: "I have so many questions that bother me! Like, there are so many systems and groups, and *our* group gets information and literature from most of them. Well, how do you choose between systems? How do you know which is the right one?"

I stared at her: she was quite serious. "Just forget the systems," I said, laughing.

"But how can I? How can anybody?" she asked, vehemently. "There's truth in all of them. They've all been worked out."

"Just take what makes sense to you, wherever you find it, and let the rest go," I said.

Then *she* stared at me. "But suppose I let the wrong stuff go? Suppose I let something go and it was the truth all along? How do I know?"

"Why be so scared of making mistakes?" I asked. "Truth comes in all kinds of packages, I suppose. So choose the wrappings you like."

Margery shrugged with exaggerated comical helplessness and looked to Rob.

He said, "What Jane means is to trust your own feelings about what you read. You don't have to take any one system if you don't want to."

She stared at both of us then and said, "I know I haven't transmuted my base qualities yet, for example. That worries me a lot. My negative qualities. I don't love everyone yet. When people come to our group, sometimes instead of being loving, I won't like one person as much as another . . . I won't like someone as much as I should. And well, I . . . retreat." Margery almost whispered the last word, her eyes lowered. She obviously considered her remark as an admission of guilt.

I was scandalized. "Why, there are people I don't like particularly," I said. "I don't try to tell myself that I should love everyone, or even *like* everyone. And I certainly don't expect everyone to love me."

She was more scandalized by my remarks than I had been by hers—if that was possible. "You don't?" she gasped. "But why don't you expect everyone to love you? Why shouldn't they? We're all one; underneath individuality—all a part of each other. So if they don't love you, it's a part of themselves they don't love." She said more calmly, "I just don't understand. Every system I know of says that you should love everyone equally."

There was a small silence. "I thought you said that you read *The Nature of Personal Reality*," Rob said, quietly.

"I did—"

"Well, you can't love everyone equally," Rob said. "And when you think that you have to, then you build up a terrific load of guilt. That's part of what *Personal Reality* is all about."

"I do feel guilty about it. Terribly," she said. She was really quite shaken.

"Look," I said. "I like you a lot, Margery. Because

you're you and I recognize your uniqueness and react to it. If I tried to love everyone, I wouldn't really love anyone at all—and if I said that I liked you, you'd be upset. It would sound like an insult because I was supposed to *love* you. But if I said that I *did* love you under those conditions, it wouldn't really mean much at all, because you'd think to yourself, 'Well, of *course*, she has to say that because she has to love everyone, no matter who they are.' " Pause. "Do you follow me?" I asked.

She shook her head; no. I took out the first pages of this present manuscript, where I described my meeting with "Mr. Junior Parapsychologist," and read her a few passages. "I didn't like him and he was bugging me," I said. "That doesn't mean that I couldn't appreciate him as a unique human being—but one who just wasn't my cup of tea."

Margery shook her head. "But it was obvious that you . . . appreciated him in some really great way—"

"Right. I appreciated his individuality *because* I let myself respond to it, to the likenesses and differences between us; *because* I was free to dislike him if I wanted to. Then I was free to see him apart from his effect on me, and even to appreciate the fact that I disliked him."

By now, Rob was laughing. In the meantime the phone rang. Rob answered it, bending down, since we'd taken the phone off the table and put it on the radiator. Willy, our cat, suddenly leapt to the radiator and began nibbling at Rob's long curly gray hair, as if it was a batch of salad. Margery and I sat, laughing ourselves, as Rob tried to speak on the phone while the cat happily chomped away on his hair. Finally I pushed Willy out of Rob's way. But the small domestic episode at least changed Margery's mood. She looked more cheerful.

Little by little, though, she came out with ideas that were appalling to me. Once, for example, she said, "I realize that we don't originate ideas; that they're all around us and we just choose the ones we want."

I thought that I'd misunderstood her. "Wait a minute," I interrupted. "Of course we originate ideas—"

"Well, we *think* we do, of course—"

"No. We do," I said, pretty flatly. I could have been more diplomatic, but ideas like that send me up the wall. "You're saying that we aren't creative, and when you do that, you're denying the validity of your own reality."

The supper I'd planned wasn't enough for three, so we fixed a meal of scrambled eggs, instant potatoes, and canned hash. Margery stopped with her fork in midair and said with utter honest astonishment: "You're saying that we *do* originate ideas ourselves?" Again, it was really difficult for me to imagine how she could seriously think otherwise. I went briefly into my ideas about models, explaining that even these were constantly refreshed by "eccentricities" or new creative variations.

But we weren't through. Over ice cream and coffee, Margery went through an entire web of beliefs involving the "gross physical plane" and the necessity of transmuting it into finer vibrations. She'd read Seth's *The Nature of Personal Reality* all right, but interpreted it through the framework of old beliefs, and she considered those beliefs as The Truth. Following these concepts, Margery believed that the body was at best an instrument; that life at its greatest was a trial, and that man was denied the joys of truly original or creative thought. At the same time, she was convinced that she had to love everyone—each of those gross uncreative people.

Yet she was a beautiful girl; a *loving* girl. When she left, though, I was exhausted. Rob and I did the dishes and then watched *Kojak* on television; and I thought that the program at least had a warm sense of humanity about it; an "aura" of creaturehood with its "ups" and "downs." Even the crooks could think for themselves, and nobody went around wailing over their mortal state: right or wrong, they tried to do something *with* it. And they weren't limp.

Not that my own thoughts weren't contradictory. They were. I've always been deeply concerned about the strange vulnerability of our human condition—but to rob it of creativity, to deny its vitality and exuberance, is hardly any help. Such attitudes can lead to a soggy spiritual sloppiness in which no action, mental or physical, is clearcut or spontaneous.

I mentioned Margery's visit to my class two days later and this apparently triggered Seth into making some new statements about his own "past". It also led into an excellent monologue on love and hate as Seth spoke about those emotions. Beyond that, though, he answered many questions that concern not only my students but people in general. For that reason, I'm describing that class in the following chapter.

Chapter 15
Seth: On Love and Hate.
Inner Codes

This was actually one of the last regular class sessions. When it was held, Rob and I were still talking about the possibility of moving. But that was all. In our normal world, we'd made no real decisions. After we moved, though, I discontinued classes to finish this book, and at this writing I haven't started them up again. I'm not even sure that I will. But since I enjoy *not* knowing what I might do tomorrow, I rarely try to precognate the events of my own life.

On ordinary levels, then, no one realized that the classes—and the class Seth sessions—would not continue indefinitely as they had over the past eight years. I'd thought that a possible move on our part might briefly disrupt class, but at that point I hadn't even considered anything over a month's break.

In regular sessions, Seth was still dictating *The "Unknown" Reality*, but often in class he mentioned visitors we'd had, and answered students' questions. That night, January 7, 1975, our living room was filled—to the ceiling, it seemed. Nearly forty people of all ages sprawled on the floor, sat on the chairs or couch, or just leaned against the walls. As he often did, Seth jumped into the general conversation; smiling, hearty, and gregarious.

We'd been discussing the mail, which had grown by leaps and bounds. I could no longer answer all of it, even with Rob's help, so the students had been answering some letters for me. Many of the letters had suggested that we set up some kind of organization or training program to help people apply Seth's ideas to their daily lives. As we spoke about this, Seth came through, speaking to the students:

"Now tell Ruburt that he does not need a foundation. As you answer the letters, you show people your own interpretation of our ideas and at least you make your own understanding clear. Then people can do as they wish. It is their right, and it is their freedom. But you are here, and you help in that you show the interpretation that we here place upon those ideas. [Humorously:] We will be an unofficial foundation.

"Often when you set up new bridges, you must help others rip down the old ones. That is what we are doing. Each of you is doing the same thing in your own way. Each of you, in your own life, looked upon the systems and found them wanting. The individual is stronger than any system, and the individual must always come first. Therefore, we will not set up another system that exists apart from the individual. Instead we will show the individual his and her proper place as the initiator of reality.

"Your vitality comes first. You form systems. That is fine, but the systems must not be allowed to rule you...."

Seth cautioned us against forming an organization in several later sessions too, but that night he switched the subject to Margery, the girl who thought she had to love everyone. This time Seth spoke quite loudly, half in a bantering tone, his full voice filling the room with the almost bombastic vitality it sometimes displays.

"I am also free to like or dislike," Seth said, referring to a similiar remark that I'd made earlier. "I am also free to love or hate. The one thing about an ancient existence, if you will forgive the term, is that old hatreds do not last because you learn to have a sense of humor. I used to think that this was highly regrettable, for at one level of reality, there is nothing more comforting than an old hate. It lets you know where you are and where you stand.

"But with a sense of humor, hate is all too funny and therefore it loses its power. Love, on the other hand, even with a sense of humor, becomes highly precious and large enough so that it can contain old hates very nicely.

"There are old hated comrades, in your terms, in past lives, whom I love dearly. We share a fine hatred. We loved each other because of that hatred that united us. We were in contact with each other beautifully, and we related. So examine what you mean by the word 'hate,' and see how related to love it can be."

There's no doubt about it: Seth enjoys himself thoroughly when he speaks to students. He doesn't speak over them but to them, individually and as a group; looking first at one and then at another; responding to their individuality in a way few people do. At the same time, he uses individual questions as ways of stating more general issues. He ended the above remarks with a smiling comment, "Now I return you to this *un*foundation," when a student interrupted him.

"May I ask a question?" The young man, whom I'll call Larry, jumped up like a jack-in-the-box to catch Seth before he turned into me again. The students grinned; lots of them had tried the same trick before. Sometimes they catch Seth while he's still "him," sometimes not. This time it worked.

"You may indeed," Seth said. "It does not mean that you will get an answer, but you may ask the question." He spoke in a gentle banter. Larry grinned in reply, then said, "It's a question about All That Is. Since All That Is is everything, does it ever get lonely?"

"All That Is is you, Larry. How can it be lonely?

That is my answer," Seth said. Yet he went on, elaborating: "All That Is is composed of each and every pigeon and wren and cardinal and bird and dog and leaf. And All That Is speaks to itself constantly through growing worlds and realities, and those whispers and those murmurs are lonely only in that they yearn for further creativity. And *that* is an answer."

I knew that Seth's presence was very powerful that evening, but I was surprised by the energy I felt collecting around me. When Seth finished talking to Larry, he turned class back to me. We got into a discussion on death when Seth came through again, and this time his voice seemed to act like a channel or carrier for energy in an even more emphatic way than usual. He delivered the following monologue in tones ranging from a whisper to a deep resonating volume.

At the very least, Seth speaks from a level of consciousness (or a kind of consciousness) not usually available to us. For this reason, I feel that the rest of the session is a beautiful demonstration of the politics of the psyche as other aspects of it view existence from a standpoint that is certainly not our own.

"What is death?" he began. "Ask *yourself* the question. But in my own way, in an answer that is no answer, I answer you. For I am death. I am myself, as you are yourself. I am a small flower on a planet you do not know, and I am myself. I am a mist over a time that you cannot understand, and I am myself. I am a god that is not yet created, and yet I am myself as you are yourself, and as you are portions of thoughts that you have not yet thought.

"You stand on the chasms of yourselves and the pinnacles of yourselves. You are death and you are life. And I am death and I am life. I am a butterfly in a world that is not yet born in your terms, and yet I am myself in this room.

"I am Ruburt and I am Jane, and I am a stone in the backyard and yet I am myself, apart from all of those other realities, for those realities are also themselves and apart from mine.

"The earth speaks through the grasses, and the

grasses flourish, and the birds come, and the snow flies: that is death and that is life.

"You sense here the energy of your being, and it is death and it is life, for the two are united. You will never know, in your terms again, the self that you are now and yet it will never end and you will always remember it. Yet in other terms there is a history to your being. In *your* terms you can look backward toward reincarnational lives, but they are not you.

"You are yourself. I am myself. I am not Ruburt. Ruburt is not me. Ruburt is me. I am myself. I am Ruburt and not Ruburt. You are death and you are life. You are more than the selves you think you are, yet the selves that you are have absolute freedom within the framework of your reality, and you can even walk out of that reality; and you do and you have.

"I am life and I am death. Now when death can talk about death, *that* is your answer. Only the living are so mute. Think of your definitions. In certain terms, you are all dead and have been for centuries. In other terms, you are not yet born and centuries will come before you walk upon the surface of the earth. Yet you are alive, and you take it for granted that I am dead, and so, what a delightful game we play!

"Death and life in your terms are relative. In those terms, to people to be born two hundred years hence, you are dead. From their reality, my dear friends, you do not exist. You are old ancient history and they read about your time in history books. Now, from *your* viewpoint, *you* read history books. Scientific men examine mountains. They look at rock strata and find only fossils. From your reality, those rock strata are dead, and only dead fossils appear. Yet those fossils live. Death and life—again in those terms—are relative. From your viewpoint you are alive. From a greater viewpoint you are alive and dead at the same time, and there is no difference.

"Now, I have spoken many times with many languages and in many places, and when I was a minor Pope, I was far from eloquent. I was a petty religious politician. I can look back, in your terms, on that existence and see a great vitality and exuberance, and that minor pope still lives. I do not have contact with him, and yet he grows and learns because of my experiences, and I remember earth life more dearly because of his continuing life.

"So you are alive and dead at once, and there is no difference. You are, again, as alive or dead now as you will ever be."

Seth paused finally and another student asked a question. "But what about focuses?" he asked. "Doesn't your focus change? Like, you still exist and the Pope still exists and once you were focused in the pope."

"He has his own reality," Seth said. "He continues to enjoy it. Examine your concept of time, for you still think that a life-span must exist between such-and-such a date, so that our dear politically minded, crooked old Pope must stop his existence at a certain time that is no longer recognized as life. Now he has chosen to continue, and some with him have chosen to continue that time period, though you would no longer recognize it."

This time another student broke in. "What would stop you from reliving your life as the Pope?"

"It is not practical. It would be boring," Seth answered. "In those terms, many people do choose to reexperience what you would think of as a past existence in order to change it as they go along. You are merely focused in a particular time period in which you recognize history . . . but as space it seems to you, extends outward, so does time. As mountains, islands, or oceans appear in space, so in the same way mountains or islands or oceans appear in time."

Seth was pausing now, giving students a chance to ask their questions. This time a young woman, Linda, spoke up.

"In this existence—and I admit I've chosen it—I've found myself catapulting forward with unbounded vitality, and it's a little frightening. I'm wondering if all I'm doing is totally valid—in my multidimensional reality."

Seth spoke soberly, but with a smile, "You would prefer to be catapulting backward, I suppose?"

Linda blushed. "I like the forward motion, but—"

"Then what is your problem?" Seth asked. "You know that your energy and vitality are good. Do not try to make a fence around the word 'validity.' That is the only answer that you will get. It is the only answer that you really want or need."

Following this, class members got into an animated discussion about reincarnation and memory. Someone wondered aloud about my connections with Seth, and if my life existed in his memory. Seth instantly returned with some comments that intrigued me later, when I read the transcript. He began by saying, "Ruburt can do many things that surprise me—that I did not do in my past, for remember that fresh creativity emerges from the past also, as in [Ruburt's novel] *Oversoul Seven*.

"My memory does not include a predetermined past in which Ruburt exists. He can do things that did not happen in my memory of that existence, and did not, in fact, occur. Now that is a 'mind-blowing' statement, and it applies to each of you. It is important in terms of your own understanding of yourself and the nature of time."

Seth paused again and looked around, locating another student, Ann, who wanted to ask a question but was timid. Seth smiled and encouraged her to speak out.

"I was thinking of probable futures," Ann said. "A future self could talk of what would be his own probable future, though he might choose to do something different. Is that what you mean?"

"Correct," Seth said, "But some class members feel as if each person has a future self like a Big Brother who looks down into each life, saying, 'Ah hah. I did this or that, so you must do the same tomorrow.'"

Another student, Len, asked a question: "But will you explain how our incarnations happen at the same time? It's a hard thing to understand."

"I've taken two full sessions in my latest book [*"Unknown" Reality*] to explain incarnations and counterparts. So I cannot explain this to you quickly. All I can tell you—and class has heard this often—is that time is simultaneous, and that there are no boundaries to creativity. So you are not at the mercy of any past life, nor are you like some vast super-self, resting on layers of past lives, so that you stand there, squashing them down.

"The nature of time speaks through your cells and molecules. The cells within your body know the proper balance to be maintained. They know your precise position upon this planet. They are each individual. The atoms and molecules within your form have their own existences. In that context they can be compared to what you think of as past lives. They exist at once, however, within the physical reality of your being.

"In the same way are all of your past and future lives simultaneous. They are connected in the same way that portions of your body are connected, and your thoughts fly from one existence to another as messages leap to the nerve ends of your body and tell your finger to move through the air.

"I am death and I am life and so are you, and you live all of your lives simultaneously. Now, you are not any of those other selves and they are not you. Yet they are related in a psychic gestalt, as all the cells in your body are."

Again we got into a discussion of Seth's statements; we ended up with questions about spontaneity and the need for discipline. Once again Seth came through. This time his energy really seemed to fill up the room.

"I have told you to trust your spontaneous self," he said. "And some of you have become daring enough to look at your own reality; daring enough to consider the possibility that you might, after all, be naturally good; scandalous enough to accept the possibility that your being might possibly be blessed; audacious enough to consider the possibility that if you let yourselves be, you will be creative, exuberant, and free.

"You have graciously listened to me. You have graciously considered what I had to say—but because you are yourselves, you have allowed yourselves to think twice. And you think, behind your thoughts, 'That is well and good for an old ghost to say, but what will really happen if I am my spontaneous self? What evils might I perpetuate or bring into existence? I might . . . speak to others honestly. I might make a blessed fool of myself by showing affection. I might open up my human vulnerability; for if I remain cool, then no one knows who I am but me, and no one can hurt me.'

"Nevertheless, you have tried, and in the backs of your minds you are beginning to consider the possibility of spontaneity, but it frightens you. You think: 'This energy and this power can be wrongfully used, and if I am an evil creature, how dare I taste my own energy? Better to hold it back.' And this applies to some extent to everyone in this room.

"But I am going a step further, for now I am telling you to be reckless with your energy, and reckless with your being, and you immediately think, 'What does reckless mean? It means out of control. Dear Lord, what could happen if I were reckless with my being?'

"The gods are reckless or you would not have a world. The flowers are reckless or you would not have a spring or an autumn. I am reckless or I would not even consider speaking under these circumstances. It is indeed reckless of me to tell you that you are blessed."

Seth looked around the room, letting his words sink in, and a student asked one of the inevitable questions that always arise whenever spontaneity is mentioned. She said, "Seth, you were talking about spontaneity and being reckless, but this my problem. I keep saying to myself, 'Gosh, you've got to be spontaneous.' And I say it to myself all the time. I mean, because I hardly ever *am* spontaneous. But how can I be, when I think about it so hard?"

A few people laughed because they had the same question. Seth said, "To you, I say forget it. Let it go. You sit and look at me, and you are a beautiful creature. Your body is doing its spontaneous best—it is keeping you alive. It makes your skin glow and your eyes shine, and it does not stop at every moment and say, 'Ah hah, I must be spontaneous.' It simply relaxes and is itself.

"So forget the issue and in your forgetting, your spontaneity will flow—as it does, whether you hassle it or not. Your lips curl. Your ears are like shells that hear my voice. They do not stop to wonder if they are spontaneous. They do not give orders to themselves. So do not give orders to yourself. And if sometimes you say to yourself, 'I will not be spontaneous, I will consider and consider again,' then that is also spontaneous!"

There were a few more remarks and questions, and Seth ended the class session with his own kind of humor and philosophy, always calculated to incite further questions and to encourage people to look at their reality in new ways. "You are in this room now," he said. "You bring your own reality here. In certain terms, of course, the room does not exist. You accept its reality, and your reality in it. In the terms in which I spoke earlier, everyone in this room is dead and gone. You are corpses. How is it that you are so dumb that you do not realize that you are as dead as I? In still other terms, you are not yet born, so how is it that you experience anything or feel the miracle of your being? Examine your definitions. Give us a moment, and then listen to a song about the examination of definitions."

With that, I came out of trance—briefly. The next moment I was singing in Sumari, my "trance language". It's impossible to describe the song, except to say that its lilting patterns and alternating rhythms seemed to rise from a state of being in which definitions are meaningless or beside the point. Being defined itself by being.

I'm certainly spontaneous when I sing Sumari. If I stopped to remember that normally I can't carry a tune, that would be the end of it. But when I read the night's transcript, Seth's use of the word "reckless" bothered me as it had some students. *Reckless*? Didn't reckless mean . . . driving cars one hundred miles an hour or taking stupid chances with your life?

Yet, singing Sumari, I knew what reckless meant; and each time I begin a Sumari chant or poem I know what it means. I know when I turn into Seth too. Thinking about it, I suspected that to some degree, at least, I'd hampered my progress in the library by not being reckless enough. I decided to really concentrate my attention there more than I had so far.

But if I hoped to just get material from the library and maintain a one-point contact with the universe, I was in for a surprise. Margery's visit not only seemed to trigger Seth's excellent class session that night, but it also seemed to touch off a new barrage of visitors and callers. It took some time before I realized how these interruptions were connected with the politics of the psyche and with this book.

From the beginning I had wondered what I'd actually find in my library: I understood that my experience there demonstrated certain politics of the psyche and represented policies of mine that made my visits possible. Beyond that, I was in the dark in many important respects and, as mentioned earlier, often it would be some time before I intellectually understood what I'd really been up to.

For example, the meaning of my encounter with the "man and woman in the sky" wasn't apparent until several months afterward, when I saw that it symbolically presented experience that wouldn't catch up to me until I was nearly finished with this book. Yet, there, it was given in a kind of concentrated capsule form.

Other hints also came that January that wouldn't make sense to me until the following July. Several nights after Margery's visit, for instance, the word "codicil" came into my mind as I sat at the table. Something about the feel of my consciousness told me that the word was important, though I wasn't at all familiar with it. It wasn't a part of my working vocabulary. In fact I was about to discount this gentle mental nudge when it came three or four times in succession. It really wanted my attention, so finally I got up and looked for the word in the dictionary, giving in to the urge much as I would have to the demands of my cat when he keeps at me about something he wants.

I didn't read the definition too carefully, noting down only that a codicil was "something appended to a will." Then, the word "polemics" came to me in the same nagging fashion so I looked that up too. The dictionary said that it was "the art of disputation, polemic theology, which has as its object the refutation of error." I didn't see how "codicil" applied to me at all until months later. But polemics made a certain sense and I thought, "Yes, in a way, that's what I'm doing." And as I thought that, suddenly I knew there was some material ready for me from the library. I sat down and wrote the following brief passage:

From the Library

INNER CODES

Inner codes of reality appear within the molecules on the one hand, and within the private and mass psyche as well. These codes get distorted through the ages, and there is a need to return to their source. The library books are my interpretation of that source. The material in these inner codes is always translated outward into the world of science, religion, politics, and law. But if these outer manifestations become too rigid or petrify, or if their inner source is forgotten, then they no longer serve the needs of the individual or mass psyche.

These codes, then, must be constantly restated, freshly experienced and interpreted, so that they emerge again to give the race new impetus and ensure that civilization follows spiritual and psychic needs. The inner codes are patterns, flexible models, carrying within them hints of man's greatest potentials and achievements, which he can then imaginatively project into the future as patterns for development. (These are to be used in the same way that a city planner uses blueprints; in the same fashion that cells know ahead of time what form to take.)

That was the end of the passage, but I made certain connections at once. As our cells have their own inner codes, directing them toward their greatest fulfillment, so do our psyches. So for me, the library and its books represented "my own true path" in the same way, acting like ... psychic chromosomes that know ahead of time the best direction for me to take; or the most fulfilling psychic "shape" for me to assume. The library also represents an individual psyche's "true source" in those terms, at least; the self returning for refreshment to its source and rediscovering its own "ancient truths."

Okay, I thought, but what are truths anyway? The chromosomes' information is certainly true in that it directs the organism and its parts to the form ultimately (and ideally?) suited to it in this reality. Are insights true in the same way, directing the self to its ideal relationship with the world?

Without knowing it I was beginning to ask some of the right kinds of questions—questions that would later trigger a new kind of psychic politics. In the meantime, other people were asking their own questions—of me—and though I yearned for some more private library experiences, I was presented with a "living library" of very human voices and problems.

Besides this, we began house hunting in earnest. My private and public world was shifting. And I worried: Would the library go with us if we did move? I didn't realize—again till some time later—that Phase One of the library and this book was finished.

Part Two

VOICES FROM THE WORLD

Chapter 16

Voices From "The Underground," and the Politics of the Focus Personality

In January 1975, the telephone kept ringing constantly, or so it seemed. People called with just about every kind of problem, so that I was forced to apply my ideas in very practical terms. Yet again, each person was almost super-real, even over the telephone. Each of their dilemmas had such an energetic "eccentric" vitality that I wondered steadily about humanity's vast creativity—and the areas in which it's focused.

A woman I'll call Molly started this "roll call" of questions. Her problem instantly gave me new insights into the various strands of consciousness and their connection with our daily living.

Molly had been hearing mental voices, or thoughts "not hers" for over a year. The voices, she said, kept going through her mind, vying for her attention. They'd changed their character during this time—and to me they presented fascinating examples of segmented strands of consciousness.

"First," Molly said, "I heard a voice in my head that was supposed to be God. Then there was a voice in my belly that said it was my father. This was right after his death. I was supposed to learn from this that my father wasn't God."

"Did you ever think he was?" I asked.

"Yes, in a way, I guess," she said. "Anyway, I didn't think he could do any wrong." Molly's voice was whiney. She sounded exhausted and weary and kept repeating herself. Yet she'd already learned a lot, because she said, "The two voices, of God and my father, taught me that one was different from the other. My father's voice—or the voice that said it was my father—always sounded as if it came from my belly, and God always came in my head. So after awhile I saw that I'd deified my father."

The two dramatizations were quite clear to her, but then she went on: "Later I really got scared, though. I read a book about possession and I thought I was possessed. Then my father and God, or the voices that said they *were*, stopped. Instead now there's a doubting voice. It's always telling me that I don't really believe what I *do* believe. And there's my good voice, the guide voice, who tries to help me. They just keep going. I believe what you say, that we create our own reality, so I keep telling the voices to go away. But they don't."

"You're going about it the hard way," I said. "Look, the voices represent aspects or parts of yourself that you're inhibiting. So they do have messages that are important. They aren't alien—just part of your own thought processes that you've denied. They've become segmented. One voice represents the doubts that you aren't expressing, that you ignore or tried to deny. The guide voice represents an idealization of the self you want to be."

Molly kept repeating what she'd already told me. I let her talk. As I listened I realized again that our normal consciousness is like an orchestra of feelings and thoughts, each blending together—strands of ideas, emotions, and value judgments intertwined and interconnected. When we become too selective; when we decide that some thoughts are acceptable and some are not, then often we pay attention only to the acceptable segments. We begin to separate the strands of our own consciousness until they no longer intermix smoothly or modify themselves as they used to. They become divided. This is what happened in Molly's case. She ignored main currents of thought and feeling until she no longer recognized them as her own.

"You're in the middle, getting it from both ends," I said. "Listen, Molly. One voice is showing you your doubts. They're exaggerated, or they *seem* to be, in contrast to the guide voice. As I listen to you, it's obvious that the guide voice is setting up a superhuman pattern of behavior that no person could achieve."

Once again, Molly started repeating her experiences, almost as if to keep me from saying anything that might help. Understandable. She'd set up a certain framework, and even though she said that she wanted help, that framework had served certain purposes. Yet, as I pointed out to her, her experiences were beautiful examples of the therapeutic nature of the self. How apt the symbolism was from the beginning! Molly, I felt, was stuck for a while with the ideals that she'd earlier assigned to her father, and I told her that when she recognized the doubting voice and the guide voice as symbols of opposing attitudes of her own, she'd be free. Then the attitudes could modify each other again and blend into the whole area of accepted selfhood.

Accepted, doubts can be encountered as a necessary part of the learning process. Molly considered the doubting voice evil, but the doubts arose precisely because her ideals were not reasonable. No one can be a "pure spirit" while living on the face of this earth, yet her guide voice set up just such impossible goals. God wasn't the "father" anymore, but the ideals she'd assigned to him were now spoken by the guide. So, as I told her, the doubting voice instantly protested whenever she denied her own emotional experience.

"I'm thinking of quitting my job and just concentrating on spiritual development," she said.

"Uh-huh. If you don't like your job, find another,"
I answered. "But don't stay at home brooding." I told her to
do the exercises in Seth's *The Nature of Personal Reality*, and
she said that she had been doing them. From her conversation, though, it was clear that she'd only pretended to
follow the instructions. Whenever she touched upon feelings
of doubt, she backtracked. If she really works with her own
beliefs, she'll be able to find the source of her incessant
impractical aspirations—because these prevent her from
seeing her own "true" reality. And that reality *is* spiritual.
Behind many of her attitudes was the distressing idea that the
self can't be trusted, and that to be human is wrong.

In Molly's case, the doubting voice is the underground of the self. Molly separated her own attitudes into the
good guys and the bad guys, and then partially personified
them. The government of the self is undermined, because she
isn't listening to all the "constituents," all of the elements of
her personality that have a stake in her life. Because she feels
so guilty, she can't be content with being a "normal," happy,
fairly satisfied person, giving and taking, at peace with her
humanity; instead, she's driven to be a saint on earth. She
was determined to pluck out all skeptical ideas or doubts,
precisely because she was really aware of the impossibility of
living up to her ideals.

The same kind of mental-voice phenomenon could
have developed with Margery, the girl who thought she had
to love everybody, except that Margery at least admitted her
doubts and kept in contact with them. Both she and Molly
shared the same belief in the unreliability of the self and the
grossness of physical existence. Unfortunately, many people
with such beliefs think that spirituality can be developed
only by accepting a very limited range of emotion. So a pall
falls over the spirit and the world as well.

Molly believed that she was being expansive
because she was trying to develop her spiritual awareness.
Whenever she examined her ideas, however, she interpreted
the self-examination as doubt and instantly tried to be more

spiritual. I finally told her that she was trying too hard. Her own self-therapy would lead her to a more expansive view of life if she'd just let it. I think that I got through to her.

Again, in *Adventures in Consciousness* I explained my theories about the source and components of personality. I saw us as coming from a source self, free of space and time, into this reality. The focus personality (or the self that we know) focuses in this life, but is also composed of other Aspects or parts of the source self that are latent within the psyche, though "alive" in other realities.

These form the basic structure of the psyche from which the focus personality emerges. I call these "prime Aspects." A harmonious working relationship between these prime Aspects results in a well-balanced focus personality—one that is reasonably happy, healthy, and creative.

These prime Aspects merge, practically speaking, into what I call earth Aspects, or the earthly versions of the prime Aspects. They show their existence as our own characteristics and tendencies—the raw psychic materials from which we form the self we know. These Aspects also reveal themselves as models or psychic patterns that can operate as indicators of progress and fulfillment. We'll also interpret their "messages" through our current beliefs about ourselves and the world.

Molly, for example, was inhibiting strong elements of her own personality. She believed that doubting was wrong to such a degree that her very intellect became suspect. I could have said as much when I finished *Adventures in Consciousness.* Yet until the library material, I didn't understand the nature of models or the way that the earth Aspects can operate within the psyche as models for achievement, as indicators of various leanings or inclinations, or as regulators. Molly not only inhibited Aspects of herself, she exaggerated the "guide"—so effectively that the psyche sent up an opposing Aspect to right the balance. So in her experience she has the guide or saint self, and the doubter. And each has a voice. These models are not just ideas. They are psychologically active and "alive." They possess certain abilities and characteristics. They interact in her psyche.

Molly disapproves of the world because she disapproves of herself. Because she's afraid of her own inner doubts, any physical data that correlates with them are also considered subversive. Books or articles that deny the validity of psychic phenomena, for example, seem like threats to her and will represent unofficial material. The inner underground will be projected into exterior experience.

On the other hand, people who rely upon limited ideas of the intellect and repress the personal psychic elements of personality will consider any psychic field of endeavor as nonsense or threatening (one or the other), but definitely as subversive. Privately, such individuals will try to inhibit intuitional experiences.

Many people, in fact, try to maintain "the establishment" of the self, and follow its conventions as rigorously as they follow the exterior manifestations of those conventions—the religious or political groups that give them voice. When we try to maintain such an unyielding stance, however, then we always have to protect our present position, put up our defenses, and in one way or another, do battle. Our psychic politics—our private policies—also reach out to touch and affect our joint world.

Let's look at Molly again. She gave me an example of the way her doubting subversive voice "tempted" her and tried to destroy her peace of mind. "I've been reading a book that says you can increase your wealth by thinking in terms of abundance," she said. "Some of your books say this too. But every time I read this, the doubting voice speaks up, saying, 'It won't work for you.' And it repeats this over and over."

And it was right! Molly really didn't believe that thinking in terms of abundance would increase her wealth, but she wanted to convince herself that she did. Besides this, the concept wouldn't produce results unless she did something that let it work. Instead she was thinking of quitting her job because her boss was "negative." She was judging him by her own unrealistic standards so that "negative" bosses would follow her from job to job. The doubting voice was begging her to examine her own misgivings so that she could see what was behind them.

Actually this doubting voice was quite instructional, showing her the difference between her attainable and unattainable goals. It pointed up the exaggerated aspirations of the guide voice, which only drove Molly to feelings of guilt. Molly can be uniquely herself, the "best" Molly, working within the framework of the practical world as she learns to work with her human nature and not against it.

But where did the guide voice come from? I believe that it is a dimly perceived, distorted, conventionalized version of the earth Aspect—the distilled combination of prime Aspects as they operate as components of the focus personality. That part of the psyche contains within it knowledge of our greatest potentials in connection with earthly existence. We interpret its messages through our beliefs, though.

Molly's conventionalized beliefs about good and evil caused her to misread the guide portion of her personality, and the doubting voice was then set up as a needed contermeasure. Molly was acting like a dictator, setting up a set of laws, and God help any portion of her personality that didn't go along! She insisted that all of her thoughts and actions conform to a rigid pattern of spiritual development as she understood it—a pattern that left no room for simply being human.

Molly closed down all methods of communication that would allow her doubts any freedom at all. She inhibited "negative" thoughts, she read only "inspirational" literature or psychically oriented magazines and papers, until finally the repressed doubts rose to consciousness in their own revolution—with their own guerrilla warfare, appearing as the unofficial voices that clamored for her attention.

Molly considered the intellect to be at fault and thought of it as the tempter who had to be quelled or conquered. I've also heard from scientists who have the same difficulty, but in the opposite direction. They insist on the prime importance of the intellect at the expense of the intuitions. They also act like dictators. They read only scientific material, and their underground is the occult. Then one way or another, the psyche reacts against such restrictions, and suddenly the scientist is faced not with Molly's jeering voice of reason, but with men from outer space or automatic writing or sudden revelations—all unofficial messages that finally sneak in to upset the psychological establishment.

The day after Molly's call, I received a letter from just such a man. Roderick, I'll call him, gave me the following story. For years he'd concentrated on his scientific career and was very critical of religion, the occult, dreams, intuitional hunches, or anything else that couldn't be produced in a test tube. Then his daughter received a copy of *Seth Speaks* for Christmas. Wondering at his own actions, he read the book. Then—boom! Out of nowhere, he said, Roderick began automatic writing. Then he experimented with a Ouija board. He assured me that Seth had reached him, communicating through the board, and to top it off, other-world intelligences wanted him to help in the development of a new kind of pyramid. "Now everything is happening at once," Roderick wrote. "Everything that I thought wasn't true, is true."

He was so used to interpreting all information in literal terms that he wouldn't even consider the possibility that the Ouija communications might be coming from portions of his psyche that he'd denied—an explanation he'd probably have applied quite quickly to other such activity only a short while before. But now the psyche was showing its incredible richness, hinting at its true dimensions—and surely that couldn't be the psyche that he'd considered so below his notice before! In his case, the other-world intelligences and his Seth were his equivalent of Molly's doubting and guide voices. They also represented Aspects that he'd denied, dramatizing themselves through the creativity of his own interests and personality.

Whenever the intellect and intuitions are considered separate opposing characteristics, and one highlighted in exaggerated manner over the other, then the inhibited one surfaces. Certainly this happens in many conversion experiences. A new self-government rises, having new policies toward the self and the world. Unless this is understood, the old dominant characteristics can easily become the new underground, suppressed as vigorously as they were once displayed. Instances of this are apparent whenever the scientist converted to occult phenomena completely loses all of his old objectivity and becomes as fervent in his new ideas as he was earlier in his old ones. The overly credulous believer, religiously speaking, becomes the avowed atheist, against all religion for the same reason.

I see the psyche as a self-governing process, with the focus personality as the head of state. The inner models are structures within the psyche, ever-changing patterns that gently direct the personality toward its fullest development, in the same way that invisible models within the cells direct their growth. So these models stand for something, though I don't think we can take them literally in our terms. Their reality helps form ours, but they can't be confined to our definitions.

Again: In our world these models usually show themselves as earth Aspects; as characteristics or qualities that seem to be our own, and do operate as components of personality. In their greater capacity, however, they represent prime Aspects of the source self, so that each prime Aspect has its own reality in another kind of existence than ours. Taken together, they represent the psyche's potentials and unique properties—and the source of our own personhood. We draw on these characteristics constantly. Often, however, we overemphasize one at the expense of the other: our beliefs cause us to lean too far in one direction, to become off-centered. Then adjustments take place to help us maintain our focus and stance in the world.

Some people are able to form a relationship with one of the prime Aspects so that it can communicate information about its own existence and also give a description of this world from its standpoint. I think that this is what I am doing with Seth. When this is done properly, the focus personality is highly benefited while keeping its own psychological focus. At the same time it begins to extend itself in other directions, alters its perception, and brings new knowledge to bear on physical existence.

In this case, the focus personality certainly changes, perhaps drastically, but in a natural evolution in which it always retains its authority in the ordinary affairs of life. I don't know why more people can't do this well. I suspect that it hints of a natural expansion of consciousness that is ours as a species and points toward a richer kind of personal consciousness, inherent but ignored, in our focus toward specialization.

The focus personality is the front of the self, the leader who deals with other people and makes personal policies in the same way that a nation's ruler deals with other countries. But the focus personality stands for other portions of the self—its advisers and countrymen at other levels of selfhood, and from these it receives messages that prepare it for its task and position. If it doesn't do a good enough job—if it is too autocratic or censors too many messages from its constituents—then there's an overthrow, according to the kind of inner politics characteristic of the personality.

There can be a gentle democratic change of government and the adoption of a new kind of constitution; a violent overthrow; a religious conversion or inquisition. Many of my phone calls and letters during this period were showing me the methods used by other portions of the self to "set things right," and these usually involve unofficial messages; that is, messages that are not accepted by the focus personality as legitimate.

It has occurred to me many times that our idea of individuality is a very thin mixture. We can't understand, for example, the rich multiplicity of psychological experience in some tribes or civilizations who felt that their selfhood, while itself, was also a part of the consciousness of their ancestors; or of others who also identify with the animals. Perhaps in some past civilizations, a person who thought he was himself or herself only would be considered mad, only half here, a person almost without a soul.

Now and then I'm struck with an odd thought: Maybe my mode of consciousness with its many facets is as natural as other people's more singular version. In fact, maybe, it's more natural, and what we recognize as normal consciousness is a very limited specialized portion of far greater abilities. I wouldn't want to go around as Seth all the time, or fall into trances at the drop of a hat. Seth's existence is his, and mine is mine. All in all, I wouldn't trade with him for the world. And I wouldn't want to go around singing Sumari verses all the time, either.

Yet once that week friends came to call. Trying to explain a difficult point, I switched to Sumari consciousness to do so, singing in the purest, happiest tones—with a range and depth that startled the musicians present. A rather complicated philosophical statement was translated into an emotional art form far more apt than a lengthy verbal explanation. And for a moment as I finished, I felt dreadfully sorry for other people who couldn't vary their modes of consciousness to suit their needs and intents.

During this time, I was having weekly Seth sessions in class as well as the private sessions in which Seth dictated his book. Again, speaking for Seth is so outside most people's experience that they attach all kinds of meanings to it. Yet until I sang the Sumari that night, it didn't occur to me to feel sorry for other people who aren't able to switch to, say, a Seth mode of consciousness, and who never sense that extra richness of perception and expression. So it seems to me that most people only sip the thinnest soup from the gourmet broth of consciousness available.

I was still thinking about this and about the importance of the focus personality as the director of activities, when the following day I sensed that there was some material ready for me from the library. I sat down and transcribed it at once:

From the Library
The structure of the psyche of the world at any given time can be ascertained by viewing its exterior condition: the various civilizations all representing actualized characteristics inherent in the world mind. The different governments act in response to inner politics, which are the result of multitudinous ones used by individuals in dealing with private inner and outer reality.

Historically, the gods of one era may turn into the demons of another; the heroes turn into the despised; the lawgivers into the lawless and vice versa, as each group of generations views reality through those Aspects of the world psyche which they have chosen to encounter. A nation will deal with other nations as it does with its own members, and project outward upon enemies those Aspects of itself that are unexpressed, where they will appear in exaggerated form.

A nation's main literature and official pursuits will faithfully mirror the main-line consciousness of its people. The unofficial or underground cultures will represent aspects unexpressed or denied by the majority. Subversive literature or art is feared precisely because it represents inner, not exterior, culture. As with personal repressions, this kind of explosive material grows the more it is denounced.

When the material stopped, I sat there, frowning. I could sense so much more from "the book," but so far all I had were fairly brief passages. I could see where this last material applied easily enough, and it was obvious that my own experiences and the book were intimately connected. But when would I get the rest of the material, and what was the whole thing leading up to? I knew that I was in the middle of something, some psychic adventure, but its overall shape and resolution eluded me. Now and again, though, the word "codicil" kept coming into my mind. I knew that the term was important, but as I read over the dictionary definition, it was still difficult to see how it applied.

I'd no sooner finished writing down the library material when the phone rang, almost as if the subject matter from the book had triggered the call. It was from a young man who told me that a friend of his had just been murdered. She had only been seventeen years old, and the police had no clues. He asked if I could get any impressions that might lead to the murderer's capture.

I'd had a few calls of this nature before, and they always upset me. Now, with the latest library material in my mind, I suddenly understood why.

Actually I handled the call in the same way I had the previous ones, but this time I didn't have divided feelings about my own attitudes. I told the boy that I'd send energy to the dead girl—because I do believe that consciousness is responsive after death—but I told him that I wouldn't get involved in trying to track down her murderer. In the past I was always tempted to help (it's impossible not be be swayed by the emotions of the people involved) but when I got to the point of saying "All right, I'll see what I can do," something always stopped me.

Now my reasons seemed so simple and clear that I wondered at my previous opaqueness: I wasn't going to use my abilities to track down another human being, no matter what he'd done. The crime-and-punishment kind of psychic politics wasn't mine. Certainly it operates in our system, and there doesn't seem to be an acceptable alternative as yet, but hunting down an assailant just isn't for me. I believe too thoroughly that we create our own reality, for one thing—an unpopular belief where violence is concerned—but I'm convinced that the victim-to-be picks out the assailant with as much skill and craft as the murderer seeks his victim, and until we learn much more about both, we'll get nowhere battling crime. I'm not justifying murder by any means, but I'm saying that the victim wants to be murdered—perhaps to be punished, if not by a vengeful god then by one of his own fellows, and that a would-be murderer can switch in a minute and become the victim instead; and that the slayer wants to be slain.

Because we've never faced such issues, we're in a position where we must turn part of our society into paid killers, either as policemen or soldiers, to protect us, hence continuing the process. I pay taxes which help to maintain the same system, of course. But I'm not going to actively hunt down anyone for any reason. An ambiguous attitude, perhaps. In the meantime, I hope that my own work will help us understand ourselves better, so that no one needs to be an attacker or a victim.

Other calls, though, led me to consider my own psychic politics, and those of others. The very next day, for example, a man I'll call Bill called. His mother was dying. Bill phoned every psychic he knew. It wasn't just that he was naturally concerned and worried. There were other issues involved that were apparent to me as I listened.

Bill's mother was a very old woman. He wanted me to send her healing energy—and to heal her if I could, whether or not she wanted to live—so that he wouldn't feel guilty about not living nearby. She felt unwanted, he said. She *was* unwanted. She knew it, and he knew it. Rather than face the fact that he really didn't want his mother, he frantically set about trying to convince himself that he wanted her desperately—that she *must* live. He was buckling under the strain, so he lied to himself and to her and to everyone he called. If the doctors couldn't save her, then surely the pscyhics could.

Honesty might have saved her; maybe not. But honesty could have cleared the air and made Bill feel a lot better about himself and his emotions. He wouldn't listen to me, though. And I thought—sardonically, I suppose—We have to *use* everything. Truths are no good unless we can make them practical in just the ways we want; if they can get us what we want. We don't seem to realize that sometimes the impractical insight might be the "truest" and even the most practical, in a different way.

Music is true. It makes little difference if you understand musical notation or not. What music is, escapes such reasoning. Poetry or sculpture or art is true in the same fashion. Art is true whether or not you can open a can with it or make someone live, or make it your servant. You can't make art your servant, or life or truth either, and you can't use psychic ability to make people do what they don't want to do: because personal reality is too vigorous for that kind of manipulation.

That call and some of the others also reminded me that each of us seems to have a main focus, a particular idea of practicality—a concept of "what we want out of life" against which we judge our experiences. Many of us study this or that subject—science, religion, or history, for example—as if it existed as something apart from the experience that makes the study itself possible. That is, we concentrate so single-mindedly on our focus that we tend to forget its connection with life itself. Yet each person is struck by that strangeness, and for all of our philosophies we move from youth to age, and our main line of consciousness is embedded in our flesh.

Our experience is inner in a way that we really can't elucidate. Look at it this way: As I type this page, it's winter in the Northeast, a cold gray day. Yet I know that the air is warm and balmy in Florida. There are well-known roads waiting for me if I should decide to travel south for a month. Yet there are no known roads connecting the summer and winter of our souls. Perhaps all I'm doing in my work is exploring these dimensions, presenting alternate paths through the unknown experiences of our living; discovering oases, inns, continents, and islands in inner lands that we all travel. There are probably all kinds of ways to go—the scenic route, the historic route, the roads that lead past old temples, the city highways or country bypasses.

There are travelers who stop at each historical monument between here and Florida. They will recount the entire journey in terms of the battlegrounds they visited—the mememtos given out with the dates of military maneuvers. They will tramp the graveyards of the Confederate dead. That's how they program their journey. Others will stop on the way to visit any fortune-teller, healer, or medium they can find in trailers or campgrounds or town houses, stopping at little out-of-the way churches, taking "development courses." Still others will head for the hotels and bars in each of the cities, concentrating on cuisine and dance bands. So although there may be only so many objective ways to Florida, there are endless ways of traveling them. The differences become far more important than the route chosen. This also applies to our inner journeys.

Chapter 17
A Probable Class

Sometimes I think that for all our talk about expansion of consciousness, we deliberately hide much of our own unorthodox behavior from ourselves simply because it's so difficult to explain or correlate with our usual activities. Each time we encounter our own unofficial experiences, we're forced to examine the rest of our lives, suspecting (probably rightly) that we're usually conscious only in the most surface of ways. Such examination means that we're faced with the job of constantly altering our ideas about reality to bring them up to our newest experiences with it; and also, of course, we must then change our mental posture in the world of accepted facts.

Such an event occurred regarding my class during this period, for instance; one that struck each of us to some extent or another, for certainly we glimpsed the wider dimensions of activity possible to the psyche, and the range of communication that goes on beneath usual perception.

The event itself straddled waking and sleep experience and involved out-of-body states. I'm going to quote my own notes written the morning after. Obviously, elements of the event still lingered, as the first paragraph shows.

Notes, January 15, 1975:
"I'm sitting here to record an experience I had during the night. Even as I write, though, everything around me seems oddly significant. In this moment, at least, I'm imbuing the world with elements of vision from other states of consciousness. An other-worldly cast falls about the room and the view outside the window. Today must be some kind of minor holiday with no school, because now and then groups of children go by, bright in winter-red scarves and mittens. Everything looks larger than usual—the house across the way, the cars, even the mountain; all filled with that strange significance that for me at least has a delightful green cast.

"And the books progress at three levels; Seth is still dictating *The "Unknown" Reality; Psychic Politics* continues with its double stages—one in which I write accounts of events, and the inspired state in which material comes from the library or I have experiences there. But last night after class left, I had an experience of a different kind.

"Rob and I didn't get to bed until past 1:00 A.M. First, we had to clean up the living room after the nearly forty people who came to class; then we had a snack. I thought that I'd fall asleep in a flash. Instead I tossed and turned, and woke every half hour or so. At 2:30, I was sitting up in bed with the lamp on. Then I turned it off.

"The next thing I knew, I was back in the living room, conducting a class. Ben was talking, and I was taking notes. I always try to give full attention to students, and someone remarked about my note-taking. I hated to be disturbed, but said, 'Look. This is important. We accept this class as, well, class. But in another probability, class is over.

You've all gone home. I'm taking notes to compare what Ben says here with what he said in that other class, so that we can pinpoint the differences.'

"The room was as crowded as it had been, I remembered, in the earlier class. From the hallway I heard Mary's voice, then I heard her sister, Jean. I tried to figure out what was happening: Mary had left early from that other class, and Jean hadn't attended at all. I made sure that I noted these variations in events. Then I called out, 'Mary, I thought you'd gone home, and Jean, I didn't know you were even here!'

"Mary yelled back, laughing, 'Oh, we were here all right. We've been around all the time.'

"I tried to hold a clear conscious focus, to discover what was really happening. At the time it seemed vital that I note down everything I could. For all of that, my memory is not clear; that is, I remember that I've forgotten as much as I recall. About this time, the lights began to go on and off. This disrupted my note-taking. As I struggled to see, voices came again from the apartment house hall. We all heard an unknown doctor discussing medicine with a young woman, and the whole class listened as their footsteps went down to the front door. Then Rob and I went into the kitchen, where we watched the doctor get into a car in the parking lot below. Some class members watched from the living room windows.

"The doctor, however, led a monkey on a leash. This was the first really jarring note to me. I stopped and tried to consider. It was possible that a doctor had a monkey on a leash in the parking lot; but unlikely. I knew that I was conscious. I was positive that I was out of my body from my usual orientation. But from the orientation of this class, I *was* in my body, and the body that must be in bed was . . . a probable one.

"I remembered even then that the earlier class had ended up with a long discussion of medicine, inoculations, and monkey donors. In this class, were we dealing with that discussion in a different way? I opened the kitchen window, feeling the cold clear winter air—that was real air, by God, I thought—and I checked the corner intersection. Everything looked absolutely normal, except for one thing: no light shone anywhere. The streetlights were off; so was the traffic light; our lights had been off for some minutes.

"I closed the window and told Rob, who was beside me, that as far as I could tell we were operating between realities somehow, but that in any case the lights were out and something must have happened to the electricity. He grinned and said, 'At least it isn't our fuses,' meaning that he wouldn't have to go to the trouble of replacing them.

"At the same time, a radio began to blare with what sounded like a weather report. Unfortunately I slipped up here; accepted the radio without wondering that we had power for it, without electricity. Then, as suddenly, we were back in bed. A radio beside me was also blaring, and I thought with dismay that with all the noise, I'd never figure out what was really happening.

"The static grew so loud that angrily I woke up. My first thought was, 'Great. At least now I can write all this down.' My second thought was: 'It will be hard as the devil to write in the dark if the lights aren't working.' Next, I realized that I wasn't sure *which* reality I'd awakened in; and until I tried the lights, I wouldn't know. My hand trembled as I reached for the switch. The light splashed out its small circle of warmth. I wrote my notes, which I'm now editing and typing.

"Now I'm certain that the night's experience represented a probable class. But while in that class, I was equally certain that the class was the real one. I'm sure that I was in an out-of-body state, in the living room—everything was physical and perfectly clear. But was I hallucinating the class members, or were they here somehow? And was I hallucinating the lack of lights, first their off-and-on flicker, and then their disappearance? Or was I literally in a probable reality that exists in this same spot of space, and there, was there a light failure? Did I switch on a radio to discover the cause and then, in my confusion, forget? Or did the lights actually fail last night? Easy enough to check by calling the power company, although our clocks seem all right."

I called the power company. No trouble with the lights that night. Then, on a bet, I called Mary. Without telling her what happened, I asked her if she'd had any dreams she remembered or any unusual experiences after she left class.

Mary is a nurse and a mother, so she's quite busy. First she apologized for leaving class early: she'd been tired and concerned about a business disappointment that her husband had just encountered. To put herself in better spirits and to gain some perspective on the affair, she'd gone to her room and leafed through copies of old class Seth sessions, telling herself that she'd know which ones to read. "I know that nothing is really accidental," she said, "so I figured that whichever sessions I chose would be the ones most meaningful to me at the time."

She picked up a session dealing with probabilities and probable selves. "I never could get probable selves through my head," she said. "Then, suddenly as I read the session, I really understood for the first time what Seth meant. Now I can't even explain how I knew. But I was really encouraged and felt triumphant."

She didn't remember any dreams, though, as I hoped she might. Still, I thought, Mary *had* been thinking about probable selves just about the time I heard her in the hallway during my probable class. (She'd finally fallen asleep around 3:00 A.M., and I'd looked at my clock at 2:30.) Interesting, evocative, but that was all. I told her then about my own experiences and asked her to keep the matter to herself, so that I could quiz students about their experiences before they heard about mine, and hung up.

About an hour later, Mary called back. She'd checked the sessions she'd read the night before. The last sentences she remembered reading outlined instructions Seth had given about dreams from "the Gates of Horn." These were supposed to be particular kinds of dreams that put the individual in touch with the universe and the inner self.

It was at that point, Mary presumed, that she'd fallen asleep. Just the same, she turned the page to see what came next. "I don't know what it means," she said, "but I really feel that this is important. The next page was a discussion of the only conscious out-of-body I've ever had, an old June session where Seth mentioned it. In *that* experience, I came to a class out-of-body and almost went crazy trying to tell everyone that I *was* present. I kept shouting, 'Look my body is asleep at home, and I know it, but I'm here.' Well," she said, "it just seems like too much of a coincidence somehow. . . ."

I agreed. There seemed to be some kind of connection, but certainly nothing really definite. So I wrote down what she told me and hoped that maybe one of my other students would come up with a more specific connection.

My experience had happened after Tuesday's class, on January 14. Wednesday I had a regular Seth session, and Thursday afternoon I held my usual creative writing class, to which Mary also belonged. Before Wednesday's session, I asked Rob to question Seth about my out-of-body and the probable class. The session was relatively short—our 730th, and Seth's version of my experiences considerably broadened my understanding. This is what he said:

"Our classes occur in your physical reality, yet the greater encounters take place in the psyche, and this encounter is free of space and time. While probabilities do operate, your consciousness usually deals with them one at a time. In your terms, then, after class broke up last night, another class began—as those class events were experienced in the private and mass psyches of those involved. This 'second' class did not actually happen after the first one, however, but simultaneously. It represented the larger dimensions of the events of the class, and those events that composed the second class *did* take place at a different level of reality.

Mary left the physical class early, but still participated at another level of reality in the entire proceedings. Her sister, who has not attended lately, psychically was present. In that dimension, therefore, Ruburt was aware of both presences. He was perceiving the greater dimensions of the physical class event. In those terms, Jean, Mary's sister, who did not attend the physical class, attended a probable one; and Mary who was not present for the end of the physical class, was a participant in the entire probable class.

"To Ruburt's experience, the classes seemed separate; one real and the other probable. But the two seemingly separate classes represented the greater, usually unperceived dimensions of any class event, or of *any* perceived event.

"To Ruburt it seemed that the lights switched off and on. This represented the switching off and on of his consciousness as it perceived usually restricted perceptions, then lost them.

"The student, Ben, does have extraordinary energy, erratically and explosively used. He does not know how to use it as yet, so it appears not as a steady but as a rambunctious and sometimes distracting quality. He has not learned how to ride it. Ruburt recognizes this, and to some degree he counted upon Ben's energy, knowing that it would pierce both levels. Then he hoped to compare what Ben said in each reality.

"Ruburt was out-of-body, as he knows. In that state he was perceiving the greater dimensions of the class event, while trying to correlate this with ordinary class perception. [To Rob:] You were also out-of-body, but do not recall the situation.

"Mary was downhearted and wanted to give herself a present. Unconsciously she chose the precise old class session that dealt with probabilities; it contained her description last June of an out-of-body episode in which she did, indeed, visit a probable class. [Though she stopped reading just before coming to that passage, and without reading the entire session.]

"That was on her mind as she fell asleep. She visited here, then, out-of-body and was perceived by Ruburt, who was in an out-of-body state himself. Mary did not come into the room, but lingered in the hall with her sister.

"As Ruburt looked out of the kitchen window he was using all of his abilities, but he could not physically keep both events going at one time; or rather, his awareness could not contain all of the perceptive information.

"Part of the landscape was blacked out. *There*, the full light of consciousness did not shine. He alerted himself through the use of the hallucinary radio that made him question why the lights were off. Then he reverted to ordinary conscious behavior, thinking, 'There must be a storm,' and that a weather report would tell him its course.

"He realized that his body was sleeping and wanted to awaken to record the events, so he had the radio blare to awaken him.

"There is more, however, regarding the doctor and the monkey. The monkey was not free but on a leash—the psyche's interpretation, in other terms, of the earlier class discussion concerning inoculations. The monkey was not free because it had been inoculated with diseased tissues, yet the doctor hoped to keep the disease in control, or leashed, through measured inoculations. Ruburt saw a real doctor and a real monkey because he wanted to bring home the point that *living* animals were involved, who were then diseased; and that real men conducted the experiments.

"In other terms, to your general way of thinking diseases represent animal afflictions, and the monkey represented that connection. No doctor stood in the parking lot with a monkey on a leash; yet in other terms the event was literal, for doctors feel that they must control the 'animal' in you to heal; and that without their leash the animal nature (as it is thought of) would run wild. The monkey was also used [as a symbol] because it is 'humanistic,' or possesses what you consider incipient human characteristics.

"The vocabulary used in the regular class was interpreted by the psyche in that manner, and it was literally and symbolically true language."

I was intrigued and surprised by Seth's explanation. I'd taken it for granted that two separate events were involved, one physical and one probable—or real in another system. He was saying that both were portions of one event. This would mean that any event and all of its probable versions were somehow part of each other. I wondered how many of these we could glimpse at any given time.

      Before sleeping that night I gave myself the suggestion that I'd have another out-of-body experience, one that would somehow help me study the nature of events from the inside out. To my disappointment I remembered only a brief fragment in the morning. I recalled standing in the middle of my workroom, and seeing my friend Sue Watkins in the hall outside the door. She wore a new slacks suit; the word "slacks' seemed so significant while I was dreaming that later I specifically mentioned it when I wrote the incident down in my notebook. Then, though, the affair seemed so trivial that I wondered why I bothered. I reasoned that if Sue remembered anything herself, she'd let me know.

      That afternoon I held my creative writing class. Mary came in, bursting with excitement. She'd had her second conscious out-of-body experience the night before. Knowing me, she knew that I'd want a written record. This was written to record the experience as simply and directly as possible. Her experience is an excellent example of the joys and tribulations of maintaining conscious focus under varying conditions of out-of-body behavior:

      "I was dozing on the bed. I repeat, dozing. I heard the national anthem play from the television set, then the TV went off. I rolled over to the edge of the bed and got up. The loud staticky sounds coming from the set after the station went off annoyed me; I switched the set off and went back to bed. I was very sleepy but to my surprise and annoyance, the TV sounds continued.

      "I got up again—and again—to turn the set off. Each time I was positive that it was off, only when I got back into bed the sound continued. I finally realized what was happening, so I tried an experiment. I rolled off the bed, stood up, and opened my physical eyes—but I was still on the bed; I hadn't moved. I tried this several times, with the same result. 'I' was out of my body and it was still on the bed. I became more alert as I experimented, going in and out several times.

      "Then I decided to stay out. 'Jane's house,' I thought. 'I've got to get there.' I imagined the inside door in the lower hall in Jane's apartment building. I was there! Now up the steps, calling as loudly as I could, 'Jane, Jane.' At the same time I wondered if my body was yelling too, so that anyone at home would be disturbed. Both thoughts amused me.

"Jane and Rob were both standing at the top of the stairs. I was laughing, showing off. 'Look at me, my second out-of-body. Aren't you pleased?'

"Jane said, 'Great,' in her usual enthusiastic manner, but I felt that a new exclamation should be coined for the occasion. I looked around, critically trying to check the environment against the usual one. I told Jane that the apartment looked different, and she asked me how. I looked around again.

"For one thing, I knew that it was night, yet here the sun was shining through the windows. For another thing, there were dining rooms all over the place. I knew that I was seeing things differently than they should be, and I thought that I should inspect the rest of the place too, to see what differences there were from usual reality.

"Jane and Rob were different, too. They looked younger. Rob began talking. He said that he was going to Ohio to a plowing contest, and I thought, 'Oh brother, Rob, you're never going to believe this probable self you have.' Then I turned to Jane. She and Rob were both smiling but they looked blank, somehow, and I knew that I was losing them. I was fully conscious, though, studying what was going on. 'Jane, do you know what a probable self is?' I asked.

"She bobbed her head up and down, saying, 'Yup.'

" 'What?' I asked suspiciously, because by then she looked to be in her early twenties; really all that remained of the Jane I know was her black hair. She looked as if she didn't know much of anything, and when she answered my question by saying, 'Slacks,' then I knew I'd lost Jane and Rob completely.

"With this, I decided that I'd go to visit my sister Jean. I had the feeling that I didn't have much time, so I visualized her kitchen, found myself there, and went up the stairs to her room, calling her name. Jean was in bed, sleepy

and confused. I tried to tell her what was happening but felt
that I had to get back. The TV signal sound that I'd heard
earlier now sounded louder. I called, 'Gotta go, Jean,' and
found myself at my own door.

"I realized that I'd probably have to look at my
body in order to get back into it and thought, 'Oh, well, I
might as well do it and get it over with. I can do it without
getting freaked, I guess.'

"I went in, bracing myself, not knowing how I'd
feel, seeing my body. There I was, on the bed, thrashing
around. That tickled me for some reason. I dived in on top of
myself. Then for a minute it was like wrestling with another
person. I thought, 'If you'd just hold still and stop fighting! I
really should be neater about this.' I wondered if I'd ever get
twisted around right, then finally I was back in. I opened my
physical eyes."

It was supposed to be a creative writing class, but
we discussed Mary's experience. She asked me if I remembered anything and I said no, nothing but a brief out-of-body
involving Sue; but it wasn't clear at all. Then I said, "Slacks!
There's something familiar about that, though," and I
checked my dream notebook. Mary and I just looked at each
other for a minute.

What on earth did *that* mean? In her experience
she asked me what a probable self was, and I answered with
the seemingly disconnected comment, "Slacks." In *my*
experience I saw Sue wearing a new slacks suit and knew that
the word "slacks" was important—so important that I wrote
it down despite its seeming nonsense. So in some fashion,
Mary and I communicated.

We didn't know until the following Tuesday that
we hadn't been alone.

I began class as I often did, by asking students
about their week's dreams. This time I asked if anyone
remembered any dreams the night after our last class. I kept
my voice as normal as possible so that no one would know I
had anything particular in mind. Ben waved both arms in the
air immediately and seemed quite excited. "I had a really
strange dream," he said. He ruffled through a messy-looking

dream notebook, found a sheet of paper, and called out, "Here it is!"

"Okay, Ben first," I said.

He read the following: "Last Tuesday night after Seth class . . . I was in a sort of half-awake, half-asleep state. In this other state of consciousness, I found myself in the ESP class, except that it wasn't the usual one but the class in another level of reality. We were discussing adjacent classes, as we had in the regular class that night. But there was a difference. Our points of view had changed so that the physical class was considered the unreal class, and this one was the real class.

"One student, Dick, made a joke about the unreal physical class, but I don't remember it. All I know is that it had something to do with a picture of a pig with stitches through its leg. Dick then tore off the piece of the picture with the pig's stitched leg. Everyone thought this was very funny—myself included. At that point I came out of the whole thing and went over it all in my mind so I would remember. I felt unusually satisfied that I had remembered being in this other reality."

Mary and I both let out delighted whoops of astonishment—and triumph. When I read my own notes detailing the "probable class," Ben was grinning all over and other class members went searching through their dream notebooks. Some people hadn't remembered many dreams for the week. Some had; but left their notebooks home.

Mary read the notes she'd made on her out-of-body experience the night of Wednesday, January 15, in which Rob told her that he was going to a plowing contest: When she read that portion everyone laughed, including Rob, because he'd never worked a plow in his life. Then one student, John, raised his hand, grinned, and read a long dream that he'd had that same night. The whole thing involved Rob and me—in a farmhouse. Class members were there also.

Still another student read a dream of the same night in which class members were all in our apartment, getting ready to move us to a farm. In John's dream the house was built into a hillside so that it looked to be two stories, but wasn't. In this student's dream, there were fields around, and a swimming pool.

The following day another student mailed me this note: "I couldn't wait until next week's class to tell you this. I didn't remember it at all in class tonight, but as I was looking through my dream notebook just now, after class, I came across this dream I had last Tuesday night. I wrote it down Wednesday morning.

"Dream January 15, 1975: I've forgotten it but repeated this phrase over and over so much that at least it remains: I attended a Seth class. This seems to coincide with the 'second class' we talked about tonight—and I'm really freaking out!"

To top it off, Mary had called her sister, Jean, the morning after she visited her in the out-of-body state. Without saying anything she asked Jean if she remembered any dreams from the night before. Jean said, "Yeah. You came and tried to get me out-of-the-body." Jean hadn't written the episode down, however.

It's almost impossible to know what really happened, or why certain data was communicated, while other, seemingly more pertinent information wasn't. The word "slacks" for example, was obviously a connective between Mary's experience and my very brief episode with Sue and the slacks of the same night. Sue remembered nothing. Yet again, I knew that the word "slacks" was very important—and in Mary's experience when she asks me about probable selves, I answer "slacks." A bleed-through obviously occurred.

The same thing happened involving the plowing contest. In some way, this was reflected in the other students' dreams where they saw us in a farmhouse, or moving to one.

Such experiences always bring me up short. It's hard to believe that we understand so little of our own activities as they relate to the dream state. Levels of interaction and communication obviously occur beyond the normally accepted ones. As long as we consider our usual line of consciousness as the only normal one, we'll never know how different levels of perception and consciousness mix and merge.

Was Ben's dream of another class just a coincidence? If so, what a marvelous, pat coincidence! I suspect that his "pig with stitching" was his interpretation of my monkey on a leash. In any case, I'm certain that any group, social or otherwise, communicates in somewhat the same fashion in the dream state; where symbols are more mobile, and associations follow a different kind of organization.

One thing I've learned: It takes a good amount of conscious time to keep up with our usually unconscious activities. Once you learn to remember your dreams, it can easily take an hour a day just to record them, and this doesn't include analysis. Out-of-body experiences are something else again; because we can be in one of many states of consciousness when we're out-of-body, just as we can when we're in it.

From the usual point of view, my doctor and monkey in the parking lot were hallucinations, forming a creative drama as the psyche interpreted certain information in its own way. Yet from the other side of the picture, in that other state of consciousness, both the doctor and monkey were real—and my sleeping physical body seemed like the hallucination. We're highly prejudiced, perhaps, of necessity at this stage of the game; but we insist on interpreting our unofficial experiences from our usually conscious standpoint.

In any case, while I was trying to write up my dream records that week and hoping to explore other states of consciousness to a fuller degree, the telephone was ringing constantly. The world as most people were experiencing it was really making itself known. And the episodes people related seemed sometimes as bizarre as any dream.

Chapter 18

Sex and Energy: Some Inventive Versions. Seth by the Ouijafuls

It was past midnight. Rob had left the house over an hour ago, driving a strange woman to a local motel. Or, so I thought. I'd expected him home within half an hour at most. I was concerned for several reasons. I kept trying not to be concerned. Besides that, the situation was ludicrous, and I knew it. So what did I do? I sat down and wrote about it, naturally; typing as fast as I could. Just to show you that I'm not blind to my own foibles, I'm including my original notes about the situation. Even as I wrote them, I cursed my sense of humor (why wasn't I more compassionate?), yet I couldn't tell which was funnier—the events or my own present reactions. This is what I wrote:

"Well, here it is, past midnight, and Rob is down at

a local motel. He's driving a woman lawyer there. She landed here out of nowhere tonight, calling, 'Jane, Jane,' at our door—our living room door after first knocking at the hallway and study doors. In other words, she just walked into the hall that divides our two apartments and went wandering around, knocking at all the doors. We were having a Seth session. The phone had rung just before we started. Usually we turn it off during a session but we'd forgotten. So Rob turned the bell off and we began.

"We'd just stopped for a break when we heard the first knock. We ignored it. Five or six more knocks at the hall door. Then we heard the door to our places open—it wasn't locked. Next, footsteps, and knocks on my closed study door just across the way, which again we ignored, growing more irritated. I reached for a cigarette—quietly—and paused as the footsteps crossed the hall; this time the knocking began at the locked door to the living room. We were seated only a few feet away.

"Rob and I stared at each other. It's weird to sit like that, hardly breathing in your own damn living room. Besides, I was remembering the phone call we didn't answer. It crossed my mind that whoever telephoned wasn't just going to call back: but were coming here instead. Then from the hall a plaintive, lost, weak voice came calling, 'Jane? Jane? Don't you expect me? You do expect me, don't you? Jane?'

"I knew that I couldn't go on with the session anyway, if I didn't let whoever it was in. I could feel the trouble. No esoteric flashes were needed; the voice was enough. I told Rob he'd better open the door. In the meantime I called out, asking who was there. She answered, but I couldn't understand her.

"I don't know if I should laugh or cry. She got on the plane she told us and came here because Seth told her to; and the Kundalini force was so strong that during the four-hour flight layoff she had to masturbate over and over—good God—And later she said that intercourse helps—and here is Rob, down at the motel with her. So what if she asks him to help her out? And today I gave an interview for the local paper on open marriage, of all things I mean, well, there are limits. And if the old Kundalini force is driving the good lady lawyer mad, well, what's a compassionate man to do?

"But regardless, I think it's hysterical that a woman lawyer should just come here and tell us how madly she masturbated on the plane; except that she's a lovely woman, in her forties and harried; in agony, and as always I was touched and wanted to help. But I thought, as she told me how sane and well balanced she was, 'Look lady well-balanced people don't go barging in on strangers because inner voices tell them to.' She tilted her head to one side and said gently, 'What? What? Am I in the wrong place? Is this the right Jane Roberts?'

"I don't know if it was the right Jane Roberts, but it's the only Jane Roberts I've got, I thought. I said, "Look, forget the inner voices. Do you want a cup of coffee?" It was a damn cold night, I kept thinking. 'Something to eat?' I asked.

"I think it's mean of me to have such a sense of humor, but there it was—the big-boned black-haired attractive woman and the ludicrous situation; a comic tragedy. And she'd been sick. But her reality was her own and she was closed to anything I might say. I knew it; felt it at once.

"And as she talked I felt that she was asking for it all; the dramatic visits to various psychics she told us about; the excitement; the combined horror and delight of her predicament; because, as she told us, she was really so fastidious. But she knew that the Kundalini force had been released in her, and now she couldn't control it and it came out in sexual pressure that had to find release.

"Rob related to her better than I did. Yet I did have a brief Seth session for her. She barely listened. She didn't want to be helped. Her situation was too deliciously dramatic to give up. Seth told her that the Kundalini force was the natural life force; that she formed her own reality; that she was fighting her own energy instead of going along with it; making divisions where there were none. But she wouldn't listen.

"Her fiancé knew where she was; this time—and all

the other times when she flew across the country to one psychic or another. Since we obviously couldn't help, she decided to visit a famous Indian guru as soon as she left us. And we weren't to worry. She'd find a place to stay for the night, walk through the cold night air till she found a taxi stand; bundle up so that she'd be warm.

"Yeah, lady-o; I suggested a taxi. Rob said that the least he could do was drive her to a motel. That was well over an hour ago. Now, writing this, I wonder what the devil is going on down at that motel. Is she trying to explain, desperately, anxiously, earnestly? Is she mentally disturbed enough to get into serious trouble? I suggested she see a psychologist, but she refused. Can Rob handle it? I feel he can handle just about anything. Just the same, I wish he'd get home. And the big question is: If the lady lawyer is in such agony, well—should Rob help out if he can; and if he did, how could a compassionate psychic wife get mad? Easy."

Well, Rob came home just about when I'd finished writing the above. Our car hadn't started. He wanted to call a taxi but she insisted that the cold night air would do her good, so the two of them had walked over a mile to the motel; then Rob had to walk back.

My feelings about the affair were highly ambiguous and contradictory. I read my original notes in my creative writing class as an example of on-the-spot writing, but I had Rob describing the episode to the expansion of consciousness class. One thing did upset me. Like so many others, the lady lawyer was afraid of the life force itself, the source of all power. She believed that it had to be handled with kid gloves or it would destroy her. There was no trust in the spontaneity of being. She couldn't take it for granted that the life force gives us life and energy easily and naturally.

Instead she followed a dogma that defines energy as Kundalini, which must be released in certain prescribed ways. Take one wrong step, get off your inner balance a figurative half inch, and that energy can destroy you. I'm convinced that such ideas are a distortion of the original revelations behind them. But whenever the lady tried to practice her profession, the Kundalini, she believed, arose to strike her down.

On the other hand, the whole thing was an emotional con game that she was playing with herself and others; and it depended upon certain other ideas and contrasts that will be discussed later in this chapter. Again, in fact, the month was going to present us with experiences that all tied in with each other. All of them showed different versions of main issues that at first seemed separate.

We were very busy. The beginning of February we decided to start house hunting in earnest. Rob finished the drawings for my poetry book, *Dialogues of the Soul and Mortal Self in Time* and the diagrams for *Adventures in Consciousness*. As soon as these were mailed we began watching ads and calling agencies.

We took afternoons to drive around the city and nearby towns, checking houses that had been listed for sale. As we did, I was struck more and more by the resemblance between our inner and exterior interests and activities. When Rob and I drove into a neat sparkling area of suburban homes, for example, seeing the ranch houses with the small yards, hedges, garages, kiddy-cars in driveways, to us they represented cozy ingrown ideas—the neighborhoods being the materialization of the beliefs of the people who lived in them. Unfair on my part, perhaps; but that's what I felt. And Rob and I would never be comfortable there.

Then there were houses more to our liking—big sprawling things with a certain antiquated style that was somehow timeless; large private yards, high-ceilinged rooms with soft white walls and rich dark wooden floors; but these required upkeep, even a maid or yard man. And the houses seemed to demand a kind of formality—hostess gowns and not my habitual dungarees. So while those houses intrigued me, the fit wasn't right.

But I saw that we're each surrounded by the materialized versions of our ideas of wealth and power, hope and despair, and the objects about us stand in one way or another for our beliefs and our methods of handling life's energy. If we're afraid of life's energy, then we hoard what we have, afraid of not getting more, yet we often use it in ways disastrous to ourselves because of our distrust. Or we hurt ourselves in such a way that our power is short-circuited.

As we were in the process of house hunting, for example, a well-known young classic guitarist attended class and visited us privately. His music was more than delightful—it was full of power and vitality. He thought of energy as the power to make music; to move others. The life force was to be expressed, not inhibited. He was free to grow into his own power. It was the repression of that force, not its release, that was bothering the lady lawyer.

But sex seemed to be the subject matter of the month. Again, from my original notes: "I just had one of the funniest, most exuberant, most tragic phone calls that I've ever received. Unbelievable, the way it relates to psychic politics and shows how our inner ways of dealing with ourselves regulate our methods of coping with the world, our families, and social lives."

The phone rang. I answered it. The woman's voice was obviously old, but strong. Her tones were imperious, demanding, expecting service, and no nonsense.

And what a tale, worthy of a novel! My caller, the heroine, was in her seventies. She started in at once, saying: 'What would you say about a situation where someone discovered that their spouse of some fifty years had, all that time, indulged himself with all the filth of the whorehouses? That he had, all that time, embarked into the underworld of homosexuality; had oral sex often, and then, not satisfied, had to masturbate? Because he knew that those women were evil, ruled by elementals, and yet he couldn't stay away from them?

I was sipping coffee. I still had over an hour of writing time to put in and the day's correspondence to do, but instantly I was caught up by the woman's vitality and fascinated by the contrasts she'd set up in her life. She went on, endlessly it seemed, to describe the husband (hers, of course) in various situations and positions, each involving remarkable sexual appetites: Satisfying them had been his hobby all those years, while hers had been joining spiritualistic and psychic societies.

Between the two of them, they'd managed to probe with energetic zeal into the two fold dimensions of soul and sex, because they saw these areas as definitely opposed to each other. She was the good woman, the family pillar, the sensitive psychic; believer in God and purity—and he was the wandering husband, caught up in the "filthy stinking holes of the prostitutes' world and the ungodly stinking playgrounds of the devil." But he bribed one attendant too many and the word got out. Worse, a whorehouse was raided, and he was nabbed with the rest of the wiggling catch. The townspeople of their small New England village were snickering, she said, and the Elks would kick him out if word got to them of his nefarious activities.

So what did I think, she wanted to know.

"About which?" I asked.

"All of it. Any of it," she said. "Oral emission. I'm an educated woman. You don't have to be afraid to use the phrase."

"Well, it's great. I don't see anything wrong with it," I began.

"Are you telling me that I have to smile and accept it when my husband does it with a girl who does it with another girl at the same time—while another one watches?"

"That's a different question," I protested. I was having trouble trying to keep up, and it was an effort to imagine all those bodies doing what she said they were doing. And I kept thinking: You form your own reality too, Jane. So why are you getting all these wild calls? In the meantime she went on describing her husband's further exploits, which were certainly remarkable for a seventy-year-old man. And it wasn't a put-on.

She mentioned now, as she hadn't earlier, the psychic visions she'd had through the years—all correct—a glimmer of the whorehouse steps, with her husband being ingloriously assisted down them, too drunk to walk alone. "I thought you insisted earlier that you hadn't known?" I asked.

"I didn't believe what I was seeing," she said.

She continued: "Then after I discovered what was

going on, when I was told, by others of course, I confronted
him, but he denied it. He lied over and over again" (here her
voice grew hard and revengeful), "so I said, 'You're lying in
the face of Almighty God, mocking His truth. He should
strike you dead where you stand, reeking in your filth.' "

"Now, just wait a minute," I cried; growing angry
myself, seeing her in my mind's eye confronting him that
way—and with both of them strangers, disturbing *my* afternoon. "That's worse than infidelity as far as I'm concerned."

She wouldn't be interrupted. "Wait," I said, sharply.
She shut up. "Listen," I said "what right have you to call
down a god's wrath to destroy a man? And why do you think
that a god would do it anyhow? What kind of a god would
strike a man dead because an enraged wife wants him
punished?"

"But he defied the truth." Then, not stopping,
voice shaking with virtuous rage, she went on: "And he said,
he said, that suddenly as I stood there he saw his entire filthy
career through *my* eyes, through *my* eyes; and even back
through past reincarnations. *Now,* how do you explain that?"

She wanted me to say that he saw his guilt in its
true light, reflected through her pure spirit or something. But
anyhow, she didn't give me a chance to answer but went on:
"And his homosexuality—"

This time she paused and I managed to say,
"Homosexuality isn't evil."

"Well, what am I to do?" she demanded. "People
are beginning to find out and I can't shield him any longer."

"Why are you still with him, if he offends you so?"

"Because I won't leave a sinking ship," she said,
bitterly. "He'll just sink to the gutter all the way. He says
that I'm the only good thing that ever happened to him."

"Well, maybe he'd be happier in the gutter," I said,
wickedly.

She snorted. "He says that the whores are controlled by elementals."

"Look," I said, "no one is wicked and evil and
lousy all through, in the terms you're speaking of. If he
thinks that prostitutes are filthy, that's his belief, and yours

too, I guess. But it has little to do with any of the ladies involved. But while each of you shares those beliefs, you'll be caught in a dilemma between purity and sex, depravity and spirituality; caught in between, where you can't win. Examine your beliefs. You said that you read Seth's *The Nature of Personal Reality*. Well, do the exercises suggested in it. Discover what you really believe, and why."

I felt slightly triumphant, just to get a word or so in edgewise. At the same time, I saw clearly how this woman and her husband stood together, between God and Satan, each of them believing that sex was sinful—good women didn't enjoy it; only prostitutes had oral sex—and husband and wife each of them played the opposing role to the hilt. But money and power and prestige were also involved: the prostitutes and homosexuals and "dirty holes of iniquity" stood in hilarious contrast to the social organizations to which they both belonged, the business and civil groups, and the wealthy, prosperous citizens. These beliefs had little to do with any particular church or club, or for that matter, with any particular pimp or prostitute. One meeting with a wealthy, well-appointed call girl would shatter the wife's stereotyped belief to some extent, because in her mind the two can't go together.

Respectability and godliness are so intertwined in her mind that it's almost impossible for her to think of one without the other. It was precisely her husband's double life that so shocked her and brought about her sense of enraged betrayal; the same double quality that probably provided the spice and forbidden sense of evil accomplishment to him—To have commerce with prostitutes and then crawl into an immaculately appointed bed with his pure wife in a house that was the material symbol of respectability! So he was "evil" for both of them and she was their joint conscience.

While she well knew what he'd been up to, she'd kept silent for some forty-odd years. And even now, recounting her visions of his iniquities, she could say that she hadn't really believed them; hadn't really known. And he, knowing of her psychic abilities, performed knowing full well that at some level she knew. So she certainly gave silent consent, growing furious only when the inner implied conditions were broken.

It became a public affair—secret no longer, out in the open. Besides, they were older now. Sexual promiscuity of that kind in a younger man can be considered manly by some; other men can envy even as they blame. But in an old man the behavior becomes something to snicker about, and therefore not quite as evil. We don't think that things are evil and honestly funny at the same time. And now the lady was also forced to publically encounter a situation she'd actually condoned in her way for years.

My recent lady caller had been a lawyer. This woman was a designer. But I couldn't help comparing them. Both were afraid of energy, both identified it to some extent as sexual and therefore bad, disastrous, degrading—the one "forced" to masturbate and the other forced to see sex ruin her good husband. These attitudes rested on beliefs taught by some religions for centuries—the self is evil, the body a vehicle of decay; the earthy must be transmuted into the pure and good. Man's natural vitality becomes a force to be feared and disciplined, a pressure, an energy to fight against, rather than a creative living power shared with all of life.

So I told her what I thought and she took it, though with a good amount of sputtering. At least I gave her my honest opinion and recommended that she work with her beliefs. I don't know if I got through to her or not, but I suspect that I did. She called me after reading my books, so she must have had some idea what my response would be. And she was a vigorous, bristly woman: There was hope for her.

As I hung up and told Rob about the call, I learned something about myself, too. Earlier I'd dubbed the first lady "the masturbating lady lawyer." Now describing the above dialogue, I found myself at my humorous best. At the same time I was thinking: "This isn't very kind of me. To her, the circumstances certainly don't seem very funny." But as soon as I thought *that*, the whole affair seemed funnier, more tragic, yet more hilarious at the same time. I'd felt guilty about the lady lawyer for the same reason.

But I understood, as I heard myself talking to Rob, that I felt guilty only when I judged myself against another definition of goodness or kindness besides my own. Whenever I did that I got off the track. My compassion and humor existed together. It's the entire human element that is so perplexing, vast, humorous, and tragic all at once. To some extent, my humor helps me avoid pitfalls, and lets me help others to see their lives in better perspective.

Then I understood something else: The phone calls, visits, and letters were falling into patterns, just as the subjective events of my life had been doing. They came in clusters, dealing with certain particular questions and subject matter. Each call gave me the opportunity to see how various people organized exterior reality according to inner politics. Amazing that I hadn't seen the connections earlier.

I'd been brooding about the writing time lost—yet I'd already begun to write up the last phone call. And presented with the voice on the phone, I'm more or less forced to deal with people directly and to put theory into practice. So I wondered: In some funny fashion do I sit waiting for the phone to ring? Number please? And for a voice from out of the universe calling with a question that I'm meant to answer?

Most of the calls never appear in my writing at all, of course. Often I take a half hour or so to help someone; wondering if I really have. And I've seen many such people make some amazing creative adjustments in their lives. Still, some part of me needs the quiet and peace of my library. I like to retreat to the psyche's secret recesses. It also occurred to me that my "double" was in the library, peacefully going about her work, even when I answered the telephone.

As I was musing about it all, the phone rang again. This time I was tempted not to answer, but I did. The caller was a man who told me that the night before Seth had communicated with him through the Ouija board. He'd read Seth's statement about communicating only through me to protect the integrity of the material. So my caller wanted to know who or what moved the Ouija for him.

I explained that since the Seth books were

published, Seths were popping up all over, which was okay, but they weren't my Seth. People were using Seth as a symbol, which was all right with him; a symbol of higher levels of consciousness. I also told him about *Adventures in Consciousness,* in which I gave my ideas about such trance or Ouija personalities.

I hung up, shaking my head. It certainly seemed that the phone was ringing more since I'd found my library. Certainly more strangers were finding their way to our apartments. People's questions were toppling over and over in my mind, and for the first time I seriously considered getting an unlisted telephone number.

In the meantime I kept thinking about the people who called or wrote, and their problems. The next day, as I reread the earlier material on strands of consciousness, some new ideas came to me: It's not so much the events of our lives that compose our mental experience, as the level of consciousness we're in when we experience the events. I remember how everything before my eyes seemed to change in my altered state in front of the supermarket. The physical data was the same as before. The contents of the world didn't gain or lose an inch, in physical terms. Yet qualitatively everything changed to such a degree that the world was entirely different and richer. The buildings and people *were* more fully dimensioned. In my altered state, more was physically apparent. Yet even then I knew that others about me, in the usual state of consciousness, were seeing the same world I had seen before the switch. Nothing was added to *their* world, and I didn't know how much I would retain when I returned to "normal" either.

What I had retained was memory and fleeting flashes in which the experience splashed out momentarily into a day and then vanished—and the library—because in some way that I still didn't understand, the library was born out of that altered vision. But I was becoming certain that states of consciousness help mold events and are invisibly a part of them.

Difficulties at one level of awareness disappear at other levels. Certain "negative" experiences simply dissolve and contradictions disappear. We just haven't been taught to vary our own experience-levels, to travel to one state of consciousness to find the answers to problems existing at another level.

From my own experiences, I also knew that these various states possess different characteristics and creative specializations. Using altered states of consciousness, we can experience events from different sides—and if we knew how to utilize these conditions, we could conceivably circumnavigate events, seeing them from inside and outside space and time, glimpsing their greater reality. It's quite possible that difficulties in our lives represent specific areas in which our vision is truly limited to a too-confined focus.

I was thinking of all this and trying to connect it with the problems people wrote or called about when—you guessed it—the phone rang. A girl said: "Have you any idea what's going on here?" Her voice brimmed with excitement, yet half-whispered, as if afraid of its own words.

"No," I said, and in hushed conspiratorial tones she told me the following story. She and her brother read my books, and got themselves a Ouija board. On the first night Seth came through. On the second, he said that he'd speak through the girl, whom I'll call Loretta. On the third night, still through the board, Seth began to dictate a novel.

"Great," I said. "A good creative product is terrific, no matter where it comes from."

There was a pause. I complimented Loretta and her brother on their creativity and inventiveness; their curiosity and flexibility of consciousness, before broaching the possibility that *their* Seth wasn't *my* Seth. "Which is all to the good," I said, "because you're opening up areas of your own psyches. That portion probably identifies itself as Seth because of your respect for the books. It's saying, 'Listen, this is important. I come from a different level of awareness than usual.' "

"But it's Seth," she said, her voice dropping.

I told her to read *Adventures in Consciousness,* and tried to explain to her in a few words how it applied to her experience, then went on. "Look," I said, "you've opened up your own creative channels. The various portions of the psyche use different languages. Don't interpret them all literally. You've been given the idea for a novel. That's an influx of creativity from one level to another."

"Wait a minute, would you please?" she asked, and then her brother, Dennis, came to the phone. He went through the entire episode again.

I tried a slightly different approach. "Look, the books are helping people realize that they have other possible mental focuses, other kinds of perceptive consciousnesses. Seth is serving as a symbol of higher levels fo awareness, which is great. Use the symbol, but don't take it literally."

Dennis kept saying that he understood, and following this by saying, "But he keeps saying he's Seth." Then he went on to say, "I've left my job and Loretta's left hers. We're going to write this novel. The whole thing is directing our lives."

"Well, it shouldn't," I said.

"It shouldn't? Why not?" he asked.

His surprise surprised me. "Why should it?" I said. "Take the material and use it, like you would any other creative product. You both probably wanted to leave your jobs and do something else. So if you decide to write a book, great. If so, the material gave you an opportunity, and an excuse if you needed it. Maybe it shook you loose from a rut. But if you treat your source as if it were omnipotent, you're in for a letdown."

I was tired explaining. My voice trailed off. They were disappointed. We hung up.

I thought about the call, decided to write notes about it, when the telephone rang again. This time I almost decided to let it ring. What the devil was going on? The calls were coming as fast as the automatic material from the library did. I had a good clue with that connection, but I didn't pick it up until the next call was over.

It was a young man's voice. "I'm Saint Paul, calling for instructions."

"What?" I asked. I'd heard him all right. I just needed a minute's time.

"This is hard to explain," he said. "But I'm Saint Paul, reincarnated. I'm ready to embark on my mission, and I'm calling you and Seth for instructions." He spoke in a quiet, quite rational voice.

And suddenly, it was simple. I knew exactly how to handle it. I said, "When I'm on the phone under such circumstances, I speak for Seth and myself too." And as I said it, I realized that it was true.

"Okay," he said. "I'll do whatever you say."

"First, get a job."

There was silence at his end, and I plunged into it. "You can't understand people and help them if you don't share their workaday world. Don't stay home, brooding about your mission."

"All right," he said bravely.

"And you must understand: Saint Paul is a symbol in your psyche. You must find out what he represents." And miraculously I got through to him.

"I understand," he said. "I understand and thank you."

He hung up, and the clues I'd sensed earlier came to the forefront of my mind. Of course! The callers and the visitors were . . . the other side of the library; they call with certain questions, and these serve as impetus for library material. That is, my desire to help propels me into the library.

All of these people in their own way were super-real; exaggerating certain normal-enough characteristics until they could no longer be ignored. The early library material said that I'd be presented with experiences I needed, to ask the proper questions. But I'd thought that psychic experiences of the more conventional kind were meant. Instead, the callers were showing me psychic politics in action in the usual world. They were showing me how *they* related psychic events to the normal framework of reality.

They were strong vigorous people in their way, taught though, to interpret all events literally. It was often this very attempt to translate psychic events into usual terms that made them appear so strange to themselves or their fellowmen.

Yet the library material that I hoped would provide some hints, came in dribbles, now and then; suddenly but in snatches. Seth continued to dictate *The "Unknown" Reality*, but Rob was so busy that he didn't get a chance to type many of the sessions, and I can't read the shorthand system he's devised. So while I suspected that Seth might be adding some highlights on the present situation, I didn't get to read those sessions until some time later.

In the meantime, we kept on house hunting.

Chapter 19

I Hear a Voice and There's No One There. Official and Unofficial Sequences

Like everyone else, I have two sources of information: inner and outer. That winter, outer data about the world came as fast as I could handle it; from the callers and correspondence, and from our experiences as we ventured into the world of real estate. Besides, we received the usual news of the world through the communications media.

When viewed through the regular focus of consciousness, all of this information adds up to a rather frightening picture: evidence of overpopulation, pollution, ignorance—the race seemingly headed toward extinction either through war or mismanagement of the planet. This picture itself generates uncertainty and fear, for within it the individual seems threatened and unsafe. The evidence is all there and constantly reinforces itself.

That is one picture of the world, legitimate enough at the usual level of consciousness. Sometimes it's all we can see, until gradually any countering data becomes invisible and no hope shows. Yet at this level, only portions of events are perceived, and the most disastrous probabilities are used in making forecasts. The same events, perceived at a different level of consciousness, might be far different, showing solutions not visible before.

In fact, I became more and more convinced that a different kind of earthly reality existed at other levels of consciousness, as legitimate as this one—the same world, really, only a better version. Granted such a world existed, tuned in to a particular level of consciousness, then how could we learn to inhabit it in normal reality?

Even at our usual level, our beliefs and attitudes permit an endless variety of experiences and alternate views. The dowager and her promiscuous husband are locked into a good-and-evil framework that crowds about them all the time, and colors their most mundane moments. They also see the world through that tint. Their ideas in politics and social matters will follow the same line, and their world will be experienced as a battleground between good and evil.

Others may focus instead upon war. A father may be in one war and his sons in succeeding ones. Other families may never have direct war experience although they live in the same historic period—to them wars will be on the sidelines of experience. But each of us, no matter how free we feel, knows that others in this world are not. And to that extent, we share the same reality.

I was thinking of all this when a really odd event happened. It was insignificant enough: many have had the same kind of experience. I was struck by its vividness, though, and as it turned out the episode triggered some library material that gave me a much better idea of alternate worlds.

It was February 15. We were tired from working and house hunting and decided to take naps before dinner. As usual, I went into our bedroom, in the east apartment, closing the apartment door. Rob napped on the cot in his studio, in the west apartment. He closed the apartment and studio doors. I puttered around a bit first, watered the plants; sat on the edge of the bed and read a few minutes. Then I lay down. The phone rang four times then stopped, and I fell asleep.

I may have half awakened once, then I had a dream that I could hardly remember. I was in a park, and thought of staying awhile but decided not to, since it was growing dark. Someone sat down on a bench with me and began to read the mail that I'd put beside me. I protested vigorously, pleased with myself for expressing my annoyance rather than hiding it. Then Rob came along and said, "Let's get our stuff together and get the hell out of here."

Then Rob's real voice called, "Hon," from the study outside the bedroom. I awakened, sat up, yelled, "Okay, I'm awake," to let him know I'd heard him. Then I got up, wondering why he didn't come all the way into the bedroom to waken me as he usually did when we took separate naps.

To my astonishment, the door to the apartment was still closed. We always left both apartment doors open unless we were sleeping, because the hallway between the two had a separate door to an outside hall. Why on earth had Rob closed it again behind him?

I opened it and saw that the other apartment door was closed too. I went inside—and Rob's studio door was closed. Just then it opened. He came out, rubbing his eyes. "Oh, you're up," he said, surprised. "I just got up myself."

"What do you mean? You just came in and called me, didn't you?"

Rob swore that he hadn't. He said that he'd awakened a few moments earlier and thought of getting up to call me, but that was all. I shook my head: I could hardly believe it, but obviously there hadn't been any voice to hear! Yet Rob's seemingly physical voice was what awakened me— from a dream in which a dream—Rob was also speaking. The real voice was easily distinguishable from the dream one. And I yelled out, physically, in reply.

After dinner, I wrote down a list of possibilities:

1. I hallucinated the voice. If so, it was a splendid hallucination, causing physical action. There was nothing to distinguish it from the real thing. If Rob had been up when I got up, I never would have questioned his calling me, granting he'd opened the doors.

2. Rob was in an out-of-body state. He came into the room while I was still asleep, spoke to me "astrally," and I translated the voice into physical terms.

3. Rob's mental intent to awaken me was transmitted telepathically and I hallucinated the voice in response.

4. Despite what I think happened, I never called out physically at all; and the voice and my reply were both hallucinary. I can't buy this.

I finally decided that telepathically I picked up Rob's intent to call me and then hallucinated the sound of his voice; reacted as if I'd heard a real sound, and awakened. But I still wasn't satisfied. Then, watching television that evening, I saw a scene in which a comedian burned his pant legs—and suddenly I was sure that I could smell the smoke. I knew that this "fake sense data," as I called it, was related with hearing Rob's voice. But how?

The next day was Sunday, usually a free day for us. Late in the afternoon when I sat down to read a magazine, I realized that there was some library material ready for me, so I went to my desk. I didn't see my double in the library or any other images. Instead I just took the material down as it came, as fast as I could type—material certainly prepared at another level of consciousness, but "packaged" for this one.

From the Library

The world as we experience it is the result of neurological conclusions reached by acknowledging certain sequences or series of stimuli and ignoring others, in line with learned models given to us in childhood. A kind of learned prejudiced is developed in which only a given series or sequence of neurological activity is accepted. The other quite-as-legitimate series remain almost as ghost images. We then organize our experience and shape events following the prime series.

There is a correlation here with infinite and infinitesimal number patterns, or what can be called unofficial
series. These, followed, would bring a different kind of events
into experience, or events that would be other versions of the
ones we recognize. The accepted, neurologically accepted
series generally become habitual, and form a kind of percep-
tual path. This path is supported to some degree by hidden
values or unofficial events and series that hide within the
prime sequence. The brilliance and immediacy of the prime
series washed out these other hidden or minor sequences. In
this way, there is little difficulty in distinguishing the biologically accepted series from those others that are biologically
latent.

We accept verbal but not telepathic communica-
tion, for example, even though telepathy is biologically built
into the body mechanism. We simply ignore those neurological stimulations and make no effort to stablize or maintain
such data. Often, however, we do use such information subconsciously, but it does not become a part of our established
sense picture. That sequence, once activated, would automatically trigger other series with which it is connected, all
dealing with what we would call unofficial information.

Usually these unofficial perceptions aren't hooked
up to our sense organs; that is, we ignore the data and the
cues: we don't plug in, so that the information doesn't become solid sense data. When it does, for one reason or
another, our lack of experience often causes us to run the
two sequences together and bring in the unofficial information on the official line: The hidden values rise momentarily
into prominence where they conflict for our attention with
prime sense data. Actually there is a clear distinction between the two. Beside this, there are many alternate series,
though many of these would make no sense in our accepted
sequences. Events, for example, might be too large in space
and time, or too small, for our comprehension.

In my experience of yesterday I switched to
another close neurological series or sequence, where telepathy is prime data and directed thoughts are heard mentally.
Through lack of experience I switched and mixed the neuro-

logical series, turning the information over to the physical senses—the ears—which then hallucinated the sound. Then I responded physically.

Sounds have to be physically heard to be considered real in our accepted framework of reality, so I switched the information from its native sequence to the official one. The episode was important, though, because I did pick up Rob's inner word and intent so clearly. His intent, to get me up, was implied in the word "Hon," so that I not only picked up the word but the intention. That particular sequence also includes precognitive information, and a host of related unofficial events that are connected with our accepted sequence.

My own inner hearing is acute. This simply means that I've activated this other sequence and then directed it through a ghost version of sound. Usually this is interpreted by me as inner sound. Yesterday my reception was so clear that in my confusion I exteriorized the data and mixed the series. It was Rob's love for me, as he awakened, that I first reacted to. This unofficial series would build up an entirely different view of reality and events. It would include some of our accepted events and exclude others, just as our series is a specialized version built up through discriminations.

In the unofficial series that I was involved with, telepathic communication is prime event and verbal communication is the ghost version: the so-called astral form is the perceived event and the physical body is the ghost version. Obviously we can become aware of the unofficial series to some extent, since it is so related to our own. In the same way, there are hidden structures in our cells, invisible in our series. They will only appear in sequences that recognize them, while some structures visible to us will be invisible in still other sequences.

So-called expansion of consciousness involves awareness of these other sequences that escape our time-space boundaries and the insertion of these into our regular series. When this is done, however, the time-space relationships within our experience will change (in the same way that added numbers alter any sequence). This addition opens up

our reality, even though it is still possible for others to follow
the old accepted series in which such experience will not
show.

I typed this material down as quickly as I could.
Then Rob and I went for a ride. When we returned, I knew at
once there that more material was ready for me. I got my
coffee and cigarettes, put another piece of paper in the typewriter, and began again:

These official and unofficial, recognized and unrecognized sequences and series are the basis for all systems
of reality, each system being cued into its own sequences,
even while ultimately each one is related to every other. The
thickness of our reality is actually composed of many unofficial realities, ghost sequences from our standpoint. A
different system of reality entirely results according to which
sequences are focused upon. That is, our prime sequence is
an unoffical part of other systems. Each of the sequences,
while being a part of others, is also (somewhere) a prime
series.

Our own physical reality of objects and time appears unofficially in other sequences, as a hidden value.

These series maintain their own integrity but they
are not closed: time-space relationships are scaled, each
system using its own sequences. If you imagine the official
numbers 1 to 10 in a row, then there would be an infinite
number of unofficial 1's hidden in the 1 you saw, and an
infinite number of spaces between the official 1 and 2. The
position of the 1 on the paper would represent our sense
data world, while the invisible 1's behind the official 1
would represent the official 1's hidden values and infinite
probabilities.

Two (2) on the paper would represent the system
adjacent to us in space-time, and behind (or within it) would
be its infinite hidden values. More than this, of course, there
would be a 1 on top of the 1 we see on the paper; that is,
above the paper; but we can't see it. We would be between
the 1 on the paper and the 1 above it, and to that 1 (above

the paper) we are a hidden value and a probable system, a variation of its own. Moving sideways from 1 to 2, again, there would be infinite spaces on a three-dimensional level separating us from 2 on the horizontal plane, representing whatever adjacent motion our universe might take in space and time as we understand it.

Within any given system, there are all kinds of choices available. Out of an infinite number of source sequences, we choose the key ones that compose our experience, bringing these into prime position. These sequences act like dimensional pointers, directing the manifestation of energy and the dimensional attitudes that it will express. The stance of space and time will change according to the sequential patterns and—important point—there are infinite chances for new tie-ins of sequences, forming new realities at both infinite and infinitesimal points.

These sequences or series form "orders." Orders are fields formed by the intersection points within sequences that, merging, give a particular dimensional picture within which certain kinds of experience are possible. The word "orders" is used here synonymously with systems, implying a quality of seeming permanence resting on infinite variables.

Sumari as I use it is a code unscrambler, breaking up data like a laser beam, showing the fragments that make up our whole, releasing the psychological components.

Aware-ized energy or consciousness is the source, and organizing element of these systems. I'm learning to experience different sequences at a primitive level, almost in leapfrog fashion.

It's significant that we apply numbers to time, but as there are unrecognized spaces between numbers, there are unrecognized spaces (psychologically invisible) between or within moments, and some of the events of our bodies are "too small" for us to follow, focused as we are in our prime series. These body events actually are "infinitesimal but infinite," following their own patterns that merge with ours. Cellular comprehension reaches into what we think of as the distant past and distant future: These form an ever-present now at that level, however, representing interactions occuring in cellular stances too small for us to follow.

There, cells are built up on one level just as universes are at another; and that sequence also has its black holes, white dwarfs, and so forth, only we perceive them from our sequence as biological structures of minute incorporation. In a manner of speaking, our kind of consciousness twinkles from that sequence, or rather rides it, aware only of certain "peaks" within it which we recognize as events because they are large enough to fit into our scale series.

I read the material over: In my supermarket experience had I mixed sequences, then? Did that seemingly superreal world exist as fact when we activated certain neurological responses? Apparently I'd done the same thing in a different way when I heard what I thought was Rob's physical voice. I still wasn't sure what happened when I smelled the smoke as the comedian on the television show burned his trousers; yet I could almost feel the connection.

Still, to help people in a practical way, you'd need some kind of permanent touch with the world that was larger than our own—not just a few glimpses. That thought reminded me of the calls and letters. But overnight, it seemed, the tenor of these changed, at least for a while. There were simple appreciative letters and calls; people telephoned to tell me how the Seth Material was changing their lives for the better. I cheered up.

Chapter 20

We Move,
in More Ways than One,
and "Special Places"

Surely we usually just skip over the surface of our own experiences and seldom see the dazzling undersides of ordinary events. All of us move from one house or apartment to another, from one neighborhood or state or country to another, so caught up in the surface issues that we never notice the even greater momentum and mobility beneath. Yet now I'm sure that ahead of time we attract the new neighborhood or location, and repel others, and that we move in our psyches long before we pack one load of books or clothes.

We only moved from one neighborhood to another, yet we traveled through endless probabilities, it seems, and we could feel the odd stretchings and snappings of inner boundaries every time we stood looking up at a strange

247

porch that could, if we wanted it, be ours. We could feel, but hardly verbalize, the symbolizing that went on constantly as we interpreted the physical locations in terms of our inner leanings; reacting to psychic magnetisms so that we liked or disliked a house at once.

Seth was still dictating *"Unknown" Reality,* and he delivered some excellent material connecting moving with probabilities, explaining how we choose one probability over another, and showing the rich psychic intertwinings that connect one probability with another. That material is in *"Unknown" Reality,* along with Rob's notes concerning our experiences as we house hunted. Seth was using our private experiences more than ever to show how even the most mundane situations are connected with our beliefs about reality in general; and how the simplest move sets the forces of the psyche into motion and stirs others to respond. We never asked Seth to direct us to a house, although he did give some fascinating background material on several places, and offered us some general advice.

In any case, we found one house that we liked particularly. It was a bungalow, about fifty years old, with a deep private yard replete with a decayed garden, and a broken statue that had once stood by a fountain in the empty cement pond.

We decided to bid on the house. The bid was turned down. The next day we were out again, driving around, checking more ads, when Rob suddenly turned up a hill and drove to an empty house we'd looked at before. Then, we hadn't even asked to go in. We'd just driven past, unimpressed. "How come you drove up here?" I asked, as we approached the place. And then—presto—I literally gasped. How had we ever discounted this lovely house, on its own little hill, overlooking the town? I could sense Rob's surprise, too. "Is this the same place we saw before?" I asked, knowing it was before he nodded, "Yes."

We were quite suddenly enchanted. The place seemed to be like a storybook house. It was almost impossible to believe that earlier we'd passed it by. We drove around the back. We parked; looked in the windows;

imagined what it would look like in the summer. Then we went home and called the real estate people.

As we returned home, the words "special space" came to me, and connections sprang into awareness so quickly that I had trouble writing them down. The material began as library material, but the shifts of consciousness were difficult to follow. I seemed to get material from the library which was then put into personal terms for me by another level of my own psyche, and sometimes the two levels merged. I was quite excited as I wrote, though, because the material was tying together so many of our current experiences. This is what I wrote:

From the Library
The library itself is a "special space" (in this case, private) in which the energy of a directed consciousness alters space's availability in a certain fashion. As there are an infinite number of moments within any given official one, so within any given point of space there are an infinite number of unofficial space relationships, or places.

These remain latent, invisible, nonexistent in practical terms as a rule. Yet they are amiable to impression (being impressed or stamped) once their availability is understood. Because they are not apparent at the living area of usual experience, the normal time-space relationships do not apply. That is, time is experienced differently in a special place, though it will resume normally at the usual level.

When I'm in the library, my body is in a different relationship with the physical environment, minutely altered, minutely out-of-gear at infinitesimal levels, with some atomic effects that are beneath our notice. That is, the changes will not show at our levels, although they are definite and quite consequential at other levels.

This different relationship is brought about because the directed consciousness is in another environment at unofficial levels, while it still retains its physical stance. In our terms, my body is still in this room while I write now, while it is still affected by an energy exchange happening between the self in the library and the self here. This is a split such as an amoeba might make, only it is consciousness—one part staying with the "parent" and the offspring stepping into a different but related special space. In such special places, the usual spatial characteristics are present but much more plastic; and time and space are used differently; consciousness playing in them in a way not normally possible.

There, the assumed body can play unhampered by usual restraints because it is projected into the special space by the consciousness, and is composed of the same characteristics. That is, consciousness stamps its own impression into that medium. (This happens in the same way that fractions fly out of a prime number, while the number remains the same and itself; the fractions within the prime number are not stationary but always going off in their own infinite directions without injuring the primacy of the integer.)

In our terms, and from our viewpoint, such special places are not stable or permanent, though they are at their own levels. I sense the library even when it seems inaccessible to me. Its reality is partly determined by my perception of it. It has other rooms, for example. On the one hand, they are there for me to find; but on the other hand, they will be partly formed by my finding of them.

Here, that seems like a contradiction. But it's as if consciousness somehow senses leniencies in space; perceptive paths that are latent; and if you gently press your consciousness into the universe, then it gives in places and opens up. After a while you get the knack of it, and know where the special places are. You learn to nudge aside the usual dimensional barriers and sneak through with the part of your consciousness that fits the conditions best—or can best work in the conditions. I use my consciousness the way a safecracker uses his fingers; and a different kind of intense listening is involved until you get the right combination and hear invisible tumblers fall.

That safecracking analogy is good here, with its numerical connotations, because these orders or systems of reality are interconnected by virtue of their relationships. New orders or special places can be set up by settling upon any hypothetical boundaries; this automatically alters the inner relationships. It's as if you used your consciousness like the stakes of a tent, providing stability—energy digging into a particular space-time medium, or inserting itself into a different space-time as stakes are driven into the ground—and then forming a new relationship in which certain kinds of experiences are possible.

For that matter, each person stamps space with his or her private symbols. This book deals with the motion of the psyche as it translates inner data and symbols into experienced reality; with the source of such symbols and their forceful activity. Symbols are not stationary ideas that are pushed about, but concentrations of energy endowed with motion. The characteristics of symbols include force, intent, identification, motion (transference), and change of form. While symbols are primarily private, at any given time private images and associations will form groupings, ever-changing, around which communities or civilizations will gravitate.

The symbols are images or representations of beliefs, charged with energy, intensely emotional. Individuals are constantly in the process of bringing these inner symbols in line with physical reality; or rather, they are in the process of turning that reality into a counterpart of the inner symbolized world. When the experienced conditions no longer reflect the inner symbolized environment, the individual sets out to achieve a new balance. This happens privately, and in terms of any group or organization.

The symbols attract models and also help form them at our level of activity. The models are self-sustaining symbols, grouped together in a certain psychic framework—stabilized symbols, in which motion is contained or held: In that way a recognizable psychic structure is formed as a constant model against which to judge the correlation between inner symbolizing and external experience. These models, then, are stabilized organizations of symbols held a while in the psyche. They change, however, as the symbols that compose them do, according to our intent, so that one model can change smoothly into another one.

When I read the material, I began to understand

the connections between my feelings toward the hill house (as we called it), special places, and symbols. We may pick up an important symbol, form it into a model, then dismiss it at a certain time in our lives, only to pick it up later where it serves as the basis for a new model. That is, we may be unable to "complete" a symbol, either because we haven't connected it with a model strong enough to contain it or simply because we haven't encountered the elements required.

It's as if we are looking for a symbol's missing ingredient, and until we find it, we can't complete the model to which it belongs. When we do, everything clicks together like the pieces of a jigsaw; the old forgotten symbol is instantly revitalized, forms its model, is activated and moves us—or we let it move through our lives. Such symbols form strong motivating elements and can mobilize abilities that lay latent.

These usually bring with them new psychic and physical organizations, different patterns of thought and activity, changes in life experience, and a recharging of psychic and creative batteries. These symbols are like living motion pictures within the psyche, and I saw how Rob and I used two separate symbol pictures that tuned us in to the hill house and brought it into focus.

The process must have begun when we started house hunting. We knew that something was going on. We were half aware of the associations that came to mind. We realized that we were throwing out reflections of inner symbols upon the various neighborhoods, and then comparing the exterior conditions with some inner prerequisites. We were attracted to the older bungalow, but when the bid was turned down I wasn't at all surprised. I would have settled for the house, I suppose, but something was missing. When we drove past the hill house that day, however, something clicked, and that something was the formation of a workable model in space and time. Inner forgotten symbols going back to childhood were suddenly activated—and projected outward. They shimmered; hovered, and made a psychic fit.

While we looked for houses, forgotten images and symbols were looking for a place to land; an environment to which they could attach themselves. Rob hadn't said a thing, but I realized that the grounds around the hill house reminded him of a nearby state park where he'd spent many happy summers. The fireplace in the yard added to the picture, and evoked memories of all the paintings he'd done outside years ago, with his small easel set among the trees in the park. I accepted his symbolism, so that the swimming pool in the next yard next door reminded me of the park too. I visualized a picnic table by the outdoor fireplace, completing the picture, because I'd written my first published novel at such a table at the same park.

For me privately the place evoked other images too, reminding me of a particular neighborhood described in a favorite book from high school years. For example, when we went inside the house with the real estate woman a few days later, I kept seeing our stereo in a certain position in the living room. Only when I wrote these passages did I realize that the book's hero kept his stereo in the same position—in a description read years before.

So we made our own special place in more ordinary terms, by symbolizing that particular house and corner, marking it ours, stamping it with the imprint of living symbols which we transposed upon it. Henceforth it had a magic quality. On February 15, we bought the place, though we couldn't move in for a month. We weren't inside over half an hour. It was probably the easiest sale the real estate woman ever made.

In the next weeks we drove up to the hill house many times, and I kept trying to understand more about the inner politics that led us to make this particular choice. Then one afternoon on returning to the two apartments on Water Street, I realized they were rapidly losing whatever magic they'd possessed; they no longer seemed to be "ours": We were draining out of them in some odd fashion. Boxes of books and papers were piled everywhere. And I suddenly understood that the new symbols we'd activated couldn't have been, earlier. We hadn't wanted the responsibility and expense of a house before, and so we'd tuned out any symbols that might form that kind of model.

As I realized *that*, further connections came to mind. I wrote them down at once, pushing aside the half-packed boxes of dishes that were stacked on the desk.

"We've already endowed the hill house and grounds with symbols from the past. In our case, these are symbols that we'd once discarded. We've set them moving again, given them a center in the house and environment—and also activated parts of the psyche that were and now are connected with them. The house looks different to us now, and we've only been inside twice, and walked around the grounds a few times. When we first saw it, it looked anonymous, although the landscape caught our eye. Perhaps then, that initial glimpse activated the inner symbols so quietly that we didn't notice, because we looked at other houses afterward; we'd nearly forgotten the place until Rob suddenly drove up there that Thursday afternoon.

"Then, we just stared. A change had come over the place. It had an almost magical air—the house nestled safely in front of the small woods, yet looking down from its hill to the valley and town, with the mountains rising beyond. The whole place could have freshly emerged from nowhere, I thought, and even the air seemed new. How could that be the same house we'd driven by and ignored just a few weeks earlier? I kept wondering and wondering.

"But during that time the symbolizing had been going on beneath our notice. The psyche's great fantasies played upon the landscape of land and mind alike, and when we drove by that Thursday the process was completed. That clicking 'yes' we felt was the clicking of inner symbol and exterior form, that transference of dream upon matter; the same thing, perhaps, that happens when we fall in love.

"But wasn't this a house in the suburbs, something we said we didn't want? Click, click, click—how could a house on a magic hill be a house in the suburbs—a house with a new sky above it? Aren't all of those other houses like super-tents squatting on the hill, chimneys in the wintertime shooting up smoke signals—the neighborhood pool a native way of evoking memories of the distant ocean? Click, click, click. I can even imagine my dead Indian grandfather, his thin bones packed in a baggy suit out of the 1940s, stalking happily out there in some odd dimension of mind and woods.

"Yet at the same time I can see my dead mother-in-law and imagine her visiting the place, too, a far more substantial ghost wearing bright red platform shoes, some sort of frilly dress, and a haughty air; peering through the trees to see double garages, and well-kept homes. I can almost hear her thinking with a solid air of satisfaction that her son finally wasn't poor; that even if he was an artist, he must have picked up some sense. I can almost hear her saying to other ghosts: 'My son, the eldest, lives in a lovely house, now, so I can rest in peace.' And I'll say amen to that.

"Yet against this rise older ideas of ours also that crop up now and then. For the hill house has its own water supply and a bomb shelter in the basement, and this reminds me of old beliefs we had years ago about surviving in an alien world. To some extent those ideas must still go with us, a stamp of probabilities that still echo, unresolved, amid our new philosophies. For behind the house the small wood could provide fuel for the inside fireplace, transformed into a main cooking area come any disaster. The well water could come in handy, too, if we ever had to hole up together, as we did in a different way during the 1972 flood.

"I'd thought we'd finished with such ideas. And yet isn't the body of Seth Material itself a handbook of psychic survival to be handed down to others: 'Look, this is what we've learned. Do what you want with it. And beyond that, even if we don't survive, we survive.' So the new house is safe and ours, no matter who it belonged to before, or who it will belong to in some future in which we no longer play a part."

So we pick and choose from probabilities, using our own symbols as measuring sticks; testing this or that environment or situation until one fits the inner model—which we then very nicely slip over the exterior conditions. It's as if we each have a multidimensional coloring book, presenting infinite sketches of any probable event. Because of our individual intents and characteristics we'll be drawn to some of these probabilities, while others will remain sketchy and unreal. We choose which pictures we want to complete in physical terms, and color them in with experience. In so doing, though, we alter the discarded events beneath, which are still active and moving. The sketches, of course, are themselves alive.

We impress our own dimensions with special places too, then, which just means that through our choices and intents we imprint certain specifics upon the dimensions we recognize; cue ourselves to respond to those while shutting out equally legitimate probable special places. In other words, we form physical reality in the same way that I form my library; by impressing upon a willing dimension the imprint of our conscious needs, beliefs, abilities, and intents.

It was no coincidence, either, that just after beginning this book on psychic politics, we moved for the first time in over ten years; we began dealing with real estate people, lawyers, and others, so that the small move reached out into the community. When I first received material from the library, I was told that both inner and outer experience would be involved; that I couldn't just stay in the library. As time went on, I was finding out what that meant.

As in the coloring book analogy, however, not only are there infinite sketches that can be colored in, but an infinite number of probable selves looking at their own coloring books. In our case, one "me" took the bungalow, bidding higher; one moved a few miles away to Sayre, Pennsylvania (where Rob grew up), as once we'd considered doing; and the me that I recognize, the "official" one, chose the hill house in which I'm now typing this manuscript.

When we did move, we were startled by the number of coincidences that were connected with the event. Coincidences? Rob began to keep notes of them. There are more than fifty at last count. We began, rightly, to suspect that such coincidences are instead the tiny multitudinous "knots" that bind one probability to another, and Seth's own book began to explain how we all move so smoothly though probabilities that we never question the coincidences that meet us on every side.

So somewhere in the winter of 1975 we changed alliances. We moved our consciousnesses along a different track. We know that we're different people than we were before. Other portions of our consciousnesses chose other routes. I'm still curious about that moment of decision, though. What elements besides the ones we know led Rob to turn up to the hill house that day? And what are the implications of such inner activity on all of the decisions of our lives? I'm not speaking of dry theory without practical application, but of rich psychological activity that goes on in our minds all the while; in ours and yours.

In any case, students helped us move, and I never went back to the apartments again. They were remodeled afterward, so they'll never look the way they did when we lived there. Yet as we took over the hill house I wondered: Would the library be there? Would I feel comfortable having the Seth sessions? Where in the house would we hold them? And more: Would I ever get *inside* the library again? All of my published books had been written in that apartment house on Water Street. The Seth sessions had begun there. Magic hill house or no—I felt transplanted.

Part Three

TOWARD
A NEW POLITICS
OF THE PSYCHE, AND
AN ALTERNATE
MODEL FOR
CIVILIZATION TO
FOLLOW

Chapter 21

The Codicils, and an Alternate Model for Civilization to Follow

We moved into our house in the middle of March 1975. It was nothing to move our household supplies, but we had cartons and cartons of Seth Material and manuscripts, not to mention all of Rob's paintings and our books. Willy, our cat, had spent all his life at Water Street, yet he took to the new place at once. It took me longer than Willy to get settled. Rob and I settled our workrooms first. After Rob put all my books in one room, I decided that I wanted to work by the large window in the living room instead, because I vaguely sensed that the library would be transposed on the east living room wall.

We left the books where they were. I ended up with my old table and typewriter stand in front of the big windows. Rob went to his new studio. Willy prowled through

261

all the rooms, meowing as he inspected. And I wrote the following:

"Now that we're here, this house and everything in it seems inevitable, as if this is one spot in space and time that we were meant to fill; one of many equally right for us, that we could have chosen. And now by hindsight it seems that we were gently led, coming upon a series of kind surprises that suddenly appeared like soft rolling hills around a curve when you only expected level land.

"So writing in front of my new picture window, it seems somehow that I've always seen those mountains from this particular privileged viewpoint; that a ghostly me waited here, that now I'm stepping into my own future shoes, giving that image flesh.

"Our winding walk curves down its own small hill to a street that is more like a secluded country lane than anything else; lined with maples and birches; our corner marked by a few clustering mailboxes. Again, each detail seems right and inevitable, as if the house and grounds existed in my library, perhaps, as a living picture book and here it's come alive.

"I feel as if I've caught up with a part of myself, as if I projected a pattern of myself here once in the past and that now I'm filling it out or stepping into it. So in our time I have to go along day by day, learning what that Jane who got here ahead of me is up to. Yet I don't mean to imply predestination when I use the word 'inevitability.' I mean a high aptness, because the Jane who's been waiting here was, projected outward by me; sent out by my hopes and dreams, searching for a place where Rob and I could live and write and paint in a house of our own 'when the time came!'

"I, she, we, did a good job, and already I sense changes as a present, past, and future me merge, do our stuff, set up a new kind of alchemy, reacting to the conditions that we set up. Some changes in my attitude are just amusing. Today it's raining as I write, for example, but instead of feeling dreary about it as I used to at Water Street I found myself looking out the window, thinking: 'Hey, the rain is great, freshening *my* trees, bringing my grass to life—and no one is going to turn *this* lawn into a parking lot because these trees have my protection.' And I knew as I looked out that the trees protected me, too, in their fashion; that our spirits and the spirits of the birches and pines met at some level and loved this small corner of the universe.

"Reality is different with each shift of space and time, and each family creates its own house, room, corner, hut; materialized splendor or squalor, in accordance with inner beliefs and intents. The artist who believes that art and riches will never mix will paint in his chosen garret; the 'lord of the manor' who believes that the world of spirit and the world of cash can't mix will choose his great estate and live in a squalor of mind, having chosen according to his beliefs. For each personal reality is unique and presents a special picture of the universe."

Well and good. But I sat at my table and waited— for the library to show, or some inspiration. In the meantime I began typing part of this manuscript, from the beginning. And as I copied the material about my first experiences with the library and my super-real view of the world, I looked back nostalgically. Suppose, just suppose, I never got anything from the library again? Suppose it just didn't click into place here? I arranged and rearranged my work area. I wrote a few poems, and brooded.

And what about Seth? We put Rob's portrait of him on the wall next to the fireplace where he smiled down, looking portly and amused. But before my worry about sessions could really settle in, Seth resumed his book, right where he'd left off. We held the sessions in the living room. At first it actually seemed odd not to hear people walking overhead, or the water rushing through the plumbing from above, or the traffic screaming from the corner below.

Seth kept telling me that new material was being prepared for me in the library, and I kept thinking, "Yeah, Seth, that's great, only where is it?" So April passed. Then the first part of May so much creative material came that literally I could hardly keep up. Even then I didn't realize what I was getting, or what the information really meant; that understanding came somewhat later. For one thing, I was so busy just writing the material down and observing my own different states of consciousness that I put off usual conscious examination. Mostly, though, I was just so delighted to be going full steam ahead again, that I didn't even second-guess the material I was getting, as I used to.

But finally one morning as I sat at my table, I saw the library transposed against the living room wall. My double sat there, reading a book. At the same time, the word "codicil" kept coming into my mind again. I heard it mentally, at first faintly and then it sounded louder and louder until I wrote the word down and waited. Then I knew that the material to come represented an alternate model for civilization to follow, and that I was transcribing my book from one depicting such a model—a model that we hadn't chosen in the past. The codicils would represent a fresh hypothesis upon which to build a new, better civilization.

I didn't realize it then, but large sections of the third section of *Psychic Politics* would be written in various altered states of consciousness. It was as if all of my earlier experiences with people and events went into some "input" slot and now the library was presenting me with answers for all the questions that had tumbled through my mind.

From the Library

Codicils

(Alternate hypotheses as a base
for private and public experience.)

1.   All of creation is sacred and alive, each part connected to each other part, and each communicating in a creative cooperative commerce in which the smallest and the largest are equally involved.

2.   The physical senses present one unique version of reality, in which being is perceived in a particular dimensionalized sequence, built up through neurological patterning, and is the result of one kind of neurological focus. There are alternate neurological routes, biologically acceptable, and other sequences so far not chosen.

3.   Our individual self-government and our political

organizations are by-products of sequential perception, and our exterior methods of communication set up patterns that correlate with, and duplicate, our synaptic behavior. We lock ourselves into certain structures of reality in this way.

4.   Our sequential prejudiced perception is inherently far more flexible than we recognize, however. There are half steps—other unperceived impulses—that leap the nerve ends, too fast and too slow for our usual focus. Recognition of these can be learned and encouraged, bringing in perceptive data that will trigger changes in usual sense response, filling out potential sense spectrums with which we are normally not familiar.

5.   This greater possible sense spectrum includes increased perception of inner bodily reality in terms of cellular identity and behavior; automatic conscious control of bodily processes; and increased perception of exterior conditions as the usual senses become more vigorous. (Our sight, for example, is not nearly as efficient as it could be. Nuances of color, texture, and depth could be expanded and our entire visual area attain a brilliance presently considered exceptional or supernormal.)

COMMENTS ON CODICILS

Acceptance of these first codicils would expand practical knowledge of the self, break down barriers that are the result of our prejudiced perception, and restructure personal, social, and political life.

Concepts of the self and practical experience of the self must be broadened if the race is to develop its true potentials. Only an evolution of consciousness can alter the world view that appears to our official line of consciousness.

COMMENT ON CODICIL 2

This next step is as important as the birth of Christianity was in the history of mankind. It will present a new structure for civilization to follow. Christianity represented the human psyche at a certain point, forming first inner patterns for development that then became exteriorized as myth, drama, and history, with the Jewish culture of the Talmud presenting the psyche's direction. The differences between Jewish and Christian tradition represented allied but different probabilities, one splitting off from the other, but united by common roots and actualized in the world to varying degrees.

The traditional personified god concept represented the mass psyche's one-ego development; the ego ruling the self as God ruled man; man dominant over the planet and other species, as God was dominant over man—as opposed to the idea of many gods or the growth of a more multi-focused self with greater nature identification.

Neurological patterning of the kind we know began with the early testament Jews (known, then, as God's people), looking forward through time to a completely one-ego focused self. Before, neurological functioning was not as set; and in our world today some minority peoples and tribes still hold to those alternate neurological pulses. These will not appear to our measuring devices because we are literally blind to them.

The Jewish prophets, however, utilized these alternate focuses of perception themselves, and were relatively unprejudiced neurologically. They were therefore able to perceive alternate visions of reality. Yet their great work, while focusing the energy of an entire race, and leading to Christianity, also resulted in limiting man's potential perceptive area in important ways.

The prophets were able to sense the potentials of the mass psyche, and their prophecies charted courses in time, projecting the Jewish race into the future. The prophecies gave the people great strength precisely because they gave the race a future in time, providing a thread of continuity and a certain immortality in earthly terms.

The prophecies were psychic molds to be filled out in flesh. Some were fulfilled and some were not, but the unfulfilled ones were forgotten and served their purpose by providing alternate selections and directions. The prophecies ahead of time charted out a people's probable course, foreseeing the triumphs and disasters inherent in such an adventure through time.

They provided psychic webworks, blueprints, and dramas, with living people stepping into the roles already outlined, but also improvising as they went along. These roles were valid, however, chosen in response to an inner reality that foresaw the shape that the living psyche of the people would take in time.

But as a snake throws off old skin, the psyche throws off old patterns that have become rigid, and we need a new set of psychic blueprints to further extend the species into the future, replete with great deeds, heroes, and challenges; a new creative drama projected from the psyche into the three-dimensional arena. For now we no longer view reality through original eyes, but through structures of beliefs that we have outgrown. These structures are simply meant to frame and organize experience, but we mistake the picture for the reality that it represents. We've become neurologically frozen in that respect, forced to recognize the one sequential pattern of sense perceptions, so that we think that the one we've chosen is the only one possible.

COMMENT ON CODICIL 3

Thus far we've projected the unrecognized portions of our greater selfhood outward into God, religion, government, and exteriorized concepts. In this existence, selfhood is dependent upon sense perceptions, so that our neurological prejudice and rigid focus have limited our concepts of identity. When we do become aware of unofficial information, coming through other than recognized channels, then it seems to come from notself, or outside.

A great deal of energy has been used to repress levels of selfhood and to project these into religious and nationalistic heroes and cultural organizations. Government and religion try to preserve the status quo, to preserve their own existence, not for political or religious reasons but to preserve the official picture of the self around which they are formed.

But the structured reality in which that kind of.ə self can exist is breaking down. The official picture no longer fits or explains private experience which is growing out of it. There is a momentary rift between the inner psyche and its creations.

Besides this, the experienced self is not the same through the ages. The experienced self is a psychic creation, responsive to exterior conditions which it creates as the psyche dives into the waters of experienced earthly selfhood. Only a portion of the potential self is experienced, but different portions as intents and purposes change. It is possible, though, to actualize more of our potential.

COMMENT ON CODICILS 4 AND 5

The answers and solutions lie in using levels of consciousness now considered eccentric or secondary. This includes far greater utilization of the dream states and altered conditions thus far thought to be exceptions of consciousness. These "exceptions" represent other kinds of focuses, greatly needed to broaden our concepts of the self, and our experience of personal selfhood by increasing conceptualization, giving direct experience of alternate views, and bringing other kinds of data to bear upon the world we know. In the past, the attitudes surrounding such perceptions brought about their own difficulties. The perceptions are biologically acceptable, however, and will lead to a clearer relationship between mind and body.

THE FOCUS PERSONALITY
AND ALTERNATE SENSING

(As I wrote this originally, I sensed my double in the library. She was reading a book and I felt that this material was my version of that book. It was twilight: the birds were singing, and a delicious relaxation overtook me. The word "codicil" kept returning strongly, so that sometimes I felt it was the sound that the birds made.)

The focus personality or experienced self is one focus through which the self knows itself; one facet of the self's relationship with other persons and the world, and represents its exteriorization. But different approaches could increase the knowledge of the focus personality and extend its scope. By providing this experienced self some conscious affiliation with the source of its own being, it could receive a sense of continuity not bounded by known time and could literally see beyond itself to the source in which it is inviolately couched.

Identifying now with current life experience only, the focus personality is limited by its chosen perceptive framework, and such additional data is unavailable in usual terms. Life after death, the existence of other valid realities, and the self's part in these, must be taken on faith—if they're taken at all—and a faith cluttered by old beliefs. This makes it extremely difficult for the focus personality to perceive any unofficial information that could contradict the current picture of reality.

The focus personality is everywhere presented with the evidence of the senses which seems to deny any such altered conditions. The senses themselves are kept restricted so that they seem to present the only possible picture of reality upon which assumptions can be made. Their view *is* valid, but other perceptive methods and modes can add to that picture, extending it to show other quite-as-valid kinds of existence. And we have a choice. We can open the doors of perception, move out into a broader mental and psychic world, as, in historic terms, at least, we left the caves to explore the physical environment. We have yet to explore the geography of the psyche.

Various altered states can provide the focus personality with the direct evidence it needs by giving it the benefit of extraordinary or eccentric sense data—data complete in itself that does not, however, fit into the established picture, and may sometimes seem to contradict it. There is no such contradiction between the official and unofficial pictures of reality, however, when each is seen as a valid alternate or parallel version. As a result of accepting such material, ordinary sense data will be deepened, its qualities enhanced, sense experience becoming super-real by our current standards as the fuller spectrums begin to emerge.

This emergence instantly triggers different body responses and corporal surprise. The change is not just metaphysical but appears in quite practical garb: the world looks different because it is different; more of its qualities are perceived and the perceiver brings more to bear upon the given objective field. (My super-real vision of the world described earlier in this book is an example.)

Such experiences, again, hint of the true potentials of human perception, but greater portions of the self must be brought into play and made available to the focus personality. Often such experience frightens the focus personality because it is hampered by old beliefs about selfhood, and feels in conflict with established culture. It is the focus personality itself that must break out of the ancient patterns, and alter its concepts of selfhood. This experienced self is not to be annihilated but fulfilled; not to dissolve into oneness but to discover its true individuality in relationship to a oneness that is always individualized.

Here the analogy of the model and its eccentricities can be of great value. The constant tension and interplay between them can hint of the mystery of individuality existing as a part of oneness; the many-in-one in which the One constantly translates itself into individuation but without destroying the original unity.

That unity seeks greater diversification, investing each part of itself with its own creativity and thrust, hence changing itself, re-creating itself constantly in a creation that is never static and always new, for the infinite eccentricities of itself are always added to its own model, multiplying probabilities of development that create further eccentricities.

THE ASPECTS AND ALTERED STATES

The Aspects are the representatives in the psyche of these alternate routes of consciousness to self-expression and experience. The Aspects, then, experience reality differently and have their own kind of subjective being. They are aware in a different context; in another kind of medium—yet their reality forms a rich unconscious bed upon which our own version of consciousness rests.

Here, the Aspects are the latent eccentric variations of our models of personhood. In their reality the reverse is true. There our kind of psychological processes serve as supportive frameworks; that is, our consciousness may serve as a part of their unconscious activity.

In dreams, visions, and altered states we lean toward their kind of organization and symbolism, which is valid in that inner order of events but not usually perceivable here. In the ordinary state of awareness we force those perceptions to flow into our symbolized structures, in which sometimes they seem to make no sense at all.

Culturally, in our society, we've neatly divided the intellectual and intuitive abilities. To that degree, we've isolated portions of ourselves and limited the practical benefits that could otherwise be provided by the intuitive parts of the self.

We've divorced ourselves from levels of awareness that have to do with the health of our own bodies, for example, turning such problems over to specialists and further separating ourselves from our own corporal competence, denying any responsibility for the state of our health. There *is* a healer within us, the same force that keeps us alive and functioning. It might be natural for us to personify that part of our consciousness, since it's difficult for us to imagine consciousness without our ideas of personhood. There is nothing unsophisticated in having an outside image, statue, or symbol to represent the self's healing Aspects, and to serve as an exterior reference point. But religions project the inner power into the images, further divorcing it from its source. In *that* kind of structure it *is* easier to go to a doctor than to attempt any self-healing.

The Aspects also serve as invisible models for self-hood, however. The healer, teacher, parent, male and female, all residing within the psyche not as rigid models but as living patterns uniquely fashioned in accord with the focus personality's interests and purposes; representing the tension between the self's immortal existence and its temporal life.

The Aspects also operate as psychic counterparts, banks of abilities and strengths from which the focus personality can choose, and in a way they represent an inner family of potential selves upon which our own personhood is firmly based.

They appear in our experience as emotional feelings, psychological tendencies, tints through which we view ourselves and the world. But sometimes they rise out of psychological invisibility with their own characteristic strands of consciousness, carrying with them views of reality uniquely theirs.

In such cases, we can view existence from a different center of the psyche. In so doing, we need not become less well focused in this world, but we can instead bring the world into a newer, fuller focus: we can become better centered, for we then have more information about the greater context in which our world rests. This can happen, however, only if we learn how to take advantage of these messages from other Aspects; only if we learn to interpret their dramatic content.

We are a multitude of selves, and the sooner we learn that, the better. And in that rich alliance of psychological Aspects lies the very secret of our practical operative stability. Only because we change our positions constantly in reference to the psyche and the world are we able to manipulate physically and translate inner experience into sense terms.

NATURE AND CONSCIOUSNESS

To attempt to protect the self in old terms or to keep the self rigidly "itself" is like holding your breath for too

long. Selves, like breaths, go through us all the time. But from
our standpoint we are the larger psychological structures that
translate these selves into ourselves; just as the body translates our breaths into our living.

Even our bodies often seem not us or not ours because we have forgotten how to identify with them, lost the
knack of following the strands of consciousness that should
connect us, so that our full experience of creaturehood itself
is further limited. We seem instead to be victims of the flesh,
at the mercy of illnesses, wars, and natural disasters, because
we have lost track of our natural selves and lost sight of our
place within nature's framework.

It seems idiotic, for example, to think that we can
cure ourselves naturally of illnesses when we believe that
disease is thrust upon us by the flesh, and has nothing at all
to do with our desires or beliefs. Until we realize that our
consciousness, working through the body, creates its state
of being, then any natural cures will be considered miraculous. Seth, for example, states that so-called miraculous cures
are simply examples of unimpeded nature.

In the same way we are part of nature; physically
as real as mountains, air currents, trees, or oceans, all of
which have their effect upon the climate and world conditions. Yet for some reason we imagine that we affect the
natural world only through our technology. But our physical
presence itself has an interaction with the earth and with the
physical elements that compose it. We are biologically connected, and this means that the chemical makeup of our
bodies is a part of the earth's contents.

Our chemical balance changes as our emotions do,
and we alter the composition of the earth. We are not at the
mercy of natural disasters. We have forgotten or ignored our
native emotional identification with the wind and with
storms, and therefore lost our part in their existence, and
whatever conscious control we may once have had over them.
Therefore we need technology—to bring rain to parched
areas, for example—and consider it the sheerest nonsense to
blame parched emotions instead.

We've lost the larger dimensions of a natural self-

hood that identifies as itself and with its position in nature.
We can if we wish command the wind, but only when we
realize that it is a part of us and we are a part of it. We can
move mountains without cranes—only when we realize that
our consciousness is itself and a part of earth at the same
time; that our breath contributes to the atmosphere and our
discarded chemicals help form the mountains.

That natural consciousness is not afraid of death. It
knows its individuality is unassailed even while its form and
experiences change. Because it can identify with earth, it is
not dependent upon corporal knowledge because earth itself
is not, and nature has always known better.

ONE-LINE CONSCIOUSNESS, GOVERNMENTS, AND SOCIAL ORDERS

If we also saw our governments and social orders as
natural elements of the psyche (as the continents and seas are
the natural phenomena of the earth), then we would also see
their seasons, their rising and falling, as a part of a cycle as
natural as spring or winter.

In the past all civilizations, Christian or otherwise,
set up a system of gods and goddesses, or mythical jouneys
and mystic cosmologies, that mirrored the structure of the
psyche, projecting its Aspects outward so that an individual
embarking upon such a religious pilgrimage actually traveled
through the inner lands of the psyche. The visit to the church
or holy shrine was an objectification of an inner state. The
objectification served as a physical signpost. These myths and
intuitive constructs worked as long as they effectively mirrored the individual and mass life of the psyche.

Unfortunately the mythical and magical elements
became dogmatized so that they no longer served as guidelines but began to program the individual in his journey, to
such an extent that original vision and spontaneity were
denied. The psyche then seeks for new routes, yearns to
shake off the rigid stylizations in which its experiences are
couched. When this happens, the old gods tumble, along with

the political and social organizations that supported them.

Since we've almost always uplifted certain parts of the self over others, the security of governments and social institutions has been dependent upon the suppression of portions of the psyche which were considered suspect. Education had to support the status quo, with only lip service being given to unofficial areas of experience, and those expressions were channeled into the backwaters of activity or to the realm of the bizarre.

Civilizations and social orders have not been geared to the fulfillment of human potential (even now, for all of our liberal thought), but to the suppression of abilities that did not fit in with the basic assumptions about the nature of the self. We inhibited any such evidence from conscious awareness, developing a kind of one-line official consciousness. Opposing data did not disappear, but formed powerful undercurrents that composed the unofficial knowledge of the race.

So we *did* become afraid. Revelatory information could lead to disruptive behavior, and to that extent challenge the beliefs of family, church and state. The Roman Catholic Church put rigid rules about the visionary, and took great pains to control its mystics. With Protestantism and private interpretations of the bible came the birth of still new religions, each bringing forth its own interpretations of the relationship between the psyche, God, and the state; and becoming nationalistically centered to some degree. Missionary fervor has always involved political goals and survival far more than visionary experience.

The official line of consciousness sees everything in black and white, good and evil; in the same manner it experiences the private self—which is, in a way, its own creation. Alternate visions of reality can't be tolerated, because in that framework one must win over the other; even as the official line of consciousness must dominate other portions of the self. Other political parties, religions, or social orders can't be seen as alternate visions of reality or as organizations dealing with experience in a different way, but as threats. This belief in competition is, in fact, one of the basic similarities that all of our current belief systems have in common.

In this century, we've lived together in an uneasy alliance. Little surprise that when Freud began his investigations, he saw the unofficial portions of the self as unsavory, so that the unconscious seemed to hold only savage, uncontrollable elements. A new Pandora's box. If some of us escaped religion's repressive beliefs, we could take our enlightened selves to a psychoanalyst for a more acceptable scientific reason for our guilt. We never understood that it was our souls that we were hiding. Our guilt was a natural reaction to make us question our concepts about ourselves and the societies that mirrored and extended them.

As I wrote down the above, I suddenly realized that the rest of the book would deal with an alternate model for civilization to follow, based on the codicils I'd just received, and others to follow. So far, we'd taken the hypothesis that the self was inherently bad and followed it to one version of reality. Government, politics, religions, and social orders have been based on that premise. Here, the opposite premise was being offered.

The rest of the material came very rapidly, and I found myself caught up in a vision of the world far different from the one we know.

The codicils, followed, would lead to a government as natural, orderly, and spontaneous as the seasons in which each individual brings personhood to fulfillment to the best of his or her ability, and in so doing automatically plays a potent role in the development of the entire society.

Such a civilization would be based upon the following codicils, added to those already given.

1.   Each person is a unique version of an inner model that is itself a bank of potentials, variations, and creativity. The psyche is a seed of individuality and selfhood, cast in space-time but ultimately independent of it.

2.   We are born in many times and places, but not in a return of identity as we understand it; not as a copy in different clothes, but as a new self ever-rising out of the

psyche's life as the new ruler rises to the podium or throne, in a psychic politics as ancient as humanity.

3. Civilizations both past and present represent projections of inner selfhood, and mirror the state of the mass psyche at any given time. We hold memory and knowledge of past civilizations as we hold unconscious memories of our private early current-life experiences.

4. From our present, we exert force upon the past as well as the future, forming our ideas of the past and reacting accordingly. We actually project events into our own new past.

5. Each generation forms such a new past, one that exists as surely as the present; not just as an imaginary construct but as a practical platform—a newly built past—upon which we build our present.

6. Options and alternate models for selfhood and civilizations exist in a psychic pattern of probabilities from which we can choose to actualize an entirely new life system.

COMMENTS ON CODICILS

As a preliminary, we must alter our concepts of the self, time, space, and the psyche so that we can envision the self or focus personality as the physically actualized version of a multidimensional psyche, equipped with freedom of choice and with greater ability to mix and match our personal characteristics than we've previously thought possible. We can bring more of the psyche's potentials to bear upon ordinary life, opening sense spectrums that will show the true significance and beauty of corporal life. We must understand that the intuitions and intellect are wedded. Only our beliefs make them appear as opposites. The "high intellect" is a perfect fusion of intuitive and intellectual qualities, merged to form what would almost seem to be a new faculty.

Left alone, the Aspects of the psyche will set up an operationally stable creative self; talents and characteristics flowing from the inner pool of being—the source self—into the focus personality as needed in response to the focus personality's beliefs, purposes, and assessments about exterior conditions.

The Aspects will also be automatically projected outward into the creation of a social order (the extended self) in the establishment of institutions, rituals, and groupings, where their distinctive and various tendencies can join with the aspects of others, therefore magnifying the purposes and values of the focus personality.

Left alone, these Aspects will flow, change, and evolve as the focus personality chooses and disregards the characteristics from its own Aspect bank. (Only when this process is frozen and barriers set about it do individuals and organizations become rigid, dogmatized, or violent.)

When we believe that the self is inherently bad and undesirable, then we set up psychic antibodies against ourselves, and impede this natural process of change. The resulting self and its behavior then often does appear "bad": our experience justifies our beliefs and leads to further restraints, thus proving the previous hypothesis.

Our beliefs concerning heredity also drastically program our behavior, which then gives effective evidence for the theory. The theory does become the reality, practically speaking; with the physical mechanisms faithfully mirroring the given information or input.

As I read the above material I wondered why we weren't more aware of the Aspects if they were so basic. Then I realized that we hide our Aspects from ourselves because we've been so used to a restricted selfhood that any extension of it actually seems threatening. For this reason, many people are afraid of their own creativity, or the thrust of the life force itself. Again, I believe that these Aspects are the components of personality, each however experiencing reality in a different fashion. They are conscious and aware at another dimension of actuality, and they experience our world from another viewpoint. In other words, our reality is different to them than it is to us. I also think that they exist independently as selves or identities in a different medium of existence than ours. Our entire psyche could consist of the totality of these Aspects.

Sometimes, as in my case, there is communication between some of these Aspects and the focus personality. Then the focus personality expands its usual abilities to join in this affiliation on a conscious basis. To some extent, it can then glimpse its own reality from a viewpoint not its own by altering its focus and taking on another kind of world hypothesis, at least momentarily. Difficulties can arise, however, if the resulting data is interpreted by the focus personality in terms of its own usual hypothesis.

The Aspects may have hidden biological connections hooked up to our neurological framework. In any case, they serve functionally to provide alternate models for the focus personality, and en masse, provide an infinite bank of potential from which the species can draw.

Chapter 22

Personal Application of Codicils. The Gods Take Off Their Clothes. Psychic Civilizations and Estates

I wrote the material on codicils in bursts of activity over a three-day period. Often I'd see the library book in my mind, suddenly, when I wasn't at my table but involved in housework, or watching television or sitting in the yard. So I kept a notebook with me, and took most of the material down in longhand. I was halfway through typing it when more came—this time it was material that showed me how to apply the codicils in my own life.

When I was getting the original codicil material, I was caught up in visionary excitement, convinced of the codicils' validity and their value in helping us to change negative aspects of civilization. As I typed them up, however, I thought, "Sure, they're valid enough. But what practical good are they *now*?"

The personal material shot in sidewards almost, just after I asked those questions. Part of it has general application so I'm including a few excerpts of it here.

From the Library
Present culture is based on the idea of a hostile universe. This concept invades all fields of thought, and brings about an exaggerated need for self-protection. Trustful, bold, innocent action becomes suspect and it seems dangerous to explore the inner reaches of the self when the whole of society is constructed to hide the self from itself; to put institutions between it and its own experiences. Yet, basically, growth cannot be impeded and consciousness will tend to blossom in its own ways regardless. . . .

The codicils are important in regard to individual action. I suggest you make up a copy of them for yourself and use them as effective new frameworks for action; that is, as a new hypothesis upon which to build your self-civilization. On a private level the codicils set a new, more effective contract between various portions of the self; and with the focus personality as it sees its position in exterior reality and understands its relationship with its own source. . . .

Each person sets up various contracts between aspects of inner and outer experience. These should be flexible, resulting in gradual change rather than, say, psychic revolutions. But some hypotheses are closer to basic reality than others, and the codicils represent the closest practical guides for behavior that are based on underlying validity: that is, they come closest to expressing man's private relationships with the psyche, and with nature. Acting in accordance with these precepts will bring about the greatest opportunities for vitality, understanding, and fulfillment. Used as cultural precepts by an entire society, they would bring about superior experience on all levels.

There was more, of a more personal nature that proved to be of great value, but it wasn't until I'd typed all the material that its implications hit me—for myself and others. Codicils; of course. I remembered getting the word months ago and looking it up in the dictionary to find "appendages added to a will." The dictionary meaning meant additions to a legal will. But these codicils were additions or appendages to the human will—suppositions for the will to build upon, new hypotheses upon which to base individual and cultural action.

   The personal material also told me that I spent too much energy worrying about any hostile reaction to my work:

   Like a country exaggerating its need for defenses, you go overboard, expending too much energy for defenses, taking it away from the arts , so to speak, and individual fulfillment. Through such misguided policies, you spend so much effort to protect your resources that you can't utilize them properly: you hide your richness so it won't be stolen, and deny yourself the pleasure of your own exuberance. In spite of this, your creativity and growth continue, but you must now accept these codicils. They are not esoteric statements having nothing to do with behavior, but will serve as a better, more creative basis for self-government, and affect behavior in the same way that a country would be changed if it adopted a new, freer constitution over a previous limiting one.

   The universe is not hostile. No one can hurt you and no criticism can hurt you—unless you stay within that level of understanding.

   Remembering this as we drove later to the post office, I thought again, "Of course," and for a few moments I felt an intense yearning, remembering once more the experiences that initiated this book. For a few days, at least, I'd never felt so unafraid of myself or others or the world in general. Had I momentarily accepted the new hypothesis then without really knowing what it was? Had I suspended the usual assumptions that most of us accept unthinkingly? Is that what the world would be like if we trusted ourselves and nature, and our relationship with life? Usually we live cozily in our codes, confused as they are, trying to find our way amid tangled concepts and erratic offshoots that arise to confront us. Thou shalt not kill, for instance—not unless we do it in a wholesale slaughter for God and country called war, when it's all right. And kill, of course, refers to our own species to begin with; the others have to take care of themselves. Thou shalt not steal. Right again. But stealing from the government or cheating on one's income tax is all right, because after all the government has all the money anyhow. Or it's okay to steal from our enemies. Then we're told to be good, which means to hate evil, and this can also be extended to mean that its good to kill the evildoers. Very confusing.

But it occurred to me that in accepting the codicils, maybe we wouldn't need any commandments because the new hypotheses would lead to a flexible framewrok in which we could safely explore our own abilities. The codicils weren't *rules*, but new *assumptions*. We believed the universe was unsafe, and it certainly seemed so in our experience. If we changed the belief to its opposite, would our experience really change too?

Yet the codicils made me uneasy in a way that I couldn't fathom at first. For one thing, they bothered me precisely because they seemed to run directly counter to general assumptions. How could you really believe that the world was safe, for example, or that the self was A-OK in the face of human experience and in direct contradiction of the basic ideas of science and religion both? Most scientists seem to think that the body is a great-enough mechanism, but that the mind or self is just a crazy chance-born by-product, while religions seem to see the body as a temple of temptation. But both certainly believe in restraining the self.

That night Rob and I were having a discussion about spontaneity, and I said, "But suppose I didn't have a writing schedule and just did what I felt like doing? I might decide to do something else instead."

He said, "You're taking it for granted that if you left yourself alone you wouldn't write enough; that you can't trust yourself to be spontaneous because, spontaneously, you might want to do the wrong thing." Rob paused, looked at me quizzically, and asked, "Just what terrible thing do you think you'd do, instead of writing? I'm always intrigued when people don't trust themselves. What on earth do they really think they'd do if they just let themselves be? Get a gun and go down the street shooting everyone they saw? Few do that sort of thing, and the people who do aren't the people who trust themselves; quite the opposite. So just what do you really fear you might do, if you left yourself alone?"

He spoke in a half-joking manner, and I answered lightly, almost without thinking. "Turn a whole civilization away from Christianity."

"Maybe you'd just offer them something better; Christianity is in pretty poor shatters," Rob said. "And besides, what makes you think that you or anyone could lead a civilization in one direction or another, or that people are going to do anything that they don't want to do?"

I was pretty embarrassed.

"Maybe the race knows that it needs to move in new directions. But why would you think *that* was bad, no matter who did it?" Rob was honestly puzzled, but I finally saw why the codicils bothered me—I was secretly worried about bucking established ideas—particularly cultural Christian ones, even though I disagreed with many of them. And the fear, hidden, was forming some truly unreasonable, hilarious images of Jane the crusader—the anticrusader—leading generations astray, down the garden path—even though the path we were on wasn't exactly the way to Paradise.

A whole swirl of memories came to mind even before I had time to speak. I remembered being a kid in fifth grade, walking with a group of girls around the block by the orphanage where I lived for two years. A nun led us. We came to a Christian Science church. The nun explained that the church was a monstrosity; formed by a woman in defiance of all Christ's rules. I can't recall her words, only their impact, her horror that a human being would dare begin a church when the Catholic Church was established by God; her scandalized derision that a woman would dare such a crime, and her perfect faith that the church members and anyone connected with the nefarious affair would be doomed to hell for all eternity.

"What utter nonsense," I thought, but even as I reminded myself that I'd outgrown such ideas, I remembered the old sayings: The worst sin of all was to lose your faith or destroy the faith of another. And knowledge was always suspect. Hadn't Eve tempted Adam; and wasn't the basic sin the desire for knowledge and the pride of the intellect, because knowledge belonged to God alone? And what was I doing, but pursuing the search for knowledge and leading my fellow beings away from Christ?

What was I doing, saying that man was good when the whole of religion shouted that he was sinful?

Because the false gods and the false prophets were always those who disagreed with the dogmas; and of course you were with Christ or against him. There was never any in-between. So I'd put myself defiantly on the other side, lined up with the false prophets. I went around looking for kinder gods, gods with some sense and dignity; but in the meantime I was taking people's comfort blankets away, and what realities would they encounter without any dogmas to give pat answers to their questions? With no sweet Jesus there and no one to put in his place?

Because I didn't believe it worked that way. And you have to tread carefully when you're ripping away such delicate psychic fabrics; but beneath his gods, it still seems to me, man might find himself, recover the lost parts that he's always projected into divinities. Man might recover his (and her) earth identity, and through spontaneously trusting the self, discover what real divinity is. I believe that the search is as natural to us as breathing; and that through knowing ourselves we'll automatically trigger responses and abilities that will lead us toward the discovering of a divinity that's been here all the while.

So why on earth did I still react to old beliefs? Was I afraid of being one more guru, mad visionary? Or was I afraid that I'd succeed so well that the old gods would strike me down? What idiotic musings! Yet ... who doesn't want the gods on his side? Who dares stand godless, searching once more? With no god with flaming sword beside us and without a hell to doom our enemies? But alone, speaking with the authority of the private psyche alone, unsupported by dogma, religious or scientific, with no credentials that the world understands?

In the beginning I could say, "No one will listen." It didn't bother me too much before Rob and I decided to make the Seth Material public: we were embarked on a private search; one I knew was tricky in our times, but I was strong and determined and I had Rob beside me. But then, being a writer, trained to describe my experiences, I had to share them. And that was the rub. Bringing possible disaster down upon my own head was one thing, a risk I was prepared to take, but what about my followers? Because soon people listened. They were trying my road. Was I then responsible for their experience? Because in that old context I didn't quite realize that we form our own reality. People will do what they want to do; and if they follow an idea it's because the idea meets an echo in their minds.

I'm still in the middle of my search, yet some are ready to set my work up as the latest dogma. I've grown to hate the term "truth-seeker," because so often it means that each new insight must be guarded, protected, turned into another rule to be followed. Seth is often seen in the light of old beliefs, so that some people use his ideas to back up old concepts with a new cement.

And behind all of this is the delegation of personal responsibility, for what use are the gods if they don't tell us how to live our lives? Any god worth his or her salt lays down a code of commandments, tells us what is right and wrong and how to treat our friends and enemies. And because we projected portions of ourselves into these divinities, they exaggerated not only our powers and abilities but our failings as well. They could be ten times as cruel, ten times as loving. They have always been personified, and so they've always reflected our state of being at any given time; or rather, our state of comprehension.

What good is a god who doesn't tell us what to do? Yet while we think in those terms, we'll always have to justify God's ways to man, for if he creates our good, then how do we explain our evil? To me, the whole structure is misleading. We create our experience on a personal and global scale—our good and our evil—through a creative energy that forms our being; that is personified in us and that is beyond our ideas of personhood. We must throw all the gods away in order to discover the mystery behind their existence, that shines through the miracle of our flesh.

I think that this is a fine sacred chase, the most worthwhile psychic endeavor, yet I'm still haunted, I suppose, by the god of my childhood. I remember the statue of the infant Jesus, and the bleeding Christ whose picture smiled compassionately from the bedroom wall—heart dripping with blood that would dissolve my sins. If my mother didn't understand, Christ did. If he was busy, there was always his mother, immaculate, safe from sex, so holy that she had a baby without ever doing it. I cried aloud to the saints, each one right there in my mind—one to find lost objects, one to keep me safe while travelling—a psychic family for the soul.

I remember the comfort; that if no one else loved me, Christ did—as long as I went to church on Sunday, didn't masturbate, kept my faith, and didn't read books that were forbidden. And he was always there, watching; the original Big Brother. It took a certain defiant daring to masturbate; lying sprawled on the child's bed, what with Christ there, staring. Even when I turned his picture to the wall it made no difference. And the simple natural act became horrid, sacrilegious, evil, because of the good it was supposed to deny. It would have to be a symbol, sometimes of humiliating acceptance of the flesh's weakness; sometimes of triumphant flaunting—because if it was wrong, why did it feel so good?

But you always knew what was right even if you strayed, and there was confession in which forgiveness was sought—forgiveness for the fact that you were human. The sacred and the profane-creations of our own thrown out into experience; our hates and loves; each seen in opposition, never fitting together, yet a part of a whole that we haven't learned to understand.

Yet I'm hardly an atheist. I'm only aghast at the kind of personifying and nonsense we've laid upon the gods; the way we've imprisoned them and us in concepts that refuse to grow, for once we decide upon a particular dogma as truth, then we stop looking in our determination to protect whatever certainty we think we've already found. Sometimes I wonder if we're strong enough to understand, because one day we're going to have to handle our own reality, stand resolute, knowing that we form our world and experience. We're going to have to take responsibility for our lives and the condition of the planet. Then maybe we'll be wise and brave enough to encounter the gods that flicker in and out of our being through the ages.

So I've been tinged by limiting concepts as much as anyone else, blinded by them to some extent. The Catholic Church is no better or worse, as far as I can see, than any other religious organization. Some fundamental Christian sects make Catholicism look liberal, for that matter; and the sciences have limiting dogmas all their own. All of these, however, share a basic distrust of the self and the very conditions of its being.

So, I wrote down the codicils and some part of me was triumphant while another part held back, thinking: but it's so hard—what would people do, denied all the old comfort blankets, taught to be free? And here *I* was, getting this material, while at the same time sticking to a tight writing schedule, as if I'd never write another line again if I gave it up. I remembered an old poem I wrote in high school:

> *I'll keep my soul in prison,*
> *She's too loving and too kind.*
> *And I'll keep her there forever,*
> *If she doesn't learn to mind.*

So, with magnificent bravery, I decided to do just what I wanted to the following day even if my "sinful" self wanted to sunbathe instead of write; or—well, anything. And faced with the day, free as a bird, I felt full of inspiration and—you guessed it—wrote all day long. But the trouble is, most of us are afraid to put ourselves on the line, even in the smallest of instances, to see what we're really like. If we leave ourselves alone, we're afraid that we won't work, won't produce: We'll lie idle, as if left alone the body and mind together won't do their thing, but need a schoolmaster or schoolmistress always on top, giving the orders. And obeying those orders without question, all we learn to do is imitate ourselves and our own living.

And I've seen many of the young, following this or that latest guru, looking for a purpose to guide their lives, searching for a sense of their own power and vitality in dogmas that encourage dependence. They ask: What is my purpose? And they have a right to ask because the beliefs we've harbored about ourselves have robbed them of the ability to find purpose in the only place it can be found—the private self.

The religions might say, "God is within you," but the "you" that He is within is such a hash of "low vibrations" or "fleshy desires," or whatever, that it seems easier to take drugs, hoping for some miraculous insight. People ask for help over the telephone and in letters, not realizing that the best thing I can do is to reinforce their faith in themselves, try to find it and pull them up by their spiritual bootstraps. Anything else only reinforces their sense of powerlessness.

So, I wrote the codicils. They led me to consider my own limiting beliefs, those tricky dogmatic leftovers that had been stewing in the back of my mind for years. With those out in the open, I could understand other people's problems better. Still brooding over the entire question of the gods and our relationship with them, I wrote the following two poems.

Will the Real Gods Stand Up

"Will the real gods stand up, please,"
I shouted, but all the prophets were yelling,
and it was hard to hear.
"Do this, do that—

or suffer divine wrath—"
like a sort of psychic nuclear reaction
aimed against souls who didn't toe the line.

I'd sooner pray
to a tiny tree toad
who at least loved the earth,
and knew what dawn was.
If he ate flies
he wouldn't pretend
that he's punishing them
for some sin
against his divine benevolence,
and his hunger is innocent.

When the Gods Take Their Clothing Off

Somewhere the gods fling off
the images we clothe them in
and swim, naked,
in the clear waters of their essence,
or twirl till their images unwind
like glimmering mummy robes
finally falling off.

Somewhere the gods hang their empty forms
on secret shores,
triumphantly stepping out of them,
wiggling their souls free
of golden coils, brocades; shaking
themselves loose of sacred hearts,
leaping boldly out of swaddling clothes,
kingly robes and blood-stained garments.

Crowns, swords and crosses
stacked in a bonfire pile and lit—
empty christs, jehovahs
slumping down into the flames,

buddhas melting, allahs burning
with a merry light
while vacant angel forms hang limply
on the tree of life,
wrinkled wings blowing
in a new spring wind.

Laughing, the gods throw in
all the emblems of their majesty.
Bibles, relics, sacred rings
go spiraling,
while in the shadows, old gods
who have gone before,
applaud and yell out advice.

What massive chuckles
as the gods rise up
and stretch right through the universe;
stamp out the fire and disperse
into everything that is.
And what divine conversation,
all public,
open as the world,
as the gods shout, whisper, chatter
their messages; disappear
into grass blades, people,
planets, dogs, molecules—
the divine camouflage.
The gods are
where we don't look.

As I read the codicils over, considered the poems I'd just written, and thought about the ways I'd been hampered by old beliefs myself, I saw the difficulties involved in trying to set up new hypotheses as a basis for action. Our culture gives official recognition only to experiences that reinforce its own belief structures. To some extent, that's fair enough. But we're taught from childhood to respect authority and to look to others to confirm our perceptions of reality; which is based on certain agreements as to what is real and what is not.

When we find ourselves having taboo experiences, or when the world seems to be behaving in a way we're taught that it can't, then we're presented with a dilemma as long as we stay in that frame of reference: Either what we perceived actually happened or it didn't—and if it didn't, then we're deluded. Our belief in ourselves and the world is shaken. Even the support we receive from other people can be withdrawn if our ideas of reality collide with the usual ones too severely.

To some, a simple precognitive dream can be shattering, not so much because of the dream's specific content as by its implications. We aren't supposed to know anything that is not immediately present to our senses. Most, though not all, conventional psychologists consider out-of-body experiences as hallucinary data, having no reference to normal behavior. Any exceptional perceptions can, therefore, be threatening at least to some degree. If our view of reality differs too much from the norm, we're considered insane: we can't cope with the real world because our private vision supersedes it. And the codicils present an alternate version of reality that would increase so-called exceptional events.

Our culture not only restricts exceptional experiences that appear to contradict accepted theories, but it often also frowns upon the development of creative abilities if they come into conflict with, say, the work ethic or any other core belief held by the society. The aspects of the psyche must be squeezed to fit this version of reality and the rich psychic mixture diluted to fit the cultural medium.

But if the focus personality has experiences that do not fit the mold, it often begins to form an interior culture of its own, in which it can use the abilities otherwise closed off. To do this it needs an inner authority for support, to compensate for the lack of usual agreement in the exterior world.

In more ideal circumstances, this subjective creation would seldom appear as itself, but flow outward naturally, projecting itself into the culture and its organizations, subtly altering them through a give-and-take of private symbolism and exterior actualization.

When culture becomes too restrictive, this flow is disrupted and the individual finds that his inner experiences no longer conform. The focus personality's sense of identity is threatened, particularly if psychic events are concerned. People who find themselves encountering revelationary material, instances of clairvoyance or telepathy, have nowhere to turn.

There *are* counterculture groups. The trouble is that most of these also set up dogmas to which their converts must conform, somewhat desperately, because where else in society can they go? Many such groups have their own newsletters, meetings, and bulletins, and some of their antics are rather ludicrous. They're no more ludicrous, though, than a science news magazine when it closes its eyes to anything outside of its own belief system, and uses its own terms as rigidly as any "fanatic."

The trouble is that we're taught that events happen—or don't happen—within a very strict framework. So if we have any visions or insights or revelations, we don't know how to interpret them. We have to prove to ourselves or others that they happened—in the normal framework—where they don't fit. For example, an engineer mentioned earlier in this book believed he saw a UFO on very flimsy evidence; then he began automatic writing, and was convinced he was receiving messages from these people from outer space. Along with this, he had some valid instances of telepathy with his wife and some excellent out-of-body experiences. His scientific background made such experiences seem impossible. On the other hand he was impelled to "prove" the data in physical terms. The spaceship was real, he insisted, so he wasn't crazy.

He wasn't crazy but the spaceship (his, at least) wasn't a physical one, either. He'd formed the entire subjective framework to try to explain legitimate subjective experiences, such as the telepathy and projections of consciousness. Finally, when no one agreed with him on the physical validity of the spaceship, he gave the whole thing up.

I tried to tell him that the UFO and the space intelligences were valid creations of the psyche, symbolic representations standing for something else, meant to lead him to other questions, but he couldn't take that. The ordinary true-and-false world can't tolerate such concepts. So, unfortunately, he wasn't able to take advantage of his telepathic experiences either, because he couldn't find a suitable framework for them. And he couldn't superimpose his subjective framework outward as physical fact.

The same thing applies, regardless of the subjective framework. I wrote earlier here about the Christ who called me off and on for a few years. His obsession was finally tempered when it no longer suited his purposes, and when I refused to accept his Christhood as literal fact. He called a few months ago. Now he realized that he wasn't Christ, he told me: he'd been confused: he was Saint Paul. Maybe it doesn't seem that he was that much better, but this was quite a jump from the omnipotent Christ he saw himself to be, to a mere physical disciple. It meant that he was seeing himself in a more realistic light. And now that he was human, he might be able to see that he was himself.

Our official line of consciousness builds up its own world view and its own group of assumptions, which then become a priori judgments. These beliefs support each other visibly and invisibly, so that to challenge one is to challenge all, and to threaten the entire framework. Yet this line of consciousness itself brings about dilemmas and contradictions that are meant to serve as impetuses for further development. I believe that the codicils by offering an alternate—even opposite—view of reality can serve as supportive guidelines that will help us bring the exterior world more in line with the psyche's potentials.

Chapter 23
The Natural Contours
of the Psyche

No one has really tried to map the *natural* contours of the psyche. Few even wonder if it can be done. You can't do it by considering the psyche a more or less local and confined phenomenon, as Freud did, wading just off the shore of our usually focused awareness. Freud rummaged about in an area between the psychic shore and ocean, examining the eddies, seeing the mud, all the while staying where he was, never going further to ride the great tidal waves of the psyche that came thundering majestically in. He examined only the natural debris that washed out from the shores of mind, but he never glimpsed the inrush of power and energy that constantly refreshes and revitalizes ordinary consciousness.

For our consciousness itself rushes in and out,

encounters physical reality, forms its three-dimensional spirals, sand castles, and rocks, and withdraws back into the depths of itself once again in gigantic and minute patterns that are etched in the very convolutions and ridges of our brains. Day—and the tide of our consciousness splashes against the objective earth, the pattern of its motion scattering the stones and pebbles of events outward, impinging in the world of time, making scrawls in historic sands: and night—when we withdraw into the depths from which the shores emerge, and from which our waking consciousness surely springs.

Carl Jung at least knew that there was such an ocean. He felt the undertow, dreamed of the distant breakers, and sensed the towering shapes that rose and fell, forming all the smaller ones. But how far can our normal consciousness go out into that figurative ocean? It *is* part of that ocean all the time, of course, composed of the same ingredients, participating in its motion. But when we travel bravely out of our usual depths and bring back souvenirs; but however strange they appear *there*, when we get them back to shore they're somehow the same old thing. They seem to go through a metamorphosis.

Intuitions and revelations that seem so sparkling and original at the time of discovery often turn seedy. It's as if we've captured a fine mysterious creature out in the depths of the ocean—a creature that seems to belong to a species we've never seen before. Triumphant, filled with hope and surprise, we bring our prize in, whatever way we can. But when we get back, before we can even shout, "Hey, look what I've found!" we see that the creature is, after all, of a well-known species; somewhat exotic, perhaps, because not too many people go out far enough to find its habitat. Yet we could have sworn—out there where we saw it—that we'd discovered something of invaluable merit and original design.

So our mystical visions escape us. When we're caught up in the tidal wave of the psyche's sudden acceleration, riding it with the heady fresh spray of insights breaking all around us, we can hardly believe the originality of our perceptions or the significance of our new knowledge. When we ride the breakers back to shore, though, grasping our new catch in the net of our thoughts, we find on examination that we have another floppy christ-fish, a seaweedy buddha that someone else has thrown away, or another crumbled virgin doll. Debris, we think, nothing new, but the old standard versions after all. Disappointed, we remember the high feeling of certainty and inspiration we felt, riding that breaker, and we wonder: Was it all a lie?

For something happens when we try to translate inner intuitive data into ordinary terms. It works, at a certain level, as instances of telepathy and clairvoyance imply. But beyond that, gross distortions seem to occur. I've read that there are strange sea creatures in the depths of the ocean, precisely attuned to their environment. But try to bring them up and you have corpses: they change from alive to dead on the way. To see them, you have to go there, to their territory. So maybe original visions change in the same way, adapting to our environment on the journey back, just in order to stay alive at all. They *may* adapt themselves to some degree to the atmosphere of ordinary consciousness.

But how much are we responsible for this unfortunate transformation? William Blake, the Eighteenth century mystic and painter, saw visions all the time. Once he painted the spirit of a flea as it appeared to him early one evening. He saw it three-dimensionally, and whatever it was, it was a personal sense experience which he then used to create a work of art. And what a remarkable and weird work of art it was! Here was no light airy vision, no fairy creature with gossamer wings. Blake drew a husky, horrible man-animal-demon, dripping blood; bloated and hairy.

As far as I'm concerned, this is perfectly legitimate as the basis for a work of art: you paint it as you see it. But why did Blake see it that way? He viewed his own visions through his religion-soaked beliefs, so that his spirit of a flea had little to do with a flea—or its spirit—but with his ideas about the grotesqueness of evil. Blake was a great mystic and artist despite all this. Yet I'm bound to wonder what he would have produced if he'd allowed his magnificient vision its own sight.

I came across his drawing of the flea's spirit as I was working on this chapter, and I thought that it was an excellent example of the transformations that can happen to visions or revelations. Someone else might have seen a nicer flea, or turned it into a romanticized fairy creature, but Blake's genius could turn even a distorted vision into art. If we could perceive the spirit of a flea, most likely we couldn't capture it anyhow. It would be an aura or atmosphere or invisible incline of being; a living knot of moving space—to be felt, perhaps, but never captured. Only we feel that we *do* have to capture our visions and cast them in physical terms. Doing so might be the one definite way of losing whatever it was we thought that we had found.

I wrote this poem about Blake and his visions after I saw the drawing of the flea, and as I was musing further about how our beliefs might program the content of our visions and insights.

Come into My Parlor

William Blake
broke the sky apart
with his visions.
Stars and planets tipped sideways,
fell into his head
in stinging fragments
till bits of gods exploded.
Hells and heavens streamed
out of his heated eyes,
spreading saints and demons
out onto his cottage floor.

Avenging angels, swords drawn,
advanced upon his garden lawn
at twilight, slaying gargoyles.
And when he opened his back door,
he never knew
who might be standing there,

ghost or demon,
black eyes swirling in volcanic sockets,
sprouting smoke,
flaming skin hotter than his kitchen stove.

He didn't care.
If they'd sit for a portrait
he'd let them in,
and invite them to say their piece
while his hell-heaven scorched fingers sketched,
or he'd turn them into poems
with a sudden flick of his magic mind,
imprisoning them in verse,
laughing when they shouted to be let out,
caught between the shining bars
of his magnetic vowels;
tricked.

All the heavenly and hellish hordes
found his humble house,
drawn down the burning chimney of his soul
as if it were a hole in the sky,
and they fell through,
till finally the heavens emptied,
and the last seraphim, devil, saint,
and every last image of God
was captured, held beyond escape
in a miniature firmament—
infinite within its frame—
but confined
to paintings hung upon a wall.

Or, maybe I'm being too hard on Blake, and all of us. The psychic or nonphysical world might not exist apart from our projections: that is, it may be so plastic, creative and psychically rubbery that it automatically translates itself into what we think it is. In other words, its responsiveness to our feelings might be so acute and accurate that it takes on the shape expected of it. If so, *then* we would always see what we believed we would see, and our visions of gods and their retinues *would* more or less agree through the centuries, providing their own separate "evidential data," just as our accepted physical world does.

We're beginning to understand that physical reality exists differently than our sense—experience with it. Our general agreement on the nature of objects betrays us to that degree, because objects just don't exist the way we think they do. On the other hand, as I write, I put my coffee cup on the table and grin, thinking that we must be pretty much all right somehow, to put solid cups that really don't exist on solid tables that aren't real either—using hands that are made up of swiftly moving molecules, with space more than anything else holding them together. A triple trick of some merit, done without the slightest strain at all.

It follows, of course, that we aren't *really* solid either, though we certainly seem to be. But the gods, demons, and other conventionalized versions of mystic experience might be psychic stereotypes, presenting their own kind of evidential material at another level of reality—no more or less valid than our solidity of cups and people, but just as handy. But . . . if atoms and molecules are behind our physical reality, what is behind the psychological reality of these other agreed-upon entities?

In our alterations of consciousness, our inner searchings, we are looking for a basic reality or the stuff out of which realities are made. For this, it's necessary to break through known patterns. If atoms and molecules are the inner components of cups and people, then what is the equivalent makeup of gods, demons, and their ensemble on another level?

We see physical reality because of neurological training and triggering. If our sense perceptions are off just a bit, we perceive a slightly different picture of a mass-accepted world. I have little depth perception, for example. In some strange manner, do I really see a truer version of space, an unofficial one, because my vision is not tuned in to the recognized pattern as clearly as usual? Is it possible that where sense patterns are eccentric, we might have a clearer point through which to view whatever it is reality *is,* apart from our normal perception?

In the same way, the visions that don't agree with the various religious and mystic dogmas, that aren't couched in terms of Christ, Jehovah, or Buddha might represent holes in the official picture through which a glimmer of inner reality seeps.

The vision that makes us uncomfortable, that doesn't fit, the one that we can't so easily explain, may give us hints and further directions in which to probe. Such visions make us uncomfortable precisely because they are unfamiliar, and this instinctively frightens us. It's bad enough to disagree with our fellows over different elements in a mass-shared reality, but unorthodox visions make us fear madness. At least the religious myths provide a framework of a kind in which reincarnated Saint Pauls, the disciples, Christ, and known saints, can find a fit, however uneasily. But true vision wouldn't provide that kind of conflict with the accepted facts of our world, because the inner reality would be seen as the source from which exterior events spring.

I'm not knocking the physical senses here, or saying that other dimensions are a priori better than ours, only that we must not automatically dress other-reality perceptions in the terms of conventional stereotypes to make them fit.

As I was working on this chapter, I received a phone call that illustrates what I mean. Lonnie, I'll call her, was a secretary in a large city on the West Coast. She'd phoned me once or twice in the past. This time her voice was excited, filled with a funny kind of wonder, with only undertones expressing a persistent sardonic questioning. "I've just been to a psychic palmist," she said, then, with a touch of skepticism, "Well, you know; that's what she's supposed to be. She reads the lines in your hand, but she really uses her psychic abilities, too. I mean, she doesn't just rely on the lines?" Her voice ended in a question.

"Go on," I said.

"Well, she read me. I mean, she *really* read me. She knew what I was like, inside. She told me that I didn't feel as if I belonged, and that I was uneasy in my environment, that I felt like an outcast. And you know, that's true."

"Okay," I said.

"Well, I was impressed by that. She'd never seen me before." Lonnie paused. She gave an embarrassed laugh that hid a hope, and went on, quickly. "Then the woman said to me, 'Of course you don't feel as if you belong because—you don't!' " Another pause. In my mind's eye I saw Lonnie sitting there, modishly thin, rather elegantly boned, chick, looking what? Modern? Sophisticated? Something like that.

Lonnie repeated the woman's words again, with a long-drawn-out mystified sigh. "You don't belong. That's exactly what she told me. Then she said that I really belonged to—the fairies! Did you ever hear anything like that? She said that they were, well, like another species, and that I belonged to them, more than anything else. That's why I've always felt as if I didn't belong."

I couldn't say anything for a minute.

"I know it sounds batty," Lonnie said. "But what do you think? Isn't it wonderful?" The wonder had broken through her voice—Santa Claus lived all over again, and she was like a kid at Christmas, given a gift too good to be true. And I was obviously the one she'd chosen to take the tinsel off the package, or she wouldn't have called: she knew me at least well enough to suspect what my attitude would be. Yet I hated to dabble with that wonder, that baby-hope. If she wanted to believe that she was part of a fairy generation, that was her business. There are worse beliefs. Except that she'd asked me what I thought.

"Well," she said impatiently. "Nutty as it sounds, I think it's true. Anything is possible."

"I think it's a psychological con," I said. Gently. "This is what I think—" And I started in.

Symbolically the statement may have accurately described the way Lonnie felt, and given her a fantasy to explain her sense of alienation—a child's dream, beautiful at age three or seven; Peter Pan who never grows old; poetic statements of inner truths—but not to be taken literally, as any child knows. Lonnie was having real problems in the workaday world: in a way, she was wandering in a fairyland, but she needed to get her footing here. She *didn't* need an excuse for not relating to the world. An imprisoned fairy who can't live in this world is a different thing than a free-flying one, comfortable in both realms—which is beside the point.

I'm not saying that the psychic was a fraud, either. She may have picked up impressions about Lonnie quite besides any clues she received from Lonnie's manner, and I'd accept her statements as creative fantasies accurately describing Lonnie's state of mind. But the psychic and Lonnie were accepting that drama at literal fact. And there I drew the line. How could Lonnie possibly believe it? How could she keep a straight face?

I'm even willing to concede that fairies might exist, as I told her. I'm not so egotistical that I believe consciousness comes only in a human package. But I don't think that people come from fairies any more than mosquitoes are born from hawks. Why couldn't Lonnie see that the whole story was like a tale told to children, with the truth *between* the words, not *in* them?

She interrupted me, saying, "Look. I know that elementals exist. I threw my consciousness into a storm and the air was full of elementals. It was wild. So if there's elementals, then why can't I be part of a species of fairies?"

Again, I didn't really know what to say, though I explained what I thought as well as I could. I talk to the spirits of the trees and the hills, and feel their response, but I know that this is a framework I'm using. I don't expect little tree people to come out in a merry parade at midnight—which doesn't mean that I don't feel the quite valid consciousnesses that form the natural world.

But so many of us think we must "see the little people," give them names and catagories, mimicking the methods of objective science in an area where such methods just don't apply. When we demand such literal interpretations, we turn emotional and psychic realities into ludicrous caricatures of themselves that rob them of whatever originality they possessed.

We end up with romantic pretenses, false in both worlds. In doing so, we destroy the natural flow of the intuitions, encasing them in yet another stereotyped form. Yet it's easy to see why so many people do this. We seem to think that if we can name and label exceptional events, they will be more acceptable and real. But the more "real" such events become, the less potent is their internal validity. They exist in a different order of events. And that order is as real or more real than the world we recognize.

That last sentence is extremely important because it implies different kinds of reality, and events that can be real in one world and perhaps not exist in another. Many of my correspondents are delightful, explorative people, privately embarking on inner roads of achievement and creative exploration, for example. Carrying on their normal pursuits, they still study their dreams, experiment with projection of consciousness, and search in their own ways for the nature of reality. But you can't use the criteria of usual fact to measure events that don't show in the fact world, any more than you can use a scale to measure a heavy mood. The heavy mood is real even if the scale doesn't recognize its reality.

But we search for certainties, and we're trained to consider physical facts as the only criteria of reality. For example, the day after Lonnie's call, another woman phoned to tell me about a situation that no longer surprised me: another instance of a Ouija-board personality insisting that he was Seth.

"Was he or wasn't he?" she wanted to know. "Was the entity lying?" Her voice was filled with hope and doubt. She took it for granted that an entity *was* communicating, without questioning that term or what she might mean by it. So some spirit out there had to be telling the truth or lying, or—worst of all, her own unconscious was lying, and was therefore mischievous and unreliable.

Years ago, I used to share the framework of concepts in which those questions have meaning, so I understood the woman's plight and did my best to explain my viewpoint. I told her that she was working through areas of the psyche;

that at some indescribable point the psyche opens up into levels usually unavailable, and that it might personify itself to get its message across. But the psyche speaks a different language, or uses our language differently. It doesn't lie; but we have to learn to decipher the language—one that is closer to the arts, with their rich pageantries of images and symbols. When we dress the psyche's multidimensional creations in old worn-out garments, we can hardly complain if they look shabby. The psyche is majestic and awesome, and our present existence springs out of its being. There's got to be a lot more there than paper gods.

But maybe our original insights and visions naturally fit themselves into the contours of our beliefs so that they blend like natural psychological scenery, highlighted only now and then precisely where our beliefs don't fit together well; or in the seams of our doubts. Perhaps if we could let our structured beliefs go long enough, we could catch ourselves transforming unofficial information into conventional garb, or even glimpse what these original perceptions are before their almost instant transformation.

Or the contours of consciousness itself might change from level to level. If our gods and religious figures are reflections of certain areas of consciousness, we might be able to follow them to their source through further alterations of focus. It's as if we've been doing number-painting translations of inner data, casting it into prearranged patterns. We're afraid not to follow the dotted lines because we might end up with a different picture of reality than the one we're used to. Our beliefs form grids, then, through which our deepest perceptions flow. Perhaps we have to suspend all beliefs momentarily, so that we can experience the original perception as it is eccentrically opposed to the model we've taken for granted.

Maybe we're afraid that reality is really formless, so we slap our own forms over whatever visions we receive. I'm personally convinced, though, that the models for everything, including ourselves, spring from this inner order of events, so it must have strong significance-forming properties. I don't imagine inner reality as a void or emptiness, but endowed with the propensity for individuation.

Those who think of it as an ocean in which all individuality is lost might be in for a surprise, for any "thing" that falls into these primordial waters may be instantly thrown up again into individuation. The physical ocean itself is composed of an infinite number of particles, even if we do think of it as one moving mass.

But I think that when we project our patterns upon inner data, we break up the greater ones that do exist.

By leaving my mind open as to the nature of Seth's reality, for example, by not imposing models taken from religion or psychology, I can let him define himself in his own way, through his actions in sessions, his interactions with others, and his own books. And I can be alert for his idea of definition, which may be far different than mine.

Yet I believe that these models in the psyche—the gods, demons, wise old men and women, fairies, and eternal children, stand for something, and reflect truths about inner reality in the same way that the natural environment tells us about the physical world we live in. So what do they mean and why do they appear so often in revelatory visions and automatic writings? And why do so many theories teach that bliss or nirvana—*sans* you, *sans* me—lies behind everything that we know? A bliss in which all knots of individual consciousness are loosened and dissolved? Again, I think *that* rich soup of creativity is more filled with alphabets than we suppose; a heady thick brew, seething with activity. But for now, I'll let that pass.

Still, maybe what we need is a cosmic rooster crowing on the rooftops of the world, or some animal god that would effectively disrupt our concepts enough so that we could at least peek through. And I've been involved with some divine father-mother visions of my own, so I know that they seem real enough. And of course, they are. It's what's *behind* them that I'm after.

In one such experience, mentioned earlier in this book, I felt myself rise to the heavens, where, as an infant, I was held and comforted by a man and woman seated in the clouds. I literally felt like a baby. Once I fell backward to earth, a frightening experience, even though I knew that "I" was seated at my desk. My sensations were inside the plummeting infant, not in my own seated physical figure.

With other beliefs, I might have seen the couple as Christ and the Virgin, or been convinced that I had been given a divine interview. Or I could have interpreted the experience to mean that God returned me to earth, to fulfill my 'mission'. In other words, I could have taken it for granted that I was literally in the sky, visiting divine relatives. The emotional validity of the experience transcends such interpretations, though.

The following is an example of what can happen when we interpret psychic data in literal terms, and get caught in what appears to be a power play between worlds. I first spoke to Dorrine one dark rainy June morning. I was typing up some notes, and looking out the front windows at the lawn and mountains. Seth had finished dictating *The "Unknown" Reality* about a month or so after we moved into the hill house, and I was wondering if he was going to begin another book, when the phone rang.

The voice on the other end of the line was feminine, young, and scared. "I don't know how to say this, but I'm in trouble. Spiritual trouble, and I need help," she said. "I wondered if you could hold a Seth session for me, or if I could attend one—"

I told her that we didn't hold private sessions for people anymore, and that Seth had written *The Nature of Personal Reality* to help people help themselves. Then I asked her what was wrong. She was a black psychologist, in her forties, doing research in racial prejudice, and she was calling from a Western state. She was also married, with two children. She told me all this in a rush. Then she said, "It was terribly hard to call you. Here I am, a black, saying that blacks can do their own thing, and I have to call a white person to ask about the nature of reality."

"Look, we're people first of all," I said, but in this case the picture *did* involve contrasts and states of mind in which everything was black or white, good or evil—and with a literal interpretation of psychic events. Dorrine had been involved with a group practicing black magic. According to her story, when she tried to leave, members directed evil energy against her. She became ill, "suffered a terrible heart attack," and was sure she was going to die.

Finally Dorrine went to a psychic, who gave her a medal to ward off the evil energy sent from the first group. This assistance only worked temporarily, however, so she went to another psychic with "still greater powers." She wanted Seth, as a still more powerful entity, to give her greater protection from the evil spirits and elementals that she believed were being sent against her.

I was appalled. I spoke to her for nearly an hour, telling her to read *Personal Reality*, reinforcing the idea that she was in control of her own life, and otherwise trying to build up her own trust and self-confidence. She hung up, and I made notes of the conversation, relating her experiences to her beliefs and level of consciousness. I kept feeling that her call contained some important hints in that regard that I hadn't crystallized.

Just then, Dorrine called back. "There are a few things I didn't tell you," she began; then she told me that she had visions herself, and one in particular in which she saw San Francisco being destroyed. Only the blacks were saved, and she was leading them to safety.

"Come on, Dorrine. You're supposed to be a psychologist, so you should know what projection is. Didn't it even occur to you that anger against the whites was erupting in your visions, so that they were being punished?"

"I know what projection is, but this is different," she protested. "I try to love all people, even if it is difficult."

"People who profess to love the world often get rid of their anger by seeing visions in which everyone in the world is destroyed except themselves and their chosen group." I said. "Skin color doesn't have to be involved. It can be a religious cult or a particular nation. Anyhow, the survivors are the good guys, vindicated."

We hung up again, but I kept thinking of Dorrine's dilemma. Her state of consciousness with its corresponding belief system results in certain kinds of experiences. The psyche's pictures are thrown outward into world events, and within that framework it all makes sense: the good spirits and bad spirits, the power plays and the sense of powerlessness beneath.

You have to change your beliefs or focus in order to escape the seeming evidence that keeps reinforcing itself. If you believe that you're harassed by evil spirits, that you're a victim; if you think that power is the answer (and you don't possess it), then you'll always have to seek out those with greater power for protection. But after a while that doesn't work either, because each reliance upon a suc-ceedingly greater power diminishes the sense of self-determination. It's easy enough to see how this works in world politics, until no projected defence against possible attack by an enemy will suffice, and finally a nation initiates aggression first—in defense.

Dorrine's revelations also symbolically represented her vision of the world. She would be a prophet leading her people to victory. But then the dilemma: How could she perform these miracles when she was herself the victim of evil elementals? The "psychic attack" was a perfect picture of the evils Dorrine saw perpetrated upon the blacks by the whites in all walks of life.

Powerful stuff indeed. As a woman and a black she felt powerless, and as a psychologist she had serious doubts that the roots of prejudice could ever be eradicated. But in her visions she was invincible. And against that psychic vision of utter triumph, anything less seemed inconsequential.

But are the devils, revengeful gods, elementals, and their kind "natural features" at one level of consciousness? I don't believe that they are archetypical elements in the psyche at all, but distorted versions of inner models or Aspects as they are reflected through certain assumptions about reality that appear valid at certain states of consciousness.

In other words, the minute we turn our focus inward, we try to interpret psychic events according to our usual assumptions, translating such data into pseudophysical terms. To many people the unseen world then becomes peopled by elementals, who can be ruled by anyone with the power to control them, in a continuation of quite human power politics. The beliefs themselves act as grids, programming inner experience. The gods and demons are already numbered patterns in the mind, waiting to be filled in by any unofficial perceptions.

These inner experiences are difficult to explain and interpret. Words are inadequate, so it may be handy to have such a stylized symbolic language—because the gods and demons *are* stylized and fairly rigid as they appear through the centuries. Perhaps that's why they seem so dependable. When we try to dispense with them, we're faced with the necessity of trying to interpret our visions and insights to ourselves without handy labels—no easy task.

As I thought about Dorrine, my own experiences, and those of my correspondents, I had the nagging thought that I knew more than I realized I did about visions and states of consciousness; that I already had some important information on the subject that I'd forgotten—information that would click into place, though earlier its significance hadn't been apparent. That material, I knew, belonged in this book. Though I'd received it some time ago, my own experience had to catch up with it. But what material? I couldn't remember anything in particular.

So, rather impatiently, I went looking through old notes. Psychic politics—a beautiful example—because I came upon some scribbled pages that instantly leapt up into significance. I stared at the material—its meaning so clear that I wondered how on earth I'd forgotten it or the events with which it was connected. The material had been there all along, waiting only for an event to trigger my full understanding.

Chapter 24
Stages of Consciousness

Several months before I began this book, I had an extremely rich perceptive experience, but it was literally impossible to describe. Being me, I wrote down what I could and ended up with a description that sounded adequate enough: it made sense; but the very sense it made was almost meaningless in other terms that escaped me once the event was over. I was so frustrated by the description, in fact, that I shelved the notes. It was these that I discovered after Dorrine's call.

The event had happened on a Friday night. Rob went to the store to pick up snacks for expected guests. I stayed home to straighten up the living room and do the dishes. When I was finished I stood at the bay windows of the apartment, brooding. I was in between books, waiting for some kind of inspiration. The scene and the circumstances reminded me of a similar evening when I'd seen my "rain creature," a vision described in *Adventures in Consciousness*. I looked back toward that experience, nostalgically. Seth, Seven, Cypris, and Helper—were they parts of my psyche? Independent? Both? Seven and Cyprus together had given my my novel, *The Education of Oversoul Seven*. Helper seemed to operate as a healer. "Well, whatever," I said mentally, "I'd like some action and help now, myself." Then I remembered the oak tree outside the kitchen window and thought of it, so secure in the earth, so in touch with its own freedom. So I said, mentally, that I'd sure like to be in touch with my own inner knowledge in the same way, or words to that effect.

I'm going to include my original notes here, to show not only what happened, but the way I described it and my frustration with the description itself.

"All at once the air and the night attained that characteristic additional beauty and significance: kids were riding bikes upon the bridge, which is not yet opened, and the new lights came flooding on, illuminating the scene with an unearthly light. I was very aware of the voices in the street and the cricket sounds—indescribably sweet and dear—and the crickets were the sounds of the gods speaking.

"Then came one of those everything-is-in-God experiences; I don't know how else to describe it. I stared at a plant on the windowsill and it was. . . . God knowing greenness but individualized greenness; greenness eternally individualized. And I knew that everything in the universe was absolutely . . . safe.

"I'm scribbling this down just after the experience, but the words don't scratch the emotional realities I sensed. But there are some kind of messages that sweep through the world constantly and help form it, invisibly, beneath what we see. And I sensed those. In a way I . . . knew that my mind's independence rises from Seth's and that this applies to other people too, with their equivalent of Seth.

"I . . . felt . . . that Seth's reality is part spiritual but partly in nature also, but mostly that there are psychological and psychic forces—a whole different category, like gravity and so forth—but on another level. These are supportive psychological forces as dependable as the physical forces we know and rely upon. They're ... substructures of personality from which our present beings spring, and they operate as the basis for our psychological life.

"The vocabulary I'm using just isn't saying what I want. In the weirdest way, the words are right in certain terms, but completely wrong in others. For example, I was going to say that I knew—while the experience was happening—that love is a force as real as gravity, operating between psyches instead of objects; but what I *felt* is so different from the word 'love' so much larger and grander and yet ... smaller, that the word 'love' as it's usually used is meaningless in the same context.

"I felt that there are states of being quite as real as the physical world, many in a given universe; sharing portions, say, of the earth at the same time, but responding to and aware of different aspects of it. While the experience was going on I sensed all this, nonverbally. I felt that I was moving toward one of those other states, a new one for me, and that an honest desire to know moves you from one state of being to another where love (that word again) is literally ... a moving force. You *do* see more clearly when you love. . . .

"I felt ... that I was being reloved, like reworked, as if this love was quickening and balancing molecular structures inside my body. As that happened I felt very sleepy. As I write up these notes, something is happening now. I'll try to describe it as I go along. If I can. All this changes to a body thing. Inside, my head swirls. The room looks new and fresh. I sense ... barely see, a giant self behind me, towering. It's in the same position I am. It's the pattern out of which I came. It's like a shadow, more defined than an ordinary shadow but not bulky. I get uneasy, thinking that I can merge with it. Decide not to. At the same time, I sense and almost see a giant cat behind Willy, our cat—it's giant-sized too, and rises from floor to ceiling or vice versa as mine does, and it's the pattern for Willy. I'm so relaxed that I'll have to stop doing these notes on the spot. . . .

"After writing the above, I lay down on the bed and suddenly felt as protected and safe as a child with loving parents nearby—though again, the words 'protected' and 'safe' just don't come anywhere near describing the kind of ... super-safety I experienced. For a moment I *was* a child in a crib. I understood what was behind the phrase 'children of God,' but also saw that the phrase was misleading in the same way the word 'love' was when I used it. At the same time, even as I felt ... the super-safety and children-of-God sensations, I felt an intellectual protest from my usual level of activity. At the super-safe level I understood why people referred to God as a father, and knew that to other kinds of consciousness one of our lives is equivalent to perhaps one year at their scale; so that after seven lives we'd still be like seven-year-olds to them."

With all my notes, the greater elements of the experience itself escaped translation. Yet as I read the notes, I realized that the giant-self-and-cat patterns were my first attempt to sense the models mentioned so often in this book.

The next day, as I sat at my desk, the following material came to me. I knew that it was connected with the previous day's experience, but somehow it didn't click for me. It wasn't until after Dorrine's call that I understood in the proverbial flash how pertinent this material was. And it had been there, all the while, waiting for me to catch up to it. Reading it over, I saw at once where the codicils fit in.

THE STAGES OF CONSCIOUSNESS

"Like many other people, I've been afraid of my own greater reality. I was used to identifying me with only a small portion of myself, 'me the writer,' because I thought in terms of me versus not-me. In our society, once you begin to glimpse the self's wider abilities and range, you're afraid that the self as you knew it earlier will be swept aside, shown to be inferior, or somehow be annihilated. Instead the 'old self' is only a small glimmer of true selfhood. The 'old self' grows

and assimilates the new knowledge and *becomes the new self.*
It is illuminated, expanded, and continues as organizer; but it
does have to open its doors to its own vaster reality and allow
itself to be illuminated by its own source. Sometimes, the
focus personality as the known self becomes frightened
because of its own beliefs, and sets up barriers to psychic
growth that are in direct proportion to the sensed expansion.

"The state of consciousness that we consider
normal, the official line of consciousness, is only a threshold
to natural "progressions." To one extent or another, each
person tries to grow out of that framework, or rather, to
expand it. In doing so, the following stages of consciousness
become apparent:

STAGE ONE

"The focus personality initiates the beginning of
the expansion process and begins to perceive unofficial
information. This usually involves some startling dream,
vision, or conversion experience. Automatic writing may be
involved, use of the Ouija board, or any process that allows
the psyche extra breathing space and motion. This stage may
or may not include checkable precognitions or telepathic
instances. There is great leeway here, and many variations in
the intensity and depth of the initial experience. While the
initial event may happen suddenly, seemingly out of the blue,
it is actually the result of a long process in which the focus
personality has been gradually casting about for new creative
expression, and some freedom from restrictions that limit its
range.

STAGE TWO

"In Stage Two the focus personality tries to continue its expansion, while attempting to maintain its previous
orientation with the world—and to correlate its unofficial
information in terms of its religious and cultural beliefs. At

this stage, for example, we will usually try to prove that our visions are true in the world's terms.

"For example, if you begin with automatic writing that gives extraterrestrials as its source, you might then try to prove that these beings exist. If the writing provides any checkable precognitions or telepathic data, then you will be convinced that the space people rather than you possess these abilities. If, like the engineer mentioned earlier, you discover that the space people don't exist in those terms, you might throw the whole thing over in disgust, at this point, and not use this opening wedge or understand that the psychic events were important even if their clothing was symbolic.

"The initial psychic event is often dramatic, even outrageous in normal terms—simply to get our attention. It may be psychological art, involving the entire personality, bringing all the senses into play in a pageantry as brilliant as any stage drama—for our eyes and experience alone. Yet we judge it—at this stage—according to the most rigid true-and-false standards. In a way such experiences (visions, revelations, and some trance personifications) are bigger than life; or rather, bigger than our ideas of what life and existence are.

"For this reason many people stay at Stage Two, in a dilemma, trying to interpret psychic events in a framework too small, or staying in fairly cozy religious or pseudo-scientific circles which provide some freedom from the official line of consciousness by allowing psychic ventures *if* they follow certain set conventions characteristic of the group.

"Unfortunately, such a course often hampers the focus personality from developing further, and if the latest unofficial data contradicts the "party line," then the person is out in the cold again. Many trance personalities developed in Stage One finally become psychologically invisible at Stage Two, or become frozen in development, mouthing the current psychic, religious, or pseudoscientific dogma.

"All of this can cloak the originality of psychic content. At the same time, genuine creativity *can* emerge; and when it does the individual is better able to cope in the normal world than before, better able to solve problems, and, perhaps, quite content to use such a dogma as a comfortable container until experience spills over the edges—and another stage is reached.

"In other words, the ready-made symbols of religion and psuedoscience are probably helpful to many people, providing them with an orientation for inner activity and growth. If the arrangement becomes permanent, however, further experiences are programmed too rigidly. Such people never work through to the truly personal, original aspects hidden within.

"These stages, left alone, will mirror the Aspects of the psyche being activated. They will show themselves in ways characteristic of the psyche and of the focus personality. Seth, Seth Two, Sumari, Seven, Cyprus, and Helper represent this kind of motion in my case. Latent creative abilities might be personified as a muse, for example, and the focus personality might be presented with new skills or interests. This personalized, tailor-made assistance of the psyche to the focus personality may not emerge, however, if rigid concepts continue to cloak the experiences. Stage Two is replete more often than not with the good and bad spirits of religion and myth.

STAGE THREE

"Stage Three is literally worlds away from stage Two. Here, the focus personality becomes reassured enough to accept new data as a part of a greater reality in which the physical world is couched. It is ready for true self-fulfillment, which means identifying with portions of the psyche formerly considered notself. The need for sacrifice or "death of the self" exists only in Stages One and Two, when arbitrary standards between self and notself predominate.

"This third stage, however, *is* the one interpreted in religious terms as the death of the self and the new birth— the death of the will, or in other concepts of similar nature. To my way of thinking, these are quite distorted. Actually, the focus personality learns that nothing works for it but the new orientation, fully accepted: this means that it expands, accepts its own larger framework, and sees that nothing is lost. In fact, the world is gained—in a new way. This stage can be a quick moment of realization, or a gradual trial-and-error process in which the focus personality fluctuates between stages One and Two until it finally receives enough momentum to break through to stage Three.

STAGE FOUR

"Stage Four is a new self-country, in which the focus personality realizes that the assumptions of the one-line official consciousness only apply *at that level*. They are dropped as valid descriptions of reality and treated as respected local ordinances. The seeming contradictions between intellect and intuitions, good and evil, object and subject, vanish—the *contradictions*. This stage can be a fleeting one of varying duration. For that matter, the divisions between the stages as given are arbitrary to some degree. Certain people will have flashes of stage Four consciousness in any of the other states.

"Overall, though, these are the stages through which we come to psychic maturity. To some extent or another, they take place in each person, regardless of culture. They represent intuitive revelation and assimilation. Again, some ancient civilizations provided mobile groups of symbols as guidelines. In our society the official line of consciousness is pre-Stage One as given—a prerequisite for the other states as it provides a sturdy physical basis. We stifle its development at this point, however, and form an entire world and culture around a specific and local area of consciousness.

"This level is particularly disadvantageous because its assumptions seem to be the only criteria for reality, since unofficial data that would show alternate patterns is discouraged. Other stages of consciousness immeasurably fill out usual reality, adding depths and nuances not generally perceivable, and provide their own kind of evidence. In a strange manner, these other stages fulfill and expand ordinary consciousness by bringing in other kinds of stimuli.

"We don't recognize such natural stages of growth and change, however. Yet a normal progression might very well lead to an understanding of death itself, for we would have evidence for the independence of consciousness from body-focus. Previously our psychological therapies have been devoted to returning the strays back to the folds of the official line, acting to reinforce the very psychological systems that retarded psychic growth—meaning the development and expression of the psyche in relationship to its inner and outer activity.

"My own experience seems to involve frequent (but never frequent enough) journeys to Stage Four, followed by assimilation of data gained there by my usual consciousness. I have discovered that now the lines tend to blur considerably, in that I regard as normal alterations of consciousness that once seem exotic. That is, I switch to various stages with relative ease. Stage Four, though, is not a steady permanent stage by any means, practically speaking, but it casts its aura over the other stages, immeasurably adding enjoyment and appreciation of the natural world.

"Again, I think that these are natural stages, experienced to some degree by everyone. Beyond are states of ecstasy, almost impossible to sustain in normal living, and the mark of the mystic state."

As soon as I came upon those notes, I saw instantly where the codicils fit in. They aren't visible at our official level of consciousness, and for that matter, at the living area or usual experience area they seem to contradict known facts. I saw where my earlier confusion originated. The codicils made perfect sense to me—were clear and apparent—when I was in the same state of consciousness in which I received them, and in all of my other altered states.

The codicils are accepted facts of existence to Seth, Sumari, Seven, and Helper, who operate at that level of reality habitually, while I experience it only in brief snatches. They exist under conditions in which space-time doesn't apply—beyond concepts of good and evil where there are no contradictions. In other words, the conditions of their reality (and of the portions of the psyche to which they correspond) are different than ours.

Seth Two—a personality allegedly more advanced than Seth, and with whom I've had some experience—seems to exist at a still more distant level. In some stages of consciousness, I've sensed realities that didn't fit my own neurological patterns. I could feel myself making all kinds of inner adjustments to bring them in, knowing that I was squeezing them out of shape to do so. But these may represent even farther-removed components of our own being, impossible to describe—"ancient" sounds, earth memories couched in an entirely different language, but alive at a molecular level in our flesh.

Seth, Sumari, Seven, Cyprus, and Helper may be Aspects of my psyche that operate at other stages of consciousness all the time, then, reflected through my experience but becoming activated *for me* only when I move to those levels myself. I'm a poet and writer, so my own interests helped activate those Aspects that suited my intents. Helper isn't utilized to the fullest, most probably because the healing abilities of my own personality are merged with the writing. Sumari definitely allows me to express musical abilities, though, that had been completely submerged and unorganized before. Other people might activate other Aspects primarily—as in spirit doctors. But even then if freedom were allowed, these Aspects would be highly individualized rather than conventionally programmed. Certainly Aspects often show themselves in dictated or automatic artistic productions of one kind or another, when such talents suddenly emerge from a previously smothered state.

Just lately a woman artist sent me two groups of snapshots—one of previous paintings done in her normal manner, and one of 'spirit paintings.' It was obvious that her earlier work was stereotyped, conventionally pretty, but lacking in any real depth. Then suddenly she was presented with mental images of pictures that she was directed to paint. These utilized geometrical figures mostly, and she 'knew' that these originated with spirit artists. She now had 'spirit commissions'. Her creativity had jumped out of previous limitations—somehow the circles and abstract shapes had more feeling in them than her previous work—but it was being experienced in another conventional framework. She was activating the creative *Aspect* of the psyche, directing it into her painting, however, and her work was charged with as much power as she could interpret and translate. Spirit artists simply seem more believable to some people than the psyche's great energy.

In any case, the focus of consciousness causes the conditions of experience. For example, at our usual level it's pretty difficult to believe that the universe is safe, and man is good. All kinds of contradictions instantly arise—contradictions that exist as conditions at that particular focus. When, in Stage Two of consciousness, you try to correlate intuitive data with the official level, these contradictions become more apparent then ever; they have to be dealt with one way or another. You almost have to move to Stage Three to make such intuitive material work—tuning in to the system of reality in which the codicils are the new facts.

Yet the Aspects, with their own distinctive levels of consciousness, are also threaded through our official focus. When we alter our focus, to some extent we tune in to these other realities that underlie our own. They usually are *not* expressed in isolated form. The Aspects merge to form our psychic and physical being. They would probably be called archetypes by some people, considered potent components of the unconscious, to be treated with kid gloves—the idea being that our individuality is so precariously posed that it is in constant danger of being submerged in its own unconscious elements.

It never seems to occur to us that our particular kind of individual consciousness is natural and rises from the psyche as easily as leaves grow from trees. The unconscious forms conscious focus; needs it, seeks it out, and operates in the objective world through its auspices. The unconscious is the constant creator of our individuality and not its great usurper; not the dark king ever ready to do us in and set up its own kingdom instead. Without the unconscious, there'd be no conscious kingdom to begin with. Such beliefs in the threatening elements of the unconscious make us fear the source of our own being and hamper the fuller facets of individuality possible with encouragement of the Aspects. Our fears and beliefs cause whatever difficulties do arise.

As a rule we just don't feel or examine the shifting guises our consciousness takes, so we can't identify with our own psychological motion. When we become aware of anything but the most usual perceptions, then our psychological mobility seems to come from outside of us. Yet the Aspects, with their own strands of consciousness, interweave just beneath our focus all the while.

The Aspects (which also operate as models) are also highly individualistic, however; unique, suited to each of us personally, and to no other. When we form them into rigid psychic molds on the one hand, or treat them as mass unconscious principles on the other, then we lose their original vision—which is also our own. We end up with a standardized package of Tibetan master, Buddha, Christ, spaceman, or whatever.

It's because the Aspects *are* basically unique that we can trust them: they're geared to our individual needs and desires, and know the extent of our abilities better than we do at our usual operating level. They *can* help solve our problems; and in reaching out beyond our own level of consciousness, we actually take the first step toward an enlarged vision in which seeming problems and contradictions dissolve. Yet in their uniqueness the Aspects are also universal, since they underlie our private and mass experience. They are, quite literally, the facets of the soul.

We follow the authority of the psyche unquestioningly as it propels us into birth, and through it, forming our very lives with exquisite precision. The child trusts the authority of the psyche, and knows that it is blessed because it exists. The child realizes that its own existence springs out of . . . something so intimate that its being is beyond question, beyond fact. We are the unknown, made known; spirit made flesh, transsubstantiation in the truest meaning of the word.

And what is "the word" we hear spoken of so frequently in various religions? It doesn't speak in syllables and vowels alone, or even primarily; but through atoms, molecules, blood, bone, and flesh. Its "sound" comes alive through the living properties of the body, just as if these letters could fly off the page, fully conscious, to form endless sentences on their own, endowed with all the abilities of this writer—able to create their own books, question their origin and mine, and speculate about the birth of alphabets.

The psyche is innocent.

My psyche is innocent and so is yours.

Our impulses are good. Left alone they'll lead us naturally toward self-fulfillment and allow us to contribute in the best way to the race at large. I believe that our impulses are as good as our cells, meant to add to our psychic development as the cells add to physical development, and that our impulses, followed with an understanding of their nature, would insure survival of the race and allow it to follow its greatest potentials.

Yet we consistently believe that our impulses are bad and that following them would lead to destruction. At our official levels of consciousness, with its prejudiced perception, this certainly seems to be the case. Yet each of us feels the burden of unrealized potential. Correspondents may write to thank me for the books, ask help, or tell their own experiences. But one thread runs through all the letters: the search for purpose. "I know I have a purpose," one woman writes. "But I don't know what it is. I know I want to help others too, but in what way?"

The individual psyche knows, and would gladly answer. Yet we ignore our own impulses—those stimuli that would set our inner purposes into motion. We've learned to doubt our own vitality. So the suggestion that we trust the authority of the psyche sounds like sheer nonsense at is best, and at its worst it suggests dangerous license, encouraging our most destructive tendencies.

Yet as we move toward Stage Three of consciousness, we see clearly that the psyche *is* innocent and that our impulses represent psychological and psychic motion leading to growth and development. At Stage Four we're able to use that knowledge to enrich normal living. While we're at Stage Four, we make the codicils work—long enough and powerfully enough so that we're certain of their validity.

Stage Four, I believe, is our most advantageous natural state of consciousness, a beginning framework, one seldom reached except in brief snatches, at least in comparison to the time spent at the official level. I'm at Stage Four often as I write. A book is a challenge: it takes physical time and effort. Yet while this time is spent in a normal way, the writing is exceptionally easy, spontaneous, and natural. In creative endeavors we're most familiar with these rhythms of consciousness, this constant translation of inner data into recognizable form. But I believe that the focus personality is meant to blend these states far more extensively than it does, merging the Aspects into a richer and more effective earth-tuned experience.

Perhaps the Garden of Eden story represents our choice of the one-line type of consciousness, stating symbolically what we were relinquishing—our innocence—and what we were gaining: the experience of duality. If so, to what purpose? Perhaps the focus personality had to concentrate on a one-line focus to establish an initial stable framework, while knowing that eventually the focus itself would recognize its limitations and seek its source.

Yet when it does, a new, unique kind of consciousness results—not simply a return to innocence, but the achievement of a knowing innocence, something quite different; an innocence that can appreciate itself, a 'youth-not-wasted-on-youth' type of psychological finesse. Such a condition weds knowledge with innocence,and merges intellect and intuitions to form a new synthesis of consciousness that is beyond the reach of intellect or intuitions alone.

When it reaches a certain point and is not allowed to fulfill itself through expansion, the linear consciousness with its assumptions leads to contradictions, illnesses, and fears. The codicils, as a new group of assumptions, release energy and dissolve the barriers of previous beliefs, unifying experience. Most illnesses, I believe, are caused by blockages of energy, resulting from linear assumptions about reality—actually by the strain that develops between the focus personality's need for development, expansion, and spontaneity, and its adherence to old beliefs that attempt to standardize and limit its experience.

As I read over my notes on the stages of consciousness, it became more obvious than ever that the level we consider normal is tension-generating after it reaches its peak of achievement, and builds up pressure meant to propel it to a new level. Again: But we inhibit this natural development, for which I believe we are biologically triggered.

Chapter 25

The Heroic Dimension
and Heroic Personages

Seth finished *The "Unknown" Reality* that spring (of 1975), a month or so after we moved. The text was so long that we decided to put it out in two volumes. Through the summer, I was working on the first draft of this book and decided not to resume regular classes for a while. Instead, I saw students about once a month.

Our first July in our new house was exceptionally hot and muggy, even though the temperature was ten degrees cooler on our hill than it was in town. I began working from three in the morning until seven, when the night air came rushing down from the hillsides and the daytime lawn mowers were quiet. In between library experiences and periods of inspiration, I'd type earlier portions of this book. I'd been typing for about a week when something clicked, and I began writing the material on codicils and the authority of the psyche. That material came all at once, in four or five days, like a package almost too big to handle. It came so quickly that I didn't have time to type it, just took it down in longhand; sometimes as I sat in the backyard.

I finished the material on a Friday. We had a busy weekend, and Monday was one of the hottest days of the year—98° and humid. I'd planned to have our usual Seth session that night. About 8:30 P.M. the phone rang—a distressing call from a young man who was contemplating suicide. I applied a psychological bandage as best I could, reinforcing his own energy and will to live. But when he hung up, I felt weary and discouraged. Why as a people did we trust anything *but* the authority of the psyche? Seth or I could only help by triggering others to use abilities they already possessed, but believed they didn't have.

Actually, most of my mail and calls are from people who are really putting Seth's ideas to work in their daily lives. Many of them have begun new businesses or creative endeavors as they examined their lives and became aware of abilities that they hadn't been utilizing before. But that night, after the young man's call, I thought angrily that lots of people didn't want to take the responsibility for their own lives: it was easier to blame their misfortunes on their backgrounds, or fate, or whatever.

Suddenly Rob and I seemed very alone, without colleagues, without ... people at our own particular focus. Twilight deepened. I put my papers away, clearing my mind for the Seth session. Still the feeling of loneliness persisted and grew. It finally developed into a kind of yearning—for what? For people who were ... wherever it was Rob and I were. A kind of homesickness for somewhere you'd never been.

I sat back at the table again, staring out the window. Without transition, I sensed other strands of consciousness, coming from all directions, for which I was the vortex. They centered in me, merged into my own stream of consciousness, which carried them out into the world. Something else was going to happen in place of a Seth session. I found my attention centered on the wall, where the library usually appeared to my inner vision.

An experience began that lasted for several hours. The trouble is that it happened at another level of activity. I could catch myself having experiences in the library . . . that were behind the events I was aware of. I sensed huge models surrounding each visible and invisible particle, that led these toward their greatest individual development, for example. But I felt as if all the knowledge of my own microscopic particles was being translated from 'their language' into symbols and images that I could understand. Each atom and molecule of my body had a psychic shape that promoted growth in different levels of existence.

While this was going on, I sensed but didn't clearly see other people in the library—colleagues of ours—waiting in other rooms through which I'd have to travel. That is, I had to go *there*. There was something different about these personalities, about the quality of their existence. The term came to me at once, seeming completely apt and inevitable: heroic personages. What I'm trying to describe now in usual terms, I knew all at once; and something escapes when the experience is described in a linear fashion.

I knew I'd been yearning toward the heroic dimension; that the library was a construct to help me in that search; and that these heroic personages existed in time and out of it. Again, I'll have to quote my original notes. I kept scribbling down what I could. Though some of the sentences are unfinished and often ungrammatical, they still retain part of my initial sense of wonder.

"I seem to be experiencing a dimension of being outside of time. The feeling of it is a lot different than just thinking that such a dimension might exist—that's for sure. I have one foot there and one foot here right now. This is a 'place' where our complete selves dwell, though 'complete' isn't the right word—our whole selves—where they exist no matter what their parts are doing in time. It's a dimension where these superpersonalities, models, or heroic personages exist and help out their selves who exist in the world.

"Even if you're in time yourself, like me, you can

go there under certain conditions, at least briefly. In fact, you can get yourself in a position where you almost have to go there to pursue your purposes and find answers that . . . aren't available where you usually are. These heroic personages aren't ghosts. It's a completely different kind of psychological existence; another version of being.

"You can't get there till you're ready, and ready means not frightened, and willing—because you see that the normal world *alone* doesn't . . . provide the . . . nourishment you want; or rather, you have to go further to learn what you want to know . . . You've gone as far as you can under the usual conditions. So your desire opens up this other heroic dimension. The heroic personages are like . . . true adults, and Rob and I in comparison are like beloved students or younger colleagues. I sense others like us there too. It is, or will be, like coming home to . . . a psychic family.

"I feel my allegiance changing, as if my reliable strong contacts are there even emotionally, at the heroic level rather than in the usual world, even though in a strange way I should be able to express my emotions more freely in normal life.

"In a way, Seth is like a traveling teacher, coming here, but now I have to go there, into the heroic dimension. Only I had to want to, and now I do. I'm not getting some of this right, but the heroic personages there, *are* . . . reflected in the psyche and help compose it in time, but their prime existence is in the heroic dimensions, outside of time.

"We've been taught to suspect . . . such otherworldly yearnings, and I suspect that I make such an effort to take these notes, just to keep up contract with known references."

I had mental experiences that I just couldn't describe or correlate—again, some seemed too fast to follow, and others seemed too slow. Somehow I connected the too-fast experiences with an accelerated time sequence, and the slow ones with my attempt to translate activity at the heroic level. Finally, I shrugged my mental shoulders and decided to go to bed. As I went to sleep, I felt as if those experiences were continuing just beneath my usual awareness.

I awakened at 5:00 A.M. Information about the heroic dimension came flooding into my mind. I got up at once. The material wasn't finished copy as it usually was from the library. Instead I knew certain things to be true. These knowings came one after another, as quickly as I could write them down.

One exception: The first paragraph came exactly as given in the following notes. After that, though, the material came as comprehensions that I translated into usual language.

"There are those who sense within the commonplace dimensions of life, the existence of a larger-than-life experience, and who feel the presence of giant events and heroic personages whose superior qualities must remain outside of the human domain, even while they are reflected in it. That is, earthly life exists under the auspices of the heroic, toward which it ever aspires. We are like children in comparison to those sensed giant consciousnesses which I'll call our own heroic selves."

That first paragraph strongly reminded me of the James material I'd received earlier. It came in a block, as if to initiate my own further experiences. As soon as I'd written it down, the comprehensions began to flow, which I then described in my own words. The paragraph also brought to mind my man-and-woman-in-the-sky experience, and several others already described in this book; all of them implied a comparison between us as children in relation to a superior kind of adulthood.

"We are one version of these heroic selves, which serve as our models. Some people have always sensed this heroic dimension, drawn upon it, and stood out in our world. The speakers [as described in *Seth Speaks*] have given evidence of its existence, interpreting it in their own time periods and inserting new models of achievement.

"Rob and I have always reacted to each other at heroic levels, besides the usual interactions. I often react to myself in heroic terms. The trouble is, this can make you terribly impatient with your own achievements. You should let yourself express the heroic in you, not try to live up to the heroic, which is the wrong approach.

"The Olympians were interpretations of the heroic personages, at a time when boundaries weren't as clearly drawn between levels of consciousness, and people were more aware of their models or heroic selves. These bigger-than-life selves can't appear in just one lifetime. Their giant capacities won't fit into that context.

"Our governments and civilizations are also eccentric, original versions of other heroic patterns. Even versions that don't work here may succeed somewhere else.

"My experience in front of the supermarket when this book began was actually an exercise in sensing the heroic proportions of objects and people in just a small section of time. Now . . . I sense the heroic from the heroic side . . . at least to what degree I'm able.

"People concerned with discovering their purpose in life are sensing their heroic nature. Only they interpret this in terms of progress: they want to know *what to do.* Instead, the heroic in those terms involves *being.* It's terribly difficult to describe what I feel, but the heroic dimension is a bigger-than-life state of being, out of which 'doing' emerges as a natural characteristic. By fully *being*, you *are* fulfilling your purpose, in those terms. When we allow the heroic elements to flow from the psyche through the models to ourselves, we feel our life in both worlds.

The models are heroic patterns in the psyche and heroic personages at the same time. But these personages are *real*; only the conditions of their existence are different than ours. When we try to pin them down to our definitions, we end up with distortions and myths.

"Again: These heroic patterns are behind everything—trees, animals, and all natural phenomena, but also behind cultural entities such as governments, families, and laws.

"While I'm sensing all this, it's quite a balancing act to keep some of my consciousness here to take these notes, or rather to translate what I'm experiencing at another level—and to choose the words themselves. I seem to throw away or discard tons of words in a minute before finally settling on one. Seth says that time is open-ended. Well, I'm experiencing these heroic personages as open-ended, psychologically. I feel them swirling into identities . . . all the time; each identity valid and eternal in a psychic or heroic space, regardless of their relative duration in our ideas of time.

"My excitement with all of this grows constantly so that my handwriting is more and more scribbled, yet I insist on getting this down. These are a kind of consciousness outside our experience. While retaining selfhood, they can mix and merge identities to get certain giant-sized effects. Our reality springs out of theirs and we're endowed with a lesser-dimensional version of their abilities and characteristics. The abilities and characteristics appear as Aspects in the psyche; but . . . on their own they live a life outside our life although connected with our lives through us.

"Yet in a way, we . . . live in their environment, unknowingly to a large extent, as maybe animals live in our environment unaware of certain aspects of it that have no meaning to them."

Dawn came. I put my scribbled notes down and stared all around: alert, excited—and angry, because I felt all my abilities stretching, to no particular avail. I sensed those other realities all about, just around the corner of my perceptions, but I couldn't bring them into focus. I sensed the support of the heroic dimensions, and the world itself took on certain properties of . . . magnificence that almost made me cry. But I wanted—more. Of course. I knew damned well that now I was trying too hard.

And I was being too serious. So I had some oatmeal and coffee, read an innocuous magazine article, wrote a note to Rob, and crawled back into bed. When I rearranged the covers Rob grunted, and the sound went right through me. Now *that* was a heroic grunt, I thought. Suddenly I felt sleepy and silly in a normally happy fashion. I fell to sleep at once.

Rob called me at noon. I ate a second breakfast while he ate lunch, and I read my notes to him. It was a lovely sunny day. I'd put a picnic table out in the otherwise empty half of our double garage, so I took out a cup of coffee and sat looking out the wide open garage door at the trees and hills across the road. Once again the world was touched by that beautiful strangeness that seemed superimposed over everything. More "comprehensions" started coming almost at once.

Again, direct knowing was involved, in which I kept receiving these comprehensions that seemed to just come. I was pretty certain that the heroic dimensions and personages were my unconscious packaging of that primary direct information; an example of the almost instant transformation of inner revelatory data into understandable terms. This surely didn't diminish my experience; the heroic dimensions *were* real, more real perhaps than the picnic table at which I sat.

I did notice something for the first time, though: The data was organized differently than usual thought processes. There was no line of thought. I seemed to get . . . all sides of the material at once, a process impossible to translate in a sentence. Literally, you can't hold that kind of information. So unconsciously I formed the heroic dimension as a symbolic framework . . . that stands for the information I received. It's the only information I'm aware of receiving, of course, but I could almost catch the symbol-building process happening beneath—and that seemed to involve a curious sense of psychological motion, familiar yet strange at once. It's as if I almost caught myself in the act of building a psychic structure to capture the information I was getting at still deeper layers. I almost heard invisible zoom, zoom, zooms until the structure—the heroic dimension—was strong enough to bear the meaning of the information, which itself could not be literally interpreted.

For all of this, to me there is a heroic dimension, and heroic personages who exist connected to each of us, reflected in our existences as we are in theirs.

The air literally shimmered in the sunlight. I felt as if the patterns for the world were just at the other side of that shimmering. I scribbled down what I was getting, and again I'm including my original notes. Their unevenness, and perhaps their circular organization itself, gives a better hint of the experience than more grammatical descriptions I might write now. To me, at least, the notes themselves seem to pucker in places, suggesting my own feelings that reality as we know it *did* pucker and wrinkle, so that I could poke my consciousness through.

I knew that I'd sensed the heroic personages before, many times, as the massive relatives I've described in some of my poetry, and that they were also connected with what I called my "massive experiences," when I seemed to expand, mentally and physically, extending out into space.

Now, the notes:

"Experience of the heroic adds the ... heroic faculty to everything else and illuminates the nature of all visible things. Nature becomes super-nature even as it's perceived by the physical eye, because the sense of sight is endowed with heroic vision. It's as if our cat, Willy, saw our living room for a moment through our eyes, and understood everything in it in the same way we do. That's how I feel just now. Only I lack the means to express what I know, as the cat's meows would be inadequate to express his new knowledge.

"The attributes of the heroic are surrounding us all the while, but we don't sense it, and ignore the obvious clues to its existence. We share part of our environment with the animals but they don't share ... what we'd call the human elements: They couldn't read time by a clock, for instance. So we share some of our environment with heroic personages, as unaware of their psychological reality ... never viewing this shared environment from their viewpoint. They know a ... time that includes ours, for example.

"And the animals share their own kind of heroic elements. (And for that matter, they have no need to tell time by a clock.)

"We come out of the heroic elements, hence the patterns for our world—the cells, atoms, and molecules and so forth—emerge from the heroic dimensions. We dwell in the heroic in that it grows our bodies, or is the medium in which our bodies grow. And we're eternal in the heroic. We touch upon it in dreams and visions, even though we view it through our own beliefs and thought-patterns.

"We're growing toward conscious awareness of the heroic dimensions. Our visions and revelations are like momentary awakenings there—distorted glimpses, as a child might just see an edge of a blanket when he awakened here, or might not focus properly, or might see his mother's face and think of her as a giant. She'd be a giant to his perception, but not to hers.

"Each lucid dream or vision or intuitive insight brings you more awake *there,* and actually wakens the heroic faculties so that this life is seen as one focus of many. Here we accept two focuses—waking and sleeping consciousness. There, our entire life experience here is just one part of a greater experience. Here, we forget most of our dreams. There, our lives here are living dreams, three-dimensional, only we waken from them there, remembering!

"Art is symbolic representation of the heroic.

"It's so damned hard to get a verbal hold on what I'm getting otherwise, but identity is both open-ended *and* formed of inviolate psychological boundaries simultaneously—and can operate in either manner without contradiction, maybe in the same way that light can act as waves or particles. This makes the God concept almost ungraspable in usual terms.

"But we feel terribly alone and cut off when we don't sense the heroic in one way or another. Children, for example, are bathed in it constantly, growing trustfully in the medium of the heroic.

"The heroic personages (of which we're part) couldn't experience earth life. They're psychologically too big to fit, so we are extensions of them, while they're extensions of us only in a different, giant-sized way. We *do* add to their experience though, and they add to ours.

"Christ's basic message was an ancient one, re-stated: that we survive death and have another existence else-where. It also dealt with heroic principles—love, devotion, honor-couched in terms that would be understood at the time. The whole idea of self-sacrifice was grossly distorted through the ages. It's based on the understanding that the self is eternal and indestructible. Only then can so-called self-sacrifice be a heroic act, done with the recognition that nothing is lost or sacrificed, since the self's basic validity rests in the heroic dimensions. But that message was and still is almost impossible to explain here, too.

"Misunderstood or half-understood, it leads to endless stupidities; for example, the belief that suffering is good for the soul—or half-cocked attempts to justify murder, since as the reasoning goes, the self is just translated neatly from one existence to another. *That* version is one of the worst instances of interpreting intuitive information in literal terms.

"Seth is right: Christ never did exist in time, but did exist (and does) as a heroic personage and as a giant-sized model for several historic persons. The myth then actualized the personage in terms we could understand. We had to believe in a literal rising-from-the-dead of a physical person. Paul tuned in to his version of that heroic personage, was blinded by the vision, and interpreted it in his terms, as a soldier—setting out to conquer the world with his truth.

"(The ancient 'divine right of kings' was a distorted attempt to synchronize the heroic and historic.)

"Pagan and Jewish sacrificial rites were also based on a literal interpretation—the idea being that in returning an animal (or person) to the heroic dimensions, you were certain of getting more of the same back; replenishing the stock by sending in a 'model' to be copied by a god or gods. The best of the crop or stock then served as the sacrifice.

"Cave drawings also represented this great love of images and patterns: Instead of sacrificing, the artist drew a replica of what was required; sometimes distorting particular desired elements, such as strength or agility. The drawings served as blueprints, requesting nature to fill them out in flesh. This could also be connected with present native beliefs concerning cameras; the fear that the soul will become confused and leap into the replica image."

(I was still at the picnic table, scribbling as quickly

as I could. As I wrote the following in response to these "comprehensions," the shimmering quality of the afternoon began to accelerate.)

ATTRIBUTES AND CHARACTERISTICS OF THE HEROIC DIMENSIONS

"The heroic dimension involves a different scale of existence, outside of time. This isn't a static sameness, frozen eternally, but a scale in which . . . action happens . . . outside of time as we know it. Not sure that I can get this straight: but it could be that change there would be so slow to our standards that we wouldn't perceive motion at all, but think everything stationary and eternal. *There*, though, motion would be happening at its own characteristic rate—characteristic of the heroic dimension.

"The heroic personages aren't dead ideals, perfection personified, but super-creative, heroic-sized psychological gestalts, and our own creative abilities are our closest connections with them. Our imaginative faculties are also important in this respect. Since it's nearly impossible for us to perceive the heroic directly even though we use our own heroic faculties, then even this material I'm getting now is bound to be a creative model or version of the heroic. We can't get a 'literal fact' interpretation because . . . the heroic exists outside of the fact framework and beyond it. Facts are materialized events from that dimension apparent in space-time as evidential.

"Something odd happens as I write this. I get a disconnected-from-time feeling which is a trifle scary. Fascinating but scary. As if while I'm writing, the garage and yard and everything that I see exists eternally, and time begins just out of my sight, around the corner maybe. But the birds are singing. A plane goes by overhead. I feel this is one eternal moment, say, called 4:30 P.M. where I am, and where everything that I can see exists. But outside of this spot, time goes on and it's 4:35 in the kitchen, beyond my sight, and outside of this crazy framework.

"But (I feel so weird) fresh action keeps coming into the scene before me from . . . nontime; flowing into this eternal moment I'm somehow in. The birds fly from branch to branch. My hand writes. I'm swinging one leg back and forth. This isn't just repetitive action. I can do anything I want. But all this—and it never gets to be 4:35. Not here. But when I lose whatever this is, this . . . heroic nontime, then I'll step right out into, say, 4:40 or whatever, without knowing what really happened.

"It's a different dimension . . . within our time (I don't know how to explain it without using the word 'time')—within any given moment that's eternal yet filled with change. Maybe it's really heroic time and only seems outside of time to me? Maybe it's just a kind of 'long time?' "

I glanced around again: everything looked so splendid, changing yet eternal. But some creature unease grabbed hold of me. I picked up my papers and went into the house where the kitchen clock said 5:00 P.M. Then, curious and safely inside time, I looked out the kitchen window at the yard—and time was outside there now, too.

Yet all the material I'd received that afternoon only represented a glimmer of the subjective comprehensions that I couldn't translate into understandable terms. And that material seemed to come from someplace else too, of course. As if there was an invisible mail slot in my mind, and foreign letters from other worlds kept dropping down. Only I had to translate them, and they kept coming.

I fixed dinner. Rob and I ate in the living room, and watched a television show. I did the dishes. Then I sat by the front windows, watching the summer twilight. Again, the comprehensions began. This time, most of them escaped my notes entirely.

We live in air, yet our breathing is automatic, and while we take air for granted, in a strange way we overlook it, too. Yet it's the medium in which we exist physically. That night, as I sat looking out the window at the mountains, it was as if I became alerted to the psychological medium in which we live. I felt a psychological support; the existence of ... an invisible something that supported my mental and emotional being in the same way that, say, the ground supports everything on top of it.

But psychologically I grew out through this medium, as a tree grows through the earth while still being a part of it. The heroic is the medium in which this existence takes place. I knew this in ways I can't explain, and I felt it sustain this world, and my own psychological existence.

Some feelings came back that I remembered having in childhood when I felt that no matter what happened in normal life, I was loved and safe "someplace else." As I sat there I felt reassured, safe, but most of all, free. Most of my early years, I realized, *had* been lived in unquestioning acceptance of the heroic. The heroic provides an emotional support that animals possess in their own way—a support that I saw I'd been missing for some time. Its lack brings about a feeling of a fall from grace. Was I in the process of regaining it?

When we lose that inner certainty, we feel abandoned no matter what our achievements. We recognize that some precious, indefinable joy not dependent upon events seems gone from our lives. Looking back, I could see where I'd regain it to some degree, only to turn back to the official line of consciousness as the criterion for reality. And then the obvious contradictions between the two approaches would reappear.

I was up again early the next morning. We went to bed around 1:00 A.M. and I awoke around 4:30. I ate oatmeal and drank some coffee and sat at my desk. At once the comprehensions started up again. I used an analogy to try to explain the concepts I was getting, and while the analogy isn't the best, it's the best I could come up with.

I compared the grown adult and its relationship with its own child-self to the heroic personage and its relationship with us. That is, children grow from fetuses to adults, led by heroic principles and patterns for development. The complicated patterns for the adult exist in the fetus then, and lead it toward adulthood. For simplicity's sake, I ignored probabilities which would also operate even at cellular levels.

In those terms, each of us is one version of a heroic personage who is leading us toward development by acting as a model in the same way that our own adulthood, in pattern form, led the fetus toward its own growth . . . into us.

In that regard the adult is always present in the child as a model, biologically and psychologically, though not historically and actually present. Yet the child grows in response, or toward that becoming, and is itself part of the overall pattern without which adulthood would be impossible.

In the same way, the heroic personages as models are present in us (adult and child alike) though not historically actualized. The child, though, trusts it will grow up, while at the one-line level of consciousness there seems to be "no place else to go" for the adult. The time-space orientation of the usual level of consciousness makes further development appear impossible.

The entire historic personality is part of an overall heroic pattern or heroic personage that (from our viewpoint) is outside of time. For that matter, the adult-to-be is outside of the child's present, too. The heroic personages operate as the Aspects of the historic personality, but they exist actualized within the heroic dimensions regardless of the posture of the historic personality in time. The focus personality is the historic personality, focused along its living area of birth-to-death reality, while the heroic personages are source selves.

I saw that acceptance and recognition of the heroic (by any name) gives a heroic cast to man, life, and the universe: but it also adds emotional richness to normal life and fills it out with that indefinable sense of basic trust, without which life itself can seem meaningless. With that feeling of the heroic, the individual doesn't feel isolated from the universe but united with it, so that its goals and the individual's are merged, not divergent—or worse, in opposition.

The presence of the heroic everywhere pervades the world, and through a constant give-and-take between historic and heroic experience, all events are formed, including our lives. The heroic dimensions are the larger-than-life source out of which our world emerges, yet our world *is* part of the heroic. It was all so simple—as I felt it—that I couldn't understand how I hadn't known all this before. It was completely obvious that all my experiences since starting this book were leading me to the heroic dimensions—that all the calls and letters led me to ask the particular kinds of questions for others and for myself that would inevitably lead me to this point—because this was the ... proper way for me to grow. I felt as if I were forming myself and also being formed into some beneficial psychic shape in the same way, say, that my hands took on the correct number of fingers.

What's important in all of this, is the emotional realization and intuitive knowledge of our roots and our constant nourishment. We feel a sense of loving direction, the assurance that we're growing toward our proper psychological and psychic shape in the same way that we grew physically into adults.

Yet many of us get unsynchronized with ourselves and nature along the way, and lose that sense of deep satisfaction. It seems that some magic and richness has vanished from life that we only dimly recall. A gap opens in our experience so that no event, however joyful, lives up to some vaguely remembered "Garden of Eden," and little by little our energy and zest diminish.

With emotional recognition of the heroic, however, we know that despite all seeming contradictions, we are each significant: our slightest motion is a vital gesture on the part of the universe. We understand that we are each part of a loving pattern—and as we *are*; rich, poor, beautiful, ugly, with our weaknesses and strengths alike—and that to rip us out of that context would do damage to the entire framework.

This recognition brings about a feeling tone that tunes us in to the heroic; replenishes, heals, and strengthens us and deepens our creativity. Therefore, it has a biological as well as psychic basis. It returns us to the feeling of a caring universe, and beautifully reconciles individual identity with its position as part of an underlying overall pattern.

Without this recognition, the historic or focus

personality defends its barriers desperately, feeling itself alone and impotent in an uncaring universe.

THE HEROIC AND THE HISTORIC

Seth says that we form our reality through our conscious beliefs, but he also stresses that the conscious mind doesn't know how this is done, and has little to do with the actual inner processes involved. Those processes are heroic, out of space-time, but ever flowing into our reality as effects. We direct them through our beliefs and intents. But how? Something gives us a life, a body, a physical world of relatedness, a historic self—the focus personality alive in time.

Seth emphasizes that all this is given. If this isn't understood, we put too much stress upon normal consciousness, forgetting the source of its strength.

We forget that the psyche or inner self is always there and available, because it seems so separated from our usual consciousness. But the psyche is as natural as a flower bulb. Watch an amaryllis plant sometime. In less than two weeks it grows a flower stalk some two to three feet high from one bulb, four giant flowers emerge, sometimes five inches across! You couldn't put the stalk back inside. How did four such large flowers spring up so quickly from a comparatively small bulb? Where did they come from? "Simple," someone says. "That's nature."

Right; and it's also heroic. The plant's reality in our world springs from its hidden heroic pattern. We get here the same way, only the mechanics are different. But besides that, and our physical growth which is perceivable, there is a development of personality that has no physical shape to keep track of: Yet it, too, follows an invisible heroic pattern and leans toward those conditions that best favor its growth. In other words, I think that the focus personality has numerous patterns of probable fulfillment from which it constantly chooses.

This became clear to me that Thursday morning. The entire week, I'd been getting this material on heroics and applying it personally. The heroic self is the original, creative, unexpected self, presenting rich patterns and alternate choices that can appear quite unconventional or unrespectable to the focus personality. And I saw how I'd often restricted its actions by my own attitudes. Most of my most creative work has come when I wasn't expecting it—when I was dallying, or daydreaming, or thinking of something else, for example. My writing production is considerable. Yet I used my writing schedule almost like a whip, as if I'd never write another word if I didn't put in so many hours a day. I mistrusted any impulse during that time that might take me from my desk. And I saw that I'd robbed myself of unexpected opportunities that might have come precisely because I forgot my ideas about my work.

The heroic provides a larger framework in which we can encounter the unexpected, and while I might be more permissive than others in that respect, I still wanted the unexpected to give proper notice! I knew that I'd have to discover more about the heroic personages, for example, and that I wanted to explore the heroic dimension. But I wasn't plunging in. I wanted the unexpected on my terms. Yet I could feel the atmosphere of the heroic all about me, so constantly that my earlier ignorance seemed incomprehensible.

While I was typing some of the week's material, two other paragraphs inserted themselves. I knew that they were from James's book:

"There is, however, within man a sense of the heroic; that is, the faculty for perceiving within himself the inner larger design or pattern of the soul. For this surrounds us always. We move in it as fishes do in the ocean, and all our actions mix and merge with the great rippling rhythms that form and support the more surface evidence of our days.

"This inner faculty allows us to glimpse those deeper currents, to plunge into living with the zest of an instinctive yet trained swimmer, who is exuberantly aware of the power and majesty of the waves, and able to identify himself with the splendor of the ocean's motion."

And I wondered: Had I pursued James's book,

would I have been led by another route to the same place—
the heroic dimension? I remembered the other paragraph that
had reminded me of James a few days previously, and the
connections became clear. The pages that I'd read from
months ago had been in the middle of the book I'd seen in
the library, and devoted to James's discussion of melancholy.
The last part that I didn't see was devoted to the heroic
faculties in man and their power to banish melancholy and
fear.

            Still ... I'd been changing myself during that
week. I could feel a new self trying to grow out of the old
one, and I kept trying to be both at the same time.

Chapter 26

Toward a
New Politics of the Psyche.
A New Allegiance,
and Heroic Impulses

Strange: Only now, finishing this book, do I see where its initial experiences were leading me. Sometime between my first visit to the library in the autumn of 1974 and my experiences with the heroic dimensions in the summer of 1975, my basic allegiance changed. I was probably aware of it to some degree when I wrote the material on codicils. It wasn't until the last of the summer, though, when I was immersed in the heroic, that I began to understand what had been going on, or what a change was taking place.

During that entire period, through June and July, I worked at night, going to bed around 1:00, rising about 3:00A.M. I worked till about 7:00. Then I'd fall asleep the minute I hit the bed, and Rob would waken me at noon when he'd finished his painting. He had lunch while I had a second breakfast. Often I'd write at the picnic table for a few hours in the afternoon.

But as I began to get the material on heroics, I realized that a change was taking place in my consciousness; a subtle alteration of focus that had been happening for some time. At night, with no exterior events to capture my attention, and no chores to do, I felt close to the undersides of consciousness. When I arose at noon, that different aura bathed my day so that the topsides and undersides of my consciousness merged. Yet I could tell them apart.

I felt exterior events riding on the top of the interior ones, and the support of the psyche beneath it all. Dawn was almost . . . dawn breaking first in the psyche, and then emerging in the physical sky. I sensed the shape of a different, larger, heroic reality in which our usual lives happen. Dream and sleep states were each more lucid; symbolic events and physical ones each appeared more clearly, yet were felt as part of each other.

In the day, I wasn't nearly as concerned with time as I used to be. I experienced it differently and went along with its apparent flow. There seemed to be more time between or within the minutes. I didn't feel rushed anymore or harried by my writing schedule. I didn't feel that I had to produce each moment I was in front of the typewriter, or think that the time was wasted if so many hours didn't produce so many pages of finished script. And I was producing like mad; as I could have all along, without hassling myself as I used to do. Distinctions were dropping away that earlier held me back.

In their place, a different kind of wholeness and relatedness emerged. An old familiar half-eerie sense of panic began to fade, that had been connected with the beliefs about time's urgency, and the exhaustion that can come of trying to make time count. It was as if the contours of my consciousness were changing. Deep feelings of connection-with-nature returned from my childhood, feelings probably impossible to describe once you've learned an adult's vocabulary.

We speak about "feeling at one with nature" as if it

were an esoteric achievement, possible only through medi-
tation; but it's a biological knowing, a creature knowledge, a
sure recognition that we're equipped to exist in our environment; that we're meant to be here because we are here. The
psyche senses its physical roots and in so doing, touches upon
its spiritual roots at the same time.

Before, I think I justified all of my psychic excursions and my study of the psyche by writing about them.
Writing was, after all, work. I wasn't being lazy, or dilly-
dallying—all abhorrent according to the beliefs of the official
line of consciousness. After all, I was *producing*. I was
brought up to believe that you had to force yourself to work
or be creative, because left alone the self just wasn't reliable.
Now those ideas were vanishing, with their effects.

But most of all, I lost my allegiance to time. I felt
in time and out of time; bathed in heroic dimensions and
appearing historically. Some ghostly strange roots of the
psyche seemed to reach ahead and in front of me in time; but
I was a great slow being that encompassed it all. The word
"slow" isn't the best one here, yet it feels right. Some underlying deep continent of myself seemed to come into view, in
which the lands of my conscious selves in time were contained. I encountered the surety of the psyche in a heroic
context.

During this period, I opened the front and back
doors because the nights were warm, and the night flowed
through the house. I felt that all times and places were
outside, in the hills: Yet the dimensions from which time
flowed—the supporting no-time was outside there too; and in
me. I happened where they merged.

I knew something was happening, though I didn't
know what it was. I only knew that I was experiencing the
motion of my psyche, and decided to go along wholeheartedly for once,. instead of intellectually questioning
myself every step of the way. In other words, I admitted that
my psyche, not my intellect, was responsible for the motion
of my being. The intellect springs out of the psyche, and not
the other way around. As a child, I trusted both; the intellect
interpreted the psyche's truth in our world, translating its

reality into terms of time and space; wondering, sure, delighted. Those feelings kept returning.

Even the weather was connected to my mood. It was hot and humid, not the kind that makes you feel energetic, and the idea of not being energetic has always frightened me a little. It was precisely then that you were supposed to really use your will, your "get-up-and-go."

But I thought: From now on I'm going to just let myself live, in the same way that I let my books write themselves. Then the obvious question came to mind: Who is this "me" I'm going to let live me? We've identified so exclusively with the main line of consciousness that there doesn't seem to be any other me to work with. We speak of the inner self, but we accept it mainly as a concept, not a part of a recognized selfhood.

The main line of consciousness identifies pretty much with the intellect and so-called ego. Once you *really* understand that your reality is more extensive, and includes other strands of consciousness, then you can at least sense the rest of your youness. These other strands, and other portions of selfhood, then constantly expand the you that you recognize. For one thing, of course, you become aware of stimuli and information that was psychologically invisible earlier.

My allegiance was turning toward the heroic, and the library was my key to it. More and more I felt the presence there of the heroic personages, some as my colleagues, and others as teachers. Some exist in time also, like me, and others are in the out-of-time context entirely. There seems to be a steady flow of information and exchange of models so that, for example, my original version of this book alters the library book that was its model. I've tuned into my space-time version of the library book, and the eccentricity of my moods and experience, being unpredictable, constantly write the book in a different way. In other words, I tune in to constantly changing probable futures, finally settling on one in which the book is the real one in our terms.

Far more is involved, though, as probabilities mix and merge, and my experience happens. Each element in my life evokes a different response that changes me, this book, and the book in the library as well. Yet somewhere along the way, the strand of awareness that connected me to the library, merged with mine. The comprehensions involving heroics were like extra strands which I accepted and claimed as my own. I think that I sent my double into the library—or into the heroic—and that what I'm learning is what she's discovering: the out-of-time context in which the library exists.

I know that I'm ready to explore the library more fully now, and realized that all along I'd been trying to form a new framework in which we could view ourselves in relation to this world, and to the heroic dimensions from which it springs. I didn't want to admit it, however. It seemed too audacious a goal. I've also been trying to rip away the superstitions that we've placed around intuitive information. The material on the codicils, the authority of the psyche, and the heroic dimension offers such a new framework, and even if the entire construct is symbolic, to me it represents basic knowledge about ourselves and the universe.

I believe that heroic impulses are those that rise from our deepest sources, uniquely fitting our individual abilities and intents, and suited to our specific needs and desires. Such heroic impulses, while individual and self-serving, are altruistic at the same time. Actions in response to such impulses will automatically trigger heroic acts on the part of others, for they will present one more piece of the heroic patterns that underlie all our lives.

Heroic impulses are self-knowing, in that they're geared also to release and activate the most fitting, most fortunate and fulfilling abilities under the circumstances at hand, and in line with present life conditions. They are pattern-activators, stimulating action in certain directions at specific times, with a view to the larger heroic pattern of our lives that is unknown at the usual level of the focus personality.

The focus personality can choose to act or not to act in response. Part of the learning process involves the acceptance of these heroic impulses after they're recognized.

First the focus personality must understand that its own existence is guaranteed and nourished by inner elements of experience and knowledge of which it is not normally aware, or which it has ignored. It then begins to accept as valid, stimuli and data that originate beyond its domain. In so doing, it increases its domain and dimishes it at the same time. Such a statement is meaningless at the usual level of consciousness, and hopelessly contradictory. It makes perfect sense at other levels, however, where it's obvious that terms like "more" or "less" cannot be applied to such issues.

Coming from the heroic dimension, such impulses may often trigger actions that seem insignificant, trivial, beside the point, or inappropriate to the official level of consciousness, while later they will be seen as highly apt. They often appear as quite simple impulses—to pick up a particular book, take a walk, call someone, change a planned outing or schedule—but followed, they lead to fortunate circumstances or encounters that might otherwise not have occurred.

My working at night during the summer was an example of such an impulse. I struggled against it for a week, thinking that it was better and healthier to be up and about in the day; feeling that there was something slovenly about sleeping in the daytime. Then I realized that I really *wanted* to wander through the house alone at night, to catch the universe or my corner of it unaware. I remembered that I'd often written nights in my childhood. The other, countering ideas had come later, through conditioning. So I went along with the impulse and as a result found myself going where I wanted to—only before I hadn't known how to get there.

Again: As I sat up nights, writing, old childhood feelings reemerged. I suppose they amount to the child's conviction that beneath any given day's difficulties, everything is okay and everything matters. As a child, I used the symbolism of the Catholic Church as a framework for that conviction.

You can hardly say that a symbol is wrong. But the church, in a psychic shorthand, insisted that the symbols were literal fact or truth, while teaching at the same time that lies or distortions of the truth were wrong. I actually remember my first problem with this. I was six, in church with my Irish grandmother. Mass was being chanted in Latin. Two altar boys stood with their backs to me, chanting the responses. My grandmother told me that God was answering, but I saw the altar boys' lips move, as their heads turned sideways.

I felt outraged that my grandmother had lied. No one explained that symbolic truth might differ from fact truth—and even, sometimes, seem to deny it.

The trend continued. I was told about a man and woman in the Garden of Eden and a God who threw them out for eating a piece of fruit, and I thought: Now if that wasn't a giant temper tantrum what was? But the apple represented forbidden knowledge. You bet your boots it did—the knowledge that there is one big difference between symbolic and literal truth, and if the two ever meet, look out! With the Garden of Eden episode, we settled for literal fact truth, a rather poor choice in many ways. And only when I see a woman come full blown out of a man's ribs (in good light) will I fall for symbolic garbs as literal fact.

The symbols are *carriers* of truths known to the psyche. They keep shoving literal interpretations aside and leaping out of them, because the symbols are only handy representations of heroic dimensions too big to appear in our fact world. Not realizing this, we who were literal-minded kept pulling the rug out from the religions, or trying to, saying, scandalized, "Now that's just not true. What kind of a God is going to throw someone into an eternal hell for not going to church on Sunday?" Or, "God is just not in that piece of bread. No way! Not unless God is in all bread."

But the churches were so involved in their insistence that symbolic truth was literal fact that they could only insist over and over again that they were right—because they'd forgotten the about the rich bed of symbolism that alone could turn much of their literal nonsense into any kind of truth.

And when you realize that symbols *are* symbols, your feelings rise up, almost touching the edges of direct knowing. Of course, instantly you make a new symbol to express what you sense, because the world itself springs from that source, and as you approach it you have to interpret it in terms of mind and flesh. But you feel some balance and support at the heart of the world, some aplomb at the center of the universe. Fleetingly, you feel yourself a part of it all: you know that it moves with your breath and that you and the universe are breathing each other in and out in some unfathomable manner; eternal yet changing. Then—pop—you're out of it; the feeling. But it's familiar from child-hood—not that you remember it, exactly, but you feel that you felt it then, and took it for granted.

So during this period, ever so briefly, that remi-niscent awareness emerged. I knew that once I'd moved through the world with that confidence, like an innocent animal, sure of my place and haunts, and certain of my ability to handle any dangers that might arise. I related that old emotional sureness to heroic spaces. I was "walking with myself" in the greater heroic pattern that surrounds me, and each of us. This brought about a kind of biological trust, the knowledge that we're each as well equipped as the animals, certainly, to deal with our lives and environment, endowed with all the energy and resources we need.

So maybe we have to return to our private psyches, as naked of symbols as possible, having worn out the ones we had. Because when we accept the symbols as literal truth in a fact world, we make lies of them or let them make lies of us, so that they stand between us and the truths they're meant to represent.

Only when we throw the symbols off do we approach the unknowable directly in whatever way we can. So what, if instantly we form new symbols to express it? They'll be rich, tinged with the original essence. They will be our touchstones. But we won't need to defend them as literal fact. We'll understand symbols as the clothing that our visions wear.

When we expand our consciousness, we enlarge our understanding, though, arriving at another level large enough to contain intuitive knowledge and facts, and we come into touch with other elements of selfhood that we've repressed.

Artists use different colors. But we have more than one self to our palette—many, dwelling (if that's the term) at other levels of reality, part of their beings meshed with ours and ours with theirs. We've denied the validity of these other selves and ignored their existence almost entirely, because while we believed in one world and one time, we needed a one-self concept and experience to go along with our world picture.

So these other selves remained psychologically invisible, like planets not yet discovered, their existence showing only indirectly as effects that we didn't understand. We dared not confront them directly because our entire picture of objective and subjective reality would have to change. Only now, when the limitations of our old world view become appallingly apparent, do we even consider alternates.

Certainly such a recognition would involve an entirely new politics of the psyche, and new methods of approaching our own reality. "Myself" would be understood to mean "ourselves" or "my selves"—many selves united like states into one psychological structure that operates for itself, and all others in the physical world. We've always known it, but we've tried to make ourselves smaller, only our consciousness and experience kept spilling over the dam we'd built around our own nature. We have no idea where the recognized myself merges with these others, yet the myself is an intersection point of cognizant energy—the focus personality through which these other selves share in corporal life and help form it (as, unconsciously, we share in their reality).

I have to use the word "selves" because we take it for granted that selves are what we are—because we've so limited our perception. We've just taken one point and said, "The self ends here, includes space-time perceptions, and no more." So we've made artificial divisions. In greater terms, we only know the earth Aspect (or focus personality) of ourselves. It's not so much that we have other selves as that these Aspects would appear separate to us, because of our concepts about selfhood. We haven't accepted our greater identities.

Trance states, conditions of high inspiration or creativity, daydreaming, sleep states--all act in a way as neutral areas. We move out of our psychologically limited centers (off focus) to form psychological platforms, travelling out into the greater psyche where other Aspects of ourselves twinkle like stars. According to our abilities, we can learn an inner travel, establishing psychological bases further from our own "home center," and send ourselves out as landing parties. Actually, these other Aspects or selves, operating in their own objective and subjective realities, send emissaries here as well. They appear to us in those neutral areas of relative psychological freedom. The conditions of the psyche might well vary at different levels so that various different atmospheric conditions might be involved that we still have to discern and evaluate.

But since these are interwoven psychological structures, they are open-ended. You can move from ... one self or Aspect to another ... without destroying the validity of private identity one whit; bringing more of your "selves" into conscious activation, adding to their experience and to your own. This is not segmentation. but the fuller dimensions of being; the exploration and cultivation of psychological assets. What we now think of as ego consciousness is broadened at its base, gaining added stability, given information denied to it before. We've kept the ego in an ignorance that alone caused it stress: Its own base was not apparent to it, and when it did briefly appear, the ego's beliefs made it fear for its identity.

We've done an excellent job along certain lines in exploring the earth. In those terms, our beliefs about the self are at "the world is flat" stage. Closed off from perceiving our own greater aspects, we projected upon the world a grid of beliefs that prejudiced the physical perception available to us. During some of my own experiences, that prejudiced perception lifted just enough so that for a few moments I saw ... what was really there ... or viewed the richness of perceptive data possible in the world we know.

The self doesn't end where we think it does, any more than the world itself ends at the horizon. We've accepted one self and thought that we'd defined selfhood. Instead, it's as if we'd explored one island and called it the world. There are other Aspects to the self that we know, whose origins and activities have never been touched upon. Our job is to understand and recognize them, to use their characteristics and abilities in an earth-tuned way, to enrich earth experience by bringing to it those other dimensions of experience; to fulfill our creaturehood.

Even with my own still-limited experiences with "the heroic," I feel more sturdily here, more sturdily myself, and at the same time I'm far freer to act, move, and interrelate with other portions of the psyche. I intend to explore these other realities with a more carefree attitude, no longer worried by what people or the world might think. On the one hand, that world is more precious as it becomes colored and filled out by other perceptions. On the other hand, my allegiance is elsewhere, so that the world's value judgments and beliefs no longer reign supreme. I see that I'm in an excellent position, since I don't belong to any already established field with its set methods or criteria.

This doesn't mean that I intend to turn into Seth or Sumari willy-nilly—and for all of my early worries, there was never even a hint of such a situation. But we are quite capable of adapting a larger description of selfhood. At childhood, I believe, we were somewhat aware of other Aspects of our being, but we were taught to form a practical self and to limit our experience to fit its mold. Many of our own talents and characteristics became invisible to us in the process.

In my usual writing, as in this book, I use my known self in that the world is viewed from my standpoint, and my excursions into other levels of consciousness are journeys from here. But I also put my writing ability to the use of other selves, with a different kind of psychological actuality, who inhabit another sort of objective and subjective environment.

Seth, for example, is not a chunk of personified psyche; not just "human but dead," and alive someplace else, but a different kind of psychological being entirely—a different species, psychically speaking—consciousness in a different context, one that I can tune in to since its strands are interwoven with mine. Something of my consciousness is also interwoven with Seth's. We are different kinds of beings, together yet apart. I am a self of Seth's and he is a self of mine.

The full orchestration of individuality would permit the playing of all the selves, with the focus personality directing the particular earth composition. Again: Our selfhood is interwoven with these other selves. We are them, focused here. They are us, focused in their reality. The strands of our own consciousness wind in and out of those other dimensions, and through them we are woven in and out of time and space but not confined to them.

These Aspects can at times seem like gods to us because of their relative freedom from our space-time system. They have a larger view of our reality. They can allow us to use abilities that seem miraculous from our viewpoint but they cannot participate in earthly experience as we do, nor know the sweet, clear focus of a life couched in time.

Yet, tuning in to those dimensions of the heroic, we *can* use time differently. Something within it opens, and I believe that what opens is the heroic medium in which time itself exists. The Aspects actually help form our own psychological solidarity, and we are what they are, in time.

For example, Seth finished The *"Unknown" Reality* in April, and in July he began another book, *The Nature of the Psyche: Its Human Expression.* I was also working on this book, which I am now preparing for the publisher. That left Rob with the two volumes of *"Unknown" Reality* to type. He also has to organize his own notes, and the nature of the book required that he include some of our personal experiences. Seth wrote the book to show how the elements of the unknown reality become known, and he used our lives as an example. Now that is fine for Seth. He isn't involved in the physical effort. In the meantime, he has an excellent start on the new book. He could dictate steadily as far as I can tell—his material seems literally endless. Only the physical mechanics and time hold that work back at all. And I'm never tired after those sessions, incidentally; never drained. Instead I'm usually refreshed.

But while Seth can do all that and while he can give us invaluable information about the nature of reality, *his* reality is focused elsewhere. His consciousness may be woven with mine and mine with his, but I'm the one who sits in the backyard these afternoons, watching the mountains. The afternoon exists in the universal brain and in my own simultaneously. But only at this level of perception does it attain its aesthetic earthly reality, achieving the dear peculiarities and details of separate leaves and trees—and this experience of personal affiliation. For we've thrown in our lot with earth, born and doomed to die within it, plunged and committed (for a *time*) to follow the rules that dictate and delineate its nature.

If life is only for a time, then death is our exit out of time, when we unscramble all the old messages and reprogram ourselves to perceive and experience other valid worlds that also lie latent in the brain of the universe, waiting only for our activation, our participation; for all possible realities exist in a gestalt of related consciousness.

As I was writing this passage originally, I was out in the yard; and if Seth was aware of my perceptions, he was not directly experiencing them as I was. I felt what I felt from my own viewpoint. And in that viewpoint I knew that my cat Willy's tour around the grounds—through the sunlight, shadows, and stiff grasses—was as legitimate and important as a planet orbiting; and the mark of the cat's paw was as significant as the tracings that our rockets make in space. Both the rocket's plunge and the cat's explorations are acts of curiosity, wonder, and expansion, in which it's evident that all consciousness seeks to outdo itself and wanders the furthest reaches of its sacred leash.

Death, I think, is such an exploration; assured by our anatomy, for all of life is a preparation for it. Death is our assurance that we won't be caught in a dimensional dilemma, trapped in a three-dimensional house with no way out of it. Granted, we choose the house and terms of rental. But no residence, however grand, could contain such freeranging consciousness for long.

It seems to me that my own books always begin with a new psychic event, and new questions that then structure my experience. I never know where they're leading me on a conscious level. So only as I was ending this book did I understand its full development, and the natural evolution of the super-real picture of the world that I saw, now over a year ago. For that picture was meant to lead me on until, gradually, the old world of assumed facts was seen as only part of a much more vast existence.

This book began when I heard my own true tone and felt that I'd found my true path; or in other words, when I began to line myself up with inner inclinations of being that seemed to know what was best for me, and followed most faithfully the contours of my psyche. I found the library, like the one magic place in the universe discovered by a child—the place of seeming miracles, the place of homecoming.

Following these experiences, I explored various states of consciousness, each giving slightly different versions of reality. People called and wrote, bringing into my life those elements of their own experience that made up their reality. Click-click-click, as I encountered the great differences and similarities of our lives. The contents of the mind and the contents of the world—where do they begin or end? Where do they merge? When are they private? When are they shared?

I've been on a long journey since this book began. I see that we form the contents of the private and shared world: We choose our focus. But all of this is not only determined by events, but by the state of consciousness with which we perceive them. The perception alters events, changes them to such a degree that only the merest of physical data remains the same, while the significant inner data escapes such classification.

Seth is right: I live in a safe universe. Each of us does. That statement is senseless at the official level of consciousness; the sheerest kind of Pollyanna. Surrounded by wars, poverty, cruelty, and prophecies of the end of the world, how can the idea of safety fit in?

Yet—when the psyche goes within itself and finds

its own true tone, discovers its private touchstone, the aura of safety spreads about it, forming special places as the psyche imprints its own private mark upon the environment; transforming it by altering the focus of consciousness and changing levels of perception, and hence coming into a world where the old laws and beliefs no longer apply.

Then and only then, going out into the world means going out into a safe universe with the way cleared and vision open, where none of the old defenses are needed and in which old fears no longer apply. As Seth humorously put it in one of our sessions, "I said it was a *safe* universe. I never said it was a perfect one." So this doesn't mean the end of challenges, but the release of energy and ability, the full use of our equipment to achieve our goals, whatever they are.

So when we go out into the world again, it is the same world—the streets and shops are there as always—but it is also a completely different world, filled out and enriched by enlightened perception, no longer prejudiced by limited beliefs. It becomes a world in which we are competent; no longer victims but creators, learning to develop an art of living hardly suspected before.

The stages between that condition and the one we have now will vary considerably, but again Seth is correct: He says that a time comes to each of us when we can no longer equivocate, when we can straddle the fence no longer. Then we truly rouse, take the leap, and replace old beliefs with the codicils or their equivalent. The codicils are my versions of the new assumptions that can lead us to such a state; sifted through my psyche and experience. Yet they will be discovered to some extent by each person in his or her way, new assumptions of consciousness—but ancient knowledge native to each of us, ready to be used in a new way.

Chapter 27

"Come to the Mountain," and Seth on the Safe Universe

A young man, a college student, just phoned. He said that he wanted to come and see me, to "come to the mountain, so to speak." Dear God—if you'll forgive the term. I'm reminded of a poem I wrote in high school:

> *A frog sat still*
> *and stared with awe*
> *at a watch that lay in the sand.*
> *"Now," he said, "I am quite sure*
> *there is such a thing as man."*
>
> *"Our priests," he mused, "have spoken*
> *of man who made our pond.*

Perhaps he left this as a token,
between us, to be a bond."

So the frog spent all his life
trying to understand
and while he grew old and tired,
the watch ticked on in the sand.

Some frogs jeered at him,
others call him great,
but he only smiled, and went off by himself,
poor lonely frog, to meditate.

Ignoring the rather miraculous ever-ticking watch, the poem wasn't too bad for a sixteen-year-old. Now I think that the frog would have done better by contemplating his frogness instead. But if that's how I saw myself back then, then it's probably connected with the kind of person I've grown to be. Only I'm happier than the frog and not all that lonely. But the young man's phone call brought to the surface of my mind some thoughts I'd been playing around with a few minutes before.

Maybe some of us are so appalled by man's condition, so aware of our vulnerability and ignorance, so conscious of the plights in which our fellow beings find themselves, that in desperation we begin, perhaps in childhood, to tell stories to ourselves and others. We tell brave tales of immortality and parades of the gods; galloping crescendos—those stories in which the lost is always found, the sick cured, and all wrongs righted. These are our own creations, spun from the yearnings and questions of the heart, magically set against the terrors and uncertainties of life—our own compensating yet daring compositions to comfort ourselves and others, yet also reproaching the universe. If *we* were doing things, it would all be different!

Perhaps the animals have their own versions of these tales, but most likely they don't need them. They accept the conditions of their lives. Don't they? Don't they?

Or does a mother wolf growl in agony at the far moon at the death of a cub, and pause with a question: Why? Probably not. I take it for granted, at least, that in that respect, the animals know better: They feel their part in life and death alike. But even if I'm wrong, they're still spared our kind of questions. They seem to escape our need to set things right.

Anyhow, some of us learn to tell these stories, and see magic visions springing up to transform the world. After a while, we believe them, at least in part; and others, listening, come to be healed, to find the answers, to see the frog's watch. But the frog can't tell what the watch is for or read the features of its face. And we can't see the real nature of our stories: They dazzle, mystify—and remain undecipherable. Their origin is undecipherable; for where does the yearning come from that we seek to assuage? If there is no immortality of a sorts, no peace, then where did the yearning for these originate? In what mold are the stories unknowingly fitted?

Now and then one of us sees, or we make the stories work. We find ourselves somehow suddenly transported to another level of being where—presto, yes—the sick are cured, the lonely comforted, and all things are made right. But when we return with our miraculous message, the miracle doesn't work at home. Bewildered, we lick our wounds, swear off! Then comes another moment of the soul, when we see how easily and clearly it all works, only to find our miracles turned once again into fairy tales told by the fireside. The young man wants to visit the mountain. Don't we all?

So I wonder: Do our yearnings actually strain our creaturehood to the limit? Do they propel us momentarily into those other levels of consciousness? A kind of consciousness that exists because we have forged it, each of us, bit by bit through the ages. Only we haven't transferred our living there yet.

Maybe what we have is all we can really expect of ourselves. Maybe one species of animal—us—gave up all of its security of instinct, its known place in the fabric of things, to forge a new kind of consciousness. Maybe, just maybe, no other species, at least in our frame of reference, had to bear the brunt of consciousness going-it-alone, so to speak; traveling outside the known rules of heritage and instinct. Maybe we took a horrible plunge and fantastic leap or ascension all at once, giving up old ordered ways by breaking loose, straying, daring to remember and anticipate ourselves.

As it's said at least, that mammals or mammals-to-be crawled up on the land from the ocean, so maybe now we're doing the same thing in a different way, climbing out of time with its limited beliefs of cause and effect. After learning to acclimate ourselves to our physical environment, after struggling even to subdue it and make it ours, maybe we're learning that on certain levels at least we've been manipulating mirages. Maybe we're learning that the real world is always inside, where the mirages are made. Perhaps we're getting ready to explore those inner landscapes and learning that the flickering lights that splash across the world come from within our own animal-gifted minds, and always have.

I really believe that my library material on codicils is true, and that Seth's statements about a safe universe are valid. Then I think: But both the library and Seth have their existence at another level of the psyche, a level at which the mirages are not so clear or vivid or convincing. To us the dangers, fears, and terrors too often seem quite real.

So is Seth just ahead of us enough in his travels so that his assumptions for existence *do* work—where he is? And now and then you or I get one foot there, or glimpse one small corner of that vaster reality, and for that moment the codicils work. We shout, "Eureka! It's a miracle!"—and in that instant take a species leap more terrifying and significant and triumphant than the reptiles' first crawling upon the land. We sense a whole new field of existence. Only it doesn't last and we're left with tantalizing images that propel us still further, roused by the memories of what we've so briefly seen.

So it seems that we're betwixt and between, and often our fine animal alignment totters. We lose the fine security of instinct and yet haven't learned to use these other faculties that still elude us.

Maybe—crazy thought—the gods are spasmodic beings. Here and there through the ages a man or woman reaches higher than most of us; climbs into a new realm of being, ascends to a peak of consciousness as yet transitory—and for that moment only he or she is a god, and shouts down what is heard or sensed or experienced. Then books are written about it and translations and transcriptions; but it's all a kind of divine gibberish. We can't really translate it here any more than a dog, suddenly comprehending mathematics, could later translate the data to his dog fellows, no matter how inspired his barks.

For the vision, however brilliant, fades. Yet the memory and knowledge of its existence remains a fact in our world, however clumsily expressed. Maybe, whenever we pay attention to the lyrics instead of the song, we make our biggest error—if you'll forgive the new analogy. Maybe when we try our hardest to make the vision work in our world, to make it practical, we distort it most of all; because what makes sense at those other levels of consciousness may sound nonsensical here.

Yet those peaks of awareness may forge their own kind of reality and continuity at other levels of consciousness, each one acting like a mental footprint in an invisible world, so that paths are made for others of our kind to follow—paths visible *there* but not here.

Maybe our successes are chalked up at those other barely glimpsed levels, and for some still unknown reason they appear only in diluted form here. I'd hate to settle for that, though. I suspect that Seth's contention that we form our own reality automatically alters our subjective state the minute we accept it, and that we're suddenly confronted with challenges we were unaware of before; that we lose an old shallow innocence to gain a new innocent wisdom, because we accept the responsibility that earlier we assigned to fate or the gods. Certainly some momentary confusion is understandable.

So is Seth's voice a message from one level of consciousness to another, echoing through the symbolic molecules of some other kind of being that is different in

Seth's time than it is in ours? Do his directions, from his "future," change the course of our present, so that we turn a different corner of consciousness? And is the same thing true of any such messages? Do they lead us to a level of consciousness where the codicils *do* apply, where we use our beliefs to form reality as expertly as we now use bricks?

Seth says that our beliefs cause our reality, whether we know it or not. But knowing it changes the game, adds an extra dimension, and one in which we're driven to find a safe universe so that our beliefs are no longer the results of fear.

The trouble is that we still use old methods to implement the new ideas, some that are probably psychologically invisible to us at this stage and no longer suited to the matter at hand. We keep checking physical reality, for example, to see if such ideas are practical, because in the past we lived by accepting the evidence of our senses alone, and that was the sane way to operate.

Now perhaps we have to do the opposite, alter our methods, and check our ideas and beliefs while ignoring the physical data for a while. This is something very difficult for us to do, yet the constant checking—am I getting the effect I want yet?—in whatever area, only brings us right back where the mirage is the reality. Most likely it's when we forget to check, when we grow weary and say "to hell with it" that things really happen. Consciousness is suddenly freed from effort, and the new beliefs click into focus, or we latch on to a new kind of instinct belonging to the hypothetically new species, where—presto—the thought *does* spring into instant reality. The difficulties are gone: we find or discover a better kind of manipulation that carries us over or above the level below.

For all my work, I've barely touched upon those other dimensions. Little by little my own prejudiced perception falls away in chunks. I only know that certain new experiences seem to be leading me further. I've had a series of extremely vivid waking-dreaming events that involved probabilities: I've managed to enter another room in the library; and already have over a hundred pages on what I call *The*

World View of Paul Cézanne. The heroic personages seem to be just around the corner of my mind. So I suppose that these events will take shape in their own way.

I haven't resumed regular classes, and have no idea when or if I will. In the meantime I see students at informal gatherings. Besides dictating his new book in our regular sessions, Seth usually speaks to my students at such times. His knowledge of our psychology is flawless. At a recent get-together, I was explaining the idea of the safe universe when Seth came through, with humor and some gentle irony, to help me out. I'd like to close this book with excerpts from that spontaneous session.

When Seth speaks to people directly, he takes their emotional states into consideration. He never speaks *at* them. In this particular instance, a student had just expressed a fear that love was smothering. Before I could answer, Seth came through:

"Now, you believe that love is smothering because you do not believe in a safe universe. And each of you, to some extent or another, believe that the universe is not safe, and therefore you must set up defenses against it.

"The one-line official consciousness with which you are familiar, says, 'The world is not safe. I cannot trust it. Nor can I trust the conditions of experience or the conditions of my own existence. Nor can I trust myself. I can look at a squirrel and rejoice, but I cannot look at myself and rejoice, for I am filled with iniquity and I am, to some extent, evil.'

Seth spoke with rich irony here, looking from one person to another. " 'I am not only evil as myself,' " he continued in his example, " 'but I come from a tainted and flawed race. My mother and my father were flawed before me and I send these tragic flaws into the future. Therefore, I must set up my defenses in whatever way I can, to protect myself in a universe that I cannot trust, and from a self that is evil and flawed.'

"Now, as long as you hold on to those beliefs, then you must indeed set up defenses. And it may seem to you"— Seth nodded to the young man—"that love is smothering.

"As long as you believe that you dwell in a universe that is a threat, you must defend yourself against it. As long as you believe that the self is flawed and that the race is doomed and evil, you must defend yourself against yourself. And how can you then trust the voice of the psyche? When I say to you, 'Be spontaneous,' how dare you take that step? To be spontaneous would obviously give rise to all the lust, passion, murder, and hatred that to *you* is inherent in the human heart.

"So you say, 'I try to be spontaneous, but how can I? I try to believe that I am good, but how can I be good when I come from a race that is evil?' You try to say, 'The universe is safe,' and then you watch the news on television or read the newspaper and you say, 'What lie is this? How can the universe be safe when I read about wholesale murder, war, trickery, and greed? How can I be myself, for if I am myself will I not unleash into the world only more of the horror I see about me? For surely human nature cannot change, and human nature is evil. Look already what evil it has worked upon the planet, then tell me, Seth, be spontaneous! What do you ask of me, and how can I stand upon the authority of the psyche or tell myself that I am good?'

"The official line of consciousness forms a world about it and you experience and perceive that world. While you devote yourselves to that official consciousness, the world will always appear the same—disastrous, bound for destruction or the greater judgment of a fundamental god.

"My last book, *The Nature of Personal Reality*, is a good book. It is a helpful book, and it is far trickier than you realize. It will lead you—automatically, if you use it well—out of the official line of consciousness. You will begin to question not only your private beliefs for your own purposes, but the *nature* of beliefs. And you will be led to discover other strands of consciousness.

"Ruburt [Jane] is working with what he calls the codicils, material he is getting from the library. Now those codicils are truths, quite apparent at another stage of consciousness. The one-line stage of consciousness was necessary, but it contained within it its own impetus for development.

It set up challenges that could not be solved at that stage, and that would automatically lead to other kinds of awareness. Only when you sense these, can old contradictions make sense.

"You need not say, 'The universe is safe,' for at your present level, that will only enrage you. Say instead, 'I live in a safe universe,' and so you shall. Those defenses you have set up will crumble for they will not be needed. The codicils are practical. They are realities, but at the official level of consciousness they sound impossible. So you must learn here and now to alter the state of your consciousness, and tune it to the state in which the codicils make sense.

"When people read *The Nature of Personal Reality* they will begin to examine their beliefs. They will think they are doing so to get rid of a problem or to gain an advantage, but they will soon find themselves involved in challenging the entire belief system that they know. When they do, they will automatically begin to alter the focus of their consciousness— and in so doing, begin to alter the nature of their world. Then, my dear friends, we will have our next book, *"Unknown" Reality*, ready for them. It will confuse them further. And then we will come out with another book, *The Nature of the Psyche*, that will help them find new footing in the world that they know. We will help them out of the confusion that we have caused, in other words."

We took a break. Then the student who was worried about love being smothering said that he had trouble relating to a girl who didn't subscribe wholeheartedly to Seth's ideas. Once again, Seth came through: this time, jovially:

"Now there are people who are quite involved with my ideas who do not know my name. There are people quite content with their lot and they do not know my name. They know themselves. They are aware of the vitality of their beings and they do not need me to tell them that they are important. The flowers and cats and trees don't need me to tell them they are important either, and there are many people who do not need me for the same reason.

"These people recognize the vitality of their

existences. They ignore the belief systems of their times. They are ancient children. They may not read philosophy, but they listen to the wind. They watch the behavior of the seasons. . . . If *you* were satisfied with the nature of your existence, you would not be here. Those who are satisfied, do not need my voice. They find sufficient reinforcement from the dawn and the twilight.

"They may build ditches or work in fields or factories. They do not need to listen to my voice because they listen to the voices of the oak trees and the birds, and to the voices of their own beings. I am a poor imitation of the voices of your own psyches to which you do not listen. I will be unneeded, and gladly so, when you realize that the vitality and reinforcement and joy are your own, and rise from the fountain of your own beings; when you realize that you do not need me for protection, for there is nothing you need protect yourself against."

Index